V-Bio

AS I REMEMBER

BY ROBERT LEONARD

BY CONRADO MASSAGUER

BY MAYNARD DIXON

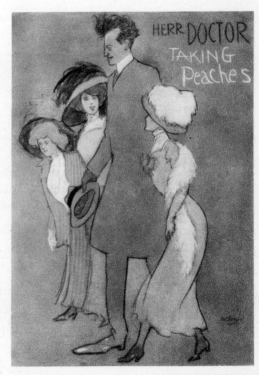

BY HAIG PATIGIAN

CARTOONS OF ARNOLD GENTHE

ARNOLD GENTHE (SELF-PORTRAIT)

ARNOLD GENTHE

AS I REMEMBER

WITH ONE HUNDRED AND TWELVE

PHOTOGRAPHIC ILLUSTRATIONS

BY THE AUTHOR

A JOHN DAY BOOK

REYNAL & HITCHCOCK : NEW YORK

Published by

JOHN DAY

in association with

REYNAL & HITCHCOCK

PRINTED AND BOUND IN THE UNITED STATES OF AMERICA
BY QUINN & BODEN COMPANY, INC., RAHWAY, N. J.
GRAVURE ILLUSTRATIONS BY THE BECK ENGRAVING COMPANY, PHILADELPHIA, PA.

Typography by Wendel Roos

FOREWORD

OFTEN after I have related a travel experience or a story about some famous person I had known, friends have said, "You ought to write that down. Why don't you get busy on your autobiography?" The idea, I admit, had been in the back of my mind for years, yet I always hesitated because by nature I am not inclined to talk about myself and in an autobiography one is supposed to talk about oneself. But when I realized that writing my memoirs—a pastime which Alexander Woollcott described once as the "favorite sport of one's declining years"—would give me the opportunity to speak of many subjects of interest to the general public, I began to think seriously about it.

The picture of my early youth would give a glimpse of family and student life in Old Germany; the story of the beginning of my interest in photography—which was responsible for my remaining in America instead of returning home (1896) to the planned career of a teacher of classical philology—would permit me to write of the efforts that were being made—and in which I had an active part—to lift photography from the mechanical, lifeless medium it had become, to the dignity and status of a real art; the personal anecdotes—often more revealing than a lengthy character study—that I could tell about the many men and women eminent in the world of art, literature, politics and society, with whom my work during the last forty years has brought me in contact, would show how simple and engagingly human most great people really are; and then comments on art, the beauty of women, incidents of travel in many out-of-way places,—all this would add color and interest to such a book of reminiscences.

And another, and more important, reason for my bringing out this volume was the opportunity it would give me of putting reproductions of some of my favorite photographs between the covers of a book and thereby letting others enjoy with me the results of my constant quest for beauty, which perhaps has been the chief aim of my life.

I want to express my thanks to Mrs. Genevieve Parkhurst for her valuable assistance in organizing the vast material that had accumulated, and in helping me to put it into shape for the book.

A. G.

CONTENTS

vii

ILLUSTRATIONS

NOTE.—*Illustrations follow text pages indicated by folios.*

xii

AS I REMEMBER

EARLY YEARS IN GERMANY

THE one memory I retain of my early childhood in Berlin is of a doll with red hair. I can see her plainly as she reposed in my arms when I sat on the sofa in the drawing room of my grandfather's house. It was not her blue eyes or her pink dress which held me, but her radiant hair. Such was her effect upon me that red hair has always fascinated me. Even today my friends tease me because of the way my eyes kindle when I see it.

At the time when I was born, my father, Hermann Genthe, was professor of Latin and Greek at the Graues Kloster (Gray Monastery) in Berlin, one of the oldest gymnasiums in Prussia. I was not yet three when in the summer of 1871 my father was called to Frankfort-on-the-Main. My first recollection there is of a bronze cat on his library desk. When I was taken in to say good-night, if I had been a good boy, I was lifted up and allowed to pet "Moepe" who had been named after my grandfather's cat. This was the beginning of my love for cats. It is told that at the age of four, when I was taken by the nurse to look at my newly arrived brother Hugo, I seriously remarked, "I'd like a little kitten better." I am fond of dogs, but cats have always meant more to me, and they have been the wise and sympathetic companions of many a solitary hour.

A third preference of mine also goes back to Frankfort. Not far from where we lived was the Baron Erlanger's estate where he kept a stable of fine horses. Often, when my grandmother took me out walking, we would go there. These visits were forbidden by my mother, but I could always wheedle Grandmother into letting me have my way. I used to wander from stall to stall petting the horses, and I still have a sense of the smoothness of their glossy coats and the fragrance of the well-kept stables.

In my later life—ever since making my home in America—I have seldom been without a mount, and horseback riding has always been my favorite exercise in town and country.

At six I entered the Wöhler Schule in Frankfort. Of my year there I retain a vivid image of the little boy who sat in front of me. He had long black curls which it sometimes amused me to pull. This boy, Rudolf Presber, is now one of Germany's most brilliant and popular novelists, but the curls, alas, are gone.

Before I was seven my father was made Rector of the gymnasium at Corbach in the Principality of Waldeck. Our home there was in a wing of the gymnasium, an old building which had been a monastery. It was a delightful place to play in. The walls were six feet thick and the windows, set deep in them, made niches and dark corners for hide and seek. And there were enormous chimneys for smoking ham, bacon and sausages. At the end of a long corridor was the *Rumpelkammer,* a large room where all sorts of mysterious things were stored, and where on rainy days my little brothers and I loved to snoop around in search of treasure to be found in trunk or chest. An ideal playground for us was the cloistered garden with its centuries-old trees.

It must have been in Corbach that my taste for books had its beginning. Testimony to this was my seventh birthday party. Receiving my little friends and graciously accepting their presents, I took a book that had been given me and went upstairs where I shut myself in my room until I was retrieved by my mother. One of the great events of my childhood had been the discovery that I could read a story book all by myself. It was about this time that I began to draw with pencil or colored crayon and to paint with watercolors. One day when my mother found me drawing something quite unintelligible, she asked me what it was. My reply was cubistic. "I don't know yet," I said, "whether it is going to be a bureau or Grandma."

But it was in Hamburg where my father became the founder and president of the Wilhelm Gymnasium that my life really began to take shape. In this I was fortunate, for Hamburg, founded as a free city, had retained its spiritual and political liberty through all the centuries, and its cosmopolitan independence of thought and liberality of outlook were a much better influence for a boy in his formative years than the bureaucracy and militarism of Prussia.

The gymnasium on the Moorweide was in a new stone building of impressive dimensions. Our home next door was spacious and comfortable. Every piece of furniture in it, even the kitchen utensils, had been designed by my grandfather, who hated the flimsy or ornate. The library was the most lived in room in the house. On its walls, reaching to the ceiling, and broken only by the wide fireplace, were rows and rows of books. In the center was a long study table, and by a mullioned window was Father's high standing desk at which he always did his writing. I often think of him standing there working at his papers, as he smoked his long pipe with the bowl resting on the floor. (It was for such desks that the *lange Pfeife* was invented.) From the time I was eleven this room was the happiest retreat of my brothers and myself. Afternoons when we came in from school we sat before the fire or at the long table carefully turning the leaves of some favorite book. We were allowed to look at any of the volumes that took our fancy, as we had been taught to treat them with respect. A treasure, brought out only on special occasions, was the illuminated vellum edition of *Theuerdank,* the romantic sixteenth-century poem of the adventures of Emperor Maximilian I written under his direction. The illustrations were by one of Albrecht Dürer's noted pupils. To us they were as thrilling as any motion picture can be to the youngsters of today. There were also some books on horsemanship—large folios with pictures of horses being trained in the complicated movements of the classical Spanish high school; of gorgeous festivals and funeral processions; of knights in armor trying to unseat one another in gala tournament. And there were the oblong volumes of Winckelmann with steel engravings of Greek and Roman sculptures; Schwind's charming illustrations of fairy stories and legends; natural history books; and the works of Wilhelm Busch, gay artist and philosopher whose delightful comic drawings and satirical poems are still beguiling to me.

In having my tastes so well directed at such an early age, I feel that destiny was as kind to me as it was to Gordon Craig, whose mother, Ellen Terry, once told me that she attributed the awakening of his instinct for color and line to the old Japanese wood-engravings with which she had decorated his nursery.

Sometimes when my brothers and I came to an exciting picture or passage, we forgot Mother's admonition that we must be silent in order not to disturb Father at his work. One look from him, however, was enough to subdue us, as we were quite in awe of him. Yet I do not think our fear could have been very real, for we always looked forward to the days when he took us on long walks through the old town, along the Fleet canals and to the harbor or out into the country on the banks of the Elbe, talking to us of many things—of history and architecture, and of ways of finding beauty for ourselves wherever we might be. As we grew older these conversations were like as not held in Latin or English or French, so that whatever we were doing, we were learning something and having a good time at it.

Father had well-defined ideas about the training and care of the body. He was himself an athlete and wished us to be the same. We were taught to fence, to shoot and to ride, and at school we had our daily gymnastic exercises, and we played strenuous games, including football.

As a rule our studying was done in our rooms, but when it was cold we went to the library, and there would be the five of us—Mother knitting by the hearth, Father standing at his tall desk, Siegfried, two years younger than I, Hugo, four years my junior, and myself, sitting at the long table. When we were permitted to stay up late, if there was time after our studying had been done, we sat around the fire for a chat. We were eager listeners when Father talked, and there were always questions to be asked and answered. Our family history interested us deeply, and we would beg to be told about it: about the first van Gents who came to notice many centuries ago in Holland; of how at the beginning of the sixteenth century they fled their native land because as followers of Luther they were open to persecution; of Baron Willem Joseph van Gent, the naval hero, whose tomb is one of the sculptural masterpieces in the Cathedral of Utrecht; and of Georg Genthius, the Persian scholar, who was sent by the Grand Elector Friedrich Wilhelm on a message of good will to the Shah of Persia. All around us on the walls of our living room were portraits of relatives, some of them painted in pastel or oil two hundred years before by Gruson, to whom my mother's family was related. There were steel engravings of my father's Swiss granduncle, Heinrich Zschokke, who won renown as a man of letters during the early part of the nineteenth century. One of his religious works, *Hours of Meditation,* was a favorite of Queen Victoria, who had it translated into English. (In the marketplace of the town of Aarau in Switzerland stands a monument to his memory.) There were also the lithographs of my father's uncle, Karl Rosenkranz, the Hegelian, who occupied the chair of Philosophy once held by Immanuel Kant at the University of Königsberg; and a portrait of my grandfather, Friedrich Wilhelm Genthe, the author of some thirty books on philological and literary subjects; and of my maternal grandfather, Hugo Zober, government architect during the reign of King Friedrich Wilhelm IV of Prussia. The stories told us of our heritage were not passed on to us with any sense of superiority, but with a feeling of responsibility, as of something of value only if we lived up to it.

A beautiful element in our home life was the relationship of our parents. Through all the years of my boyhood, and up to the time of his death, I never heard my father say a discourteous word to my mother. His devotion to her was touching. Whenever he brought her a gift, no matter how small it was, flowers, a book or a pretty scarf, it was always accompanied by a bit of "homemade" poetry. She was indeed a rare and lovely character. Her tact and sympathy were unfailing. We boys could always go to her about anything, and we would leave with the feeling that our problem was on the way to its best possible solution. All children loved her because of her understanding of them. An instance of this was the manner in which, when we were quite young and groups of our little playmates came to visit us after school, she persuaded them to leave before Father came in for his hour's study. Not wishing to hurt their feelings, and knowing how the slightest present excites the heart of a child, she tied up little gifts for them bearing a card which read: "To be opened at home before five o'clock."

My father had no income except the modest stipendium from the gymnasium. Under Mother's skilful budgeting it was translated into fine and graceful living. Our home was admirably run. In the cellar was a variety of good wines, and there was always a margin for the amenities of life, for hospitality, amusement, music, and dancing for us children.

The real event of the year was Christmas. I remember how astonished I was when, reading my first English book, I came to a passage in which one of the children remarked in the most casual manner, "Tomorrow will be Christmas." With us Christmas was a glorious holiday, to be looked forward to and prepared for months ahead. In September we began to put by a little of our pocket money each week for presents for the family. Then there were the lists to be made up, one of the things we wanted to give, and the other—it was called the "wishing list"—of the presents we hoped to receive. The former required a great deal of mathematical calculation, and whether we could spare twenty-five pfennigs for a present to a brother was often a serious problem.

More important to our parents than the presents we had for them were the evidences of the progress we had made in our studies. There were drawings to be done, musical compositions to be practiced and recitations in various languages to be memorized. On Christmas Eve in the afternoon we children were sent out with the two maids to distribute gifts to the poor. And very superior we felt tramping along through the snow, our arms filled with bundles, quite puffed up at the thought that we were public benefactors.

In the evening the whole household, including the servants, who were that night members of the family, gathered in the living room. First came the recitations and the piano pieces, and afterwards the exhibition of our drawings. Then Mother played the accompaniment while we all sang "Holy Night." At the last note Father opened the door into the library and there was the Tree! When we had exhausted our adjectives on its beauty, our attention was turned to the long table piled high with presents for everyone. The servants received theirs first, and when our turn came there was much eager inspection of one another's gifts, and always some real surprise in the way of something we had wanted very badly but had not dared to place on the "wishing list." And of course everyone received a *Naschteller*—a plate of Christmas cakes, lebkuchen, marzipan and chocolates.

German education in those days was still influenced by the monastic traditions of the medieval schools. We took up Latin at nine, French at ten, English at eleven, and Greek at twelve. Hours were long and discipline rigid. In my teachers I had unusual advantages. Professor Rambeau, who taught English and French, had evolved an original method of imparting the correct knowledge of phonetics and would not tolerate the slightest carelessness or inaccuracy in pronunciation. Professor Schader was my teacher in mathematics, for which I had no talent whatsoever. Algebraic and geometrical problems were more or less a nightmare to me. Knowing that I would carefully prepare myself for it, the wise professor arranged for me to coach a younger student. This I did for several semesters and so managed to acquire enough knowledge to pass the very severe examinations for university entrance. Professor Reinsdorf and my father were my instructors in Latin and Greek. Well they understood how to make what might have been dull and tedious lessons both fascinating and inspiring.

In 1886, when I was seventeen, my father died. It was hard for us to realize that we had to go on without his wise guidance. Although my mother had never talked to us about money, we knew that aside from her government pension there was little capital. Some good friends had suggested that my mother take *pensionnaires*. It was through their influence that a number of distinguished young foreigners found their way into our home. At one time we had with us, besides two Indian princes, the son of the ex-King of Burma, and the son of the president of Venezuela, all eager to learn German. Siegfried interrupted his studies for a whole year to follow one of the princes as his private secretary to his domain in East Bengal.

One New Year's Eve we decided that instead of going out to celebrate we would have a different kind of party. So we sat around the large table in the living room, finding out how many languages we could muster to our credit. Altogether we managed recitations in fifteen languages: six European, several Indian dialects, ancient and modern Greek, Latin, Persian and Hebrew. This may sound like a very dull New Year's Eve for a group of lively young men, but, thanks to the Christmas punch which my mother had brewed, we had a gay evening.

The day came when it was necessary to take thought of my future. I had always wanted to be a painter. My mother said that if her cousin, Adolf Menzel, one of Germany's foremost painters, thought my drawing and painting worth while, I might study art. Taking my sketches with me, I went to Berlin to see him. After looking at them critically, he said, "You have some talent, but considering the finances of your family, I feel it would be advisable for you to follow in the footsteps of your father and grandfathers. You will paint, of course, but not for fame or profit."

It was then that my mind turned toward Jena, one of the oldest and most picturesque seats of learning in Germany. I knew that later I would have to spend some semesters in Berlin where we had many friends and relatives, but I was eager first to know something of the charm of student life in an old university—one where freedom of thought was permitted and where there was a close relationship between students and professors. My intentions were further bound to Jena through what might be called the early American influence in my life. One of its distinguished graduates, for whose books I had great admiration, was Andrew D. White, who for many years was president of Cornell University and later the American Ambassador to Germany. Besides his daughter, whom I had met, I had other American friends who were living there, among them the sisters of Professor Huss and Professor Andrew F. West, both of Princeton.

In order to qualify for any university in Germany at that time it was necessary to take the *Abiturienten Examen,* a severe test in a variety of subjects. There were lengthy Latin and German essays to be composed, a Latin translation from a Greek text to be made, a series of advanced problems in algebra and geometry to be worked out, and oral exercises in Latin, Greek, French, English and General History. Having been amply prepared for this ordeal, I passed without difficulty, and was ready to begin my university life as a student at Jena.

M Y entrance to Jena in 1888 had a humorous touch. The student corps, or fraternities, had no houses for living quarters. Nor were there college dormitories. The students, no matter what their position or means, had to rent their rooms from the townspeople who were known as "philisters," to mark them as outsiders from the noble body of students. These philisters played an important part in the life of the university, as they were often the bankers as well as the landlords of the students. The best I could find was the town coffin-maker. To get to my room I had to pass through a dark, narrow hallway flanked on each side with his *memento mori* achievements. My humble lodging was scantily furnished and the bed was so short that I had to put a chair at the end.

Chapter Two

These minor hardships were of little significance, for I was happy to be living in a town where so many of Germany's great poets and scholars had lived and worked. Everywhere one walked tablets set in the walls called them to mind. Here Goethe had written his *Hermann and Dorothea,* or Schiller his *Wallenstein.* There Hegel had made his home when he was a professor at the university, or Fichte or Schelling had clarified some perplexing concept. In the Black Bear Inn Luther had halted for a brief respite on his flight to the Wartburg. The medieval architecture of both town and university could not have failed to fascinate me after a city like Hamburg where most of the old buildings had been destroyed in a great fire seventy years before. A favorite rendezvous of the students was the Town Hall, celebrated to them not so much for its sixteenth-century clock as for its wine-cellar. And the surrounding hills, crowned with the ruins of many a feudal castle, invited one to long and romantic rambles.

The fraternity I joined was the Gothania, an unassuming and

modest corps in which one could enjoy life and yet devote more time to study and athletics than to the drinking of beer.

But if we worked hard we played hard, and I have a happy recollection of the numerous pranks which are ever the bright spots in student life. In the center of the marketplace stood a monument to the founder of the university, the Grand Elector Johann Friedrich of Saxony, irreverently called "Hanfried" by the students. Frequently on Saturday nights or on the eve of a holiday, our return from the *Kommers* (beer drinking bout) through the streets to our rooms was neither quiet nor orderly. At such times we had to be on the lookout for the police, who as representatives of the long arm of the law were called by the students "Polyp," which is slang for octopus. One night late, after a revel, in passing through the marketplace, I could not resist the temptation of climbing to the top of the monument and placing my hat jauntily on "Hanfried's" august head. I was about to descend when Nemesis, in the shape of the police, bore down upon us from around the corner. As my companions had their backs turned and could not see the approaching menace, I called out the customary warning, "Polyp! Polyp!" They scattered, leaving me, as I came to the ground, in the hands of the enemy. Firmly collared I was taken to the police station and booked to appear the next day for sentence, when I was found guilty of "applying to one in the lawful pursuit of his duty engaged, Grand-Ducal constable, a from-the-animal-kingdom-derived expression." Given the choice of spending three days in the student jail or paying a fine of forty-five marks, I chose the latter.

In a class in archeological field work, our professor had taken us to the site of an old Roman encampment about an hour's walk from the town, where ancient Roman coins, pots and implements of various kinds had been found. Our digging had brought forth no results. We felt that something had to be done about it. Securing a plain earthen beer mug, we engraved on it in classical Roman lettering a Latin dedication: "Caius Julius Caesar to his dear Professor Klopfleisch, in fond remembrance." Burying it in the ruins, we removed all traces of our duplicity. That afternoon we maneuvered things so that the professor made his excavations in the spot where the stein reposed. When he struck its hard surface a beatific expression lighted up his face. Suddenly it gave way to a look of tragic disappointment as he lifted the stein to the light. After silently returning it to the grave we had dug for it, and without looking at us, he said, "It's time to be going." A thoroughly sheepish and dejected group of students followed him back to town. From then on we were the assiduous and devoted pupils of this fine old professor.

It was not often that we had the time for playful interludes of escape, for the discipline was strict and the curriculum heavy. Although there was no roll call or checking up of our attendance at the lectures, we had to work conscientiously if we hoped to get a degree. Unlike the system in American universities, the object of all teaching was not merely to pour a definite amount of knowledge into our heads, but rather to train us to carry out independent research and to use the knowledge thus gained as an approach to a problem. Having decided on classical philology as one of my major studies, I attended a series of lectures by Professor Georg Goetz, the great authority on Plautus. Also I became a member of his Philological Seminary, where a small group of students, not more than ten or twelve, exercised their minds and their linguistic abilities in discussing with him the difficulties presented by the Greek and Roman classics. The discussions were always conducted in Latin, and though I doubt that it was Ciceronian in purity and elegance, the method developed the habit of logical thinking and clarity of expression.

Rudolf Eucken, who ten years later was awarded the Nobel prize in literature, was my professor of philosophy. His lectures on psychology were stimulating and inspiring. I had wanted to know more about Darwin's theories, so, although they were outside of my curriculum, I attended Professor Ernst Haeckel's lectures. From him I learned a lesson which was to be of significance in later years. He never tired of impressing his pupils with the necessity of training the eye so that it would really see things. He constantly admonished us to draw with pencil or chalk the objects before us, no matter how imperfect the result might be. This was at a time when photography had not become easily accessible to everyone. I am sure that today Professor Haeckel would urge his pupils to train their eyes by making photographs. This great scientist loved the old university and he consistently refused many flattering offers from larger and wealthier institutions because he did not wish to leave Jena.

The relationship between professor and students was much closer at Jena than in the larger universities, as the classes were small, which made it possible for a teacher to take an interest in the individual pupil. Sometimes when a particularly puzzling question was under discussion he would say, "I think we will get along better if we take our problem out into the open." Then we would go to some garden restaurant where over a stein of beer the solution would be clarified. In one of my classes there were only three students. The first morning our professor took his place on the platform, and looking at us over his glasses, said, "Three is always an audience." Then coming down from his desk, he added, "Since we are such a little family, I will just sit here and talk with you. You can interrupt me whenever you like, and I will be glad to answer your questions."

Almost every week one of our professors would ask a few of us to his home for dinner and we would sit around the table for hours, talking and asking questions. It got to be so that we knew just what we were going to have for dinner and it became quite a joke with us. "Professor Gelzer's? Ah, then we shall have veal." Or, "Professor Goetz's?—Roast beef." Professor Haeckel sometimes invited us to his home to meet his daughter, who was the ideal Gretchen type—buxom and ruddy and the perfect picture of health —but so shy and reticent that none of us could get as much as a word out of her except when we were arriving or departing.

In order to pay my expenses at Jena, it had been necessary for me to enter competitions for some of the many scholarships that were available. In some cases to qualify meant only the recommendation of one or two professors. For others there were examinations. A memorable experience of this sort had to do with one of the most desirable scholarships, for which I had to prove a thorough knowledge of Latin, Greek and Hebrew. I had devoted two years of study to Hebrew, scarcely enough for such a difficult language. When the time came for the examination I was at home on vacation in Hamburg, and I had to make the journey to the little town where the distinguished clergyman in charge of the competition lived. The Latin and Greek tests went off quite smoothly. As we came to the ordeal of Hebrew I was very nervous. I knew I would probably be lost if I were given an unfamiliar passage from the Old Testament. A kind fate induced him to give me a psalm that I had studied thoroughly, and I was able to answer all his questions correctly. He did not express either satisfaction or disapproval, but suddenly climbed on a chair, reached to the top of a high stove in the corner—it was summer and there was no fire in it—and took down a box of special cigars. Offering me one he asked, "Do you enjoy smoking?" I knew then that I had won the scholarship, and I bravely smoked that cigar—one of the few I have smoked in my whole life.

Although I had attended several courses of theological lectures, chiefly to please my mother whose grandfather had been a well-known clergyman, I had never had ecclesiastical tendencies. Shortly after graduating from Jena, I took a walking trip in the Thuringian Mountains. Late one Saturday afternoon I came to a village where I found to my surprise that its pastor had been a fellow student of mine. He and his wife insisted that I stay over and spend the night as their guest. "You have come at just the right moment," he said. "I have finished my sermon for tomorrow and now we can celebrate."

After a good dinner we sat long over our wine talking about old times. At breakfast next morning my hostess was almost in tears. "I wish you could see Peter," she exclaimed. "He looks terrible. He simply can't conduct the services. What are we to do?"

There was nothing to be distressed about, I consoled her. The rôle of a guest preacher was one that I could easily assume. I knew the ritual, and Peter's robes would fit me, as we were about the same size. No one would know that I was not a duly ordained minister of the gospel, since there was no newspaper in the village and it was off the beaten track. She was skeptical, but as there was no other way out, she consented to my plan. After an hour spent memorizing the sermon, I took my place in the pulpit. Everything went well, until, thinking that Peter had not been quite emphatic enough, I added a few exhortations of my own. For a moment I thought my hostess was going to faint. But when the old peasant women in the congregation were touched to tears, she smiled reassuringly at me, and Peter's face was saved.

While I was studying Anglo-Saxon with Professor Heinrich Kluge, who wrote the most authoritative German etymological dictionary, I had become interested in a mode of speech, known in America as slang, which had been neglected by our German philologists. Often Americans at the university asked me to explain some of these German phrases which they heard every day but could not find in the dictionary. This gave me the idea of making a collection of them. After two years' work I had compiled a list of about fifteen hundred of the most expressive. As there was no word for them in German, I had to call the collection *Deutsches Slang*.

With youthful temerity I submitted the manuscript to Karl Truebner of Strassburg, an important philological publisher of Germany. He not only accepted it but paid me an advance royalty of two hundred marks, a considerable sum for a German student in those days. In the introduction I had pointed out that some of the most picturesque terms owed their popularity to Prince Bismarck, then Chancellor, who occasionally used them in his speeches in the Reichstag. A few weeks after its publication, I received a letter bearing his beautifully embossed coat of arms. It was dated Friedrichsruh 1892 and read: "I have received with thanks your compilation of German slang and am looking forward

GRANDPARENTS OF ARNOLD GENTHE

GENTHE FAMILY CREST

TOMB OF LT.-ADMIRAL WILLEM J. VAN GENT IN THE CATHEDRAL OF UTRECHT (1672)

GERMANY: LOOKING ACROSS THE RHINE FROM COLOGNE

MARKET DAY IN MARBURG

with interest to your further studies in this hitherto uncultivated field. v. Bismarck."

The book created quite a stir in philological circles. The reviews were favorable and Professor Huss of Princeton devoted several articles to its discussion. My American friends in Jena were delighted. On the other hand my fellow Gothanians were puzzled. "What has gotten into you?" one of them asked. "I thought you were a philologist and now you have written a book on German snakes." He had mistaken the word "Slang" for *"Schlange"* which is German for snake.

Another token of my American friendships is the scars of my only duel. One afternoon while sitting in a beer garden listening to the music with some American girls, a member of a corps not well disposed toward the Gothania in passing our table made some remark in a loud voice about those "conceited Americans." The criticism constituted a point of honor. It could not go unchallenged. There was an exchange of cards and subsequently a duel of thirty rounds with rapiers was arranged.

While the wounds from a rapier are mostly surface cuts which are not dangerous unless an artery is severed, yet in thirty rounds much blood can be spilled. My opponent, who was two inches taller than I, inflicted eight cuts on the top of my head, so that I was not sorry when he passed out at the end of the twentieth round.

A few days previously one of the girls had asked me to name my favorite flower. In fun I had told her it was the sunflower. The morning after the duel a wagonload of enormous sunflowers drew up before the house, much to the disgust of my landlady who delivered the card and went away muttering over the "strange ways and crazy extravagance of those foreigners."

When I was able to be about again I went home to Hamburg for my vacation. In order to prevent infection the whole top of my head had been shaved, the scars giving it the appearance of a railway chart. My mother was horrified. "No one must see you," she declared. Much to my delight I was banished for two weeks to the beautiful island of Helgoland.

During my second year in Jena I was translating some articles from American and English medical journals into German for Dr. Otto Binswanger, the head of the Neurological Institute. One day he told me that Friedrich Nietzsche had been brought to the institute by his mother for observation. "Would you like to go with me when I visit him?" he asked.

As Nietzsche was then the most important philosopher in Europe, it was an event for an obscure student to have the opportunity of seeing him. When we went in he was crouched in a corner of his room, a strange and spectral figure. His face was livid. His enormous mustache seemed to have grown limp under its own weight. Beneath his bushy brows his glowering eyes looked out into space as if they were seeing things beyond human understanding. Dr. Binswanger spoke to him several times. There was no answer. He was so completely detached from the outside world that neither sight nor sound made any impression upon him.

Upon leaving I said to the doctor, "He looks like a captive eagle."

"Yes," was the response, given with a sad shake of the head, "an eagle that has flown too high."

One of the members of the Philological Seminary was Lucien Waggener of St. Louis, a Princeton graduate. He had a good knowledge of Latin and he got along well in his classes. On the outside it was rather difficult for him as he knew little German. Because of my early training in phonetics, I felt that I could teach him enough of the language in a month to carry on an ordinary everyday conversation. Some of my fellow students declared such a feat was impossible and made a little bet with me.

The first thing I did was to transfer him from his lodgings, where English was spoken, to the home of a clergyman where no one could speak it, and where there was a beautiful young daughter. This was in a village about three miles from the university. Every day we walked back and forth together, conversing in German. I insisted upon his pronouncing each word correctly, as it is much easier to learn a new tongue in this way. At the end of three weeks he spoke German with a fluency and a feeling for idioms that quite astonished me. His vocabulary was not large but his pronunciation was faultless and he gave the impression of knowing the language perfectly. After he left Jena I lost track of him until 1932 when I received a letter from him. In looking through *Who's Who in America* he had come upon my name and the memory of old Jena days had impelled him to write a poem which he enclosed.

An occasional visitor to the lectures when he was in residence at the Schloss on the hill was the Grand Duke Karl Alexander, ruler of Saxe-Weimar and the honorary "Rector Magnificentissimus" of the university. Although advanced in years, he always preferred to sit on the hard wooden benches with the students. Then, taking out his pencil and notebook, he would jot down a few notes, after which he would indulge in a nap, much to the amusement of the students, who would whisper to one another, "Look, His Royal Highness is now governing his realm." A grand old soul, he had his eccentricities which were often material for anecdotes in the old *Simplicissimus,* a journal renowned throughout Europe for its trenchant satire.

He was related to nearly every ruling family on the Continent, and on his seventieth birthday a brilliant gathering of royalty came to the capital at Weimar for the ceremonies. The program included a grand parade and a court ball to which representatives of all the student bodies of Jena were invited. With two others I was selected to appear for the Gothania, all decked out in the gala costume of the corps: black velvet coat crossed by the green, white and red sash of our colors, green velvet barret with white ostrich feather, white riding breeches, high patent leather boots, and rapier at the side. The parade was attended by kings and queens, princes and dukes and their consorts. Near the Grand Duke, in the center of the reviewing stand, sat his nephew, Kaiser Wilhelm, engaged in animated conversation with young Wilhelmina of Holland. Remote from his mind then was the thought that thirty years later, as an exile from the Fatherland, he would find refuge and security in her little kingdom.

The student division of the parade was equestrian. Good horses were scarce in Weimar, and they had all been commandeered by the members of the wealthier student bodies. I had to be content with an old nag evidently more accustomed to wagon harness than to the saddle. Directly ahead of me on a fine mount rode the representative of the smartest corps. When he got to the reviewing stand and was about to make a salute in a grand manner, his horse shied, throwing him ignominiously to the ground, while my old Rosinante walked quietly along with head high.

That night there was a reception at the castle to which all officials and dignitaries, professors, student representatives, and the tradespeople who were purveyors to the court were commanded. One by one we were formally presented to the Grand Duke, who had a gracious word for everyone.

At the ball which followed, all of those who did not belong to court circles had to stand on the side awaiting the command of any royal lady who might fancy one for a partner. After the first dance the Court Chamberlain approached me and said, "Her Royal Highness, the hereditary princess, graciously commands you to dance with her." It was more of an honor than a pleasure, for the lady was distinguished neither by charm nor beauty. Since one was not allowed to speak unless the royal dancing partner opened the conversation, and the "ugly duchess" was not in an expansive mood, the dance was something like a song without words.

Some months later I had another grand-ducal experience. Visiting me in Jena was Abu Achmed Ghuznavi, the prince from East Bengal who had spent some time in our home in Hamburg. His visit was the cause of some excitement in the town and in due time the Hof-Marshal appeared with an invitation from Karl Alexander for luncheon at the castle in Weimar. The Prince said he would be delighted to come, but he would like to bring his private secretary, meaning me, who was no such thing. The Hof-Marshal signified that the wish of the Prince was a command.

The Grand Duke's English was unintelligible, to say the least. The Prince's German was little better. The day was saved by the young princesses who spoke English fluently. They were fascinated by their guest, who was unusually handsome and, to their restricted lives, like a figure out of the *Arabian Nights*. It was not so easy for the Grand Duke, who had such a time meditating about what to say and how to say it in English that he forgot to eat. At the Court table etiquette demands that the plates of each course are removed the moment the royal host has finished with his. As he ate very little, the guests had no chance to do justice to the grand-ducal cuisine.

After four semesters at Jena I went to the University of Berlin for a year. The student life there was something of a letdown, as it had little of the light-hearted gayety and freedom characteristic of Jena. The best one could do was to spend most of the time studying and visiting the museums. Among my professors were some of the greatest scholars in the Empire whose lectures attracted students from all over the world. There were Friedrich Paulsen, Heinrich Treitschke, Adolf Furtwängler, and Wilhelm Wattenbach.

Theodor Mommsen, the historian, who had been a friend of my father's, went out of his way to be hospitable to me. I can still see him, with his piercing eyes and straight white hair, peering over a pile of books in the university library. He was over seventy and he hated the thought of growing old. One afternoon, when we happened to be leaving the library together, I noticed that he was having a hard time getting into his coat and offered to help him.

Turning around he glared at me, declaring, "I am in the habit of helping myself."

He had a number of children—nine or ten I think it was—several of whom were quite young. One day when I had an appointment with him, he was returning to his house and was walking a few yards ahead of me. As he came to the door, a little boy was ringing the bell.

"Whom do you want to see, little one?" Mommsen asked.

The boy looked up at him in amazement. "Don't you know me, Father?" he asked.

Living in Berlin was expensive and the money I had from scholarships and what I had saved from tutoring was not sufficient for my needs. Short stories for family papers and jokes for *Die Fliegende Blätter* and an occasional poem filled in the deficit. Other students, who were friends of mine, were in the same predicament and we had some good times out of our impecunity. We used to have our dinner at a round table in a restaurant where the food was good and the prices fair. Sometimes for relaxation we went to the races where we could not withstand the temptation to bet. If we lost, as was frequently the case, we did not let it affect our spirits. When we were entirely cleaned out, we would spend our last mark on a flower for the buttonhole, and go to the terrace of the Kranzler Café, on Unter den Linden, where as a noble gesture over an ice or a cup of coffee we looked down in a superior manner at the passersby, all the while listing our possessions which might have some value with the pawnbroker.

As we could not then afford to join our companions at the round table, we made the excuse that we were tired of the food there and wanted to try another restaurant. When they insisted upon knowing where we were going, we told them to the Fürsten Halle (Prince's Hall), the name we had given to the public soup kitchen where the knives and forks and spoons were attached to the table by little chains—a practice which did not appeal to us. After some discussion as to ways and means, we would appear in our best afternoon outfits, high hats and all, and explain to the manager that we had been commissioned by an American magazine to write some articles on the public soup kitchens of Germany. We were then permitted to use our own silverware which we had brought with us.

We were past masters at skimming the cream from life at

little cost to our always dwindling finances. During the season, when funds were low, we were able to enjoy the opera and to be paid for doing so, by acting as "supers," carrying banners or spears, and marching on and off the stage with the knock-kneed army in *Aïda*.

One of the group at the round table was Hermann Sudermann, who had not yet made his mark as a dramatist. One night he came with tickets for all of us for the opening performance of *Die Ehre,* his first play. "They are scattered all over the house," he informed us, "and I expect you to applaud vigorously at the end of every act." It was a thrilling evening. The play was a great success and we saw our dear friend rise, in a few hours, from obscurity to lasting fame. Shortly before his death he sent me an affectionately inscribed copy of his novel, *The Mad Professor*.

A pleasant change from the daily grind was the weekly dinner at the home of my mother's cousin, Adolf Menzel. These invitations came, I am sure, from his desire to help out with my budget. Sometimes he took me with him when he went sketching. On one of these outings we went to the bicycle track where he made innumerable drawings, particularly of the hands of a bicycle-rider, for a canvas he was working on. When it was finished, one had a hard time finding the bicycle-rider, it was such a tiny figure. This detail was an example of the man's thoroughness, a quality which some of our modern painters seem to consider superfluous.

At an official banquet where I was his guest, he was wholly indifferent to the members of the court and other dignitaries who were there in all their splendor. Scarcely touching his food, he spent the evening making sketches in a small book. On one of his birthdays, the Emperor, who esteemed him highly, held a parade of the Grenadiers of the Guard in his honor. Menzel was less than five feet tall and he made a curious contrast walking with the Emperor before the troops in review, all of whom were six feet or over, their helmets adding another foot to their height.

Another little incident of my days in Berlin is what seems quaintly Victorian in the light of present day manners. I happened to be quite devoted to a young girl whose parents had very strict ideas of the proprieties. We were not allowed to be alone together except for an occasional walk in the afternoon. As we were keen about each other, this was a deprivation. We had a happy thought. At the railroad stations couples were always coming and going, and their greetings or leave-takings were accepted as a matter of course. With the aid of a time table we spent the hour allotted for our walk hurrying from station to station, pretending that one of us was about to take the train, thus enjoying many a tender farewell.

Back in Jena, after a year in Berlin, a subject for my doctor's thesis became a great problem. The solution came from a chain of unexpected circumstances. After the death of my father, there had come into my possession a number of the unpublished manuscripts of the great Hegel, whose widow had given them to my granduncle, Karl Rosenkranz, who had been a disciple of Hegel and was preparing his biography. I had never given them thorough attention as they were harder to decipher than a Greek palimpsest. Going through them again, I came across the first drafts of three letters to Goethe, which so interested me that I set myself the task of deciphering them. They were concerned with Goethe's Theory of Color, and shed an entirely new light upon one phase of Hegelian philosophy. Through the courtesy of the Grand Duchess of Saxe-Weimar, who was the custodian of the *Goethe und Schiller Archiv,* I was permitted to search through Goethe's unpublished letters, finding not only the three of which I had first drafts, but five others of which no record had been made.

Not long after I received an emphatic letter from Hegel's son, Professor Karl von Hegel, who occupied the chair of Medieval History at the University of Erlangen. He declared that whatever manuscripts I had of his father's belonged to him, as they had been entrusted by his mother to Professor Rosenkranz merely for use in the biography. With misgivings I journeyed to Erlangen, expecting to encounter a stern and imposing personage. Instead I was greeted by a genial old gentleman who invited me to lunch.

"We can talk better after we have had a glass of wine," he said with a kindly smile.

During the meal he did not mention my mission. When it was over he took me into his library. "Now," he said, "let us see what you have to show me."

I had carefully arranged the manuscripts so that the most illegible were at the top of the pile.

He looked them over for a few minutes, then turning to me, inquired, "Do you mean to say you can really read these?"

Explaining that it had taken me several weeks, I added, "If it had not been for your colleague, Professor Wattenbach, with whom I studied paleography, I could never have done so."

"Well," he laughed, "since you can read them and I am sure I cannot, you may keep them," and he gave me permission to use them for publication. The eight letters to Goethe, with my notes, were published in the Goethe *Jahrbuch*. After coming to America, feeling that the manuscripts should be kept in a safe place where they would be accessible to students, I transferred most of them to the Harvard Library.

It was during my visit to Erlangen that my attention was drawn in the university library to a tenth-century codex of Lucan, the importance of which had never been investigated. Since my father had chosen for the theme of his doctor's thesis the "Life of Lucan," I thought that a critical analysis of this manuscript, establishing its relation to the other codices through which Lucan has been handed down to us, might be a good theme for my thesis. Professor Goetz liked the idea, and the volume was sent to Jena for my use. When one considers that Lucan, a contemporary of Vergil, was after all a minor poet whose only contribution to literature was the lengthy epic *Pharsalia* (commemorating the victory of Caesar over Pompey in 48 B.C.), the discovery of a few variant readings which might prove a closer relation to the original text, would hardly change the poet's place in the world's literature. But the subject furnished a good theme for a doctor's thesis.

The task I had set myself involved, first, an accurate word-for-word comparison with the published versions, then a detailed description of the manuscript and finally an argument endeavoring to ascribe to this codex a definite place in the text tradition. Since I had to write it in Latin, it was at least a good discipline in concentration and logical argument. It meant a whole year of cloistered seclusion. There were weeks when I went out only for fresh air and exercise, cooking my meals on an alcohol stove in my room. One evening when I was scrambling some eggs, the pan slipped and its contents were spilled on a page of the priceless manuscript. After a good deal of frantic experiment all traces of the disaster were removed, and I blessed that marvelous tenth-century vellum and ink which so nobly withstood the onslaught of nineteenth-century butter and eggs.

That winter, having to devote all my time to work on my thesis, I did not go home for Christmas. Resisting the sentimental temptation to have my solitude brightened by a Christmas tree, I celebrated by brewing myself a punch and unpacking the presents which my good mother had sent me from Hamburg. I had just settled down to read, when I was startled by a strange sound coming from the stairway. The little house, of which I was the sole occupant, was supposed to be haunted. It was for that reason I had been able to rent it for a very small sum. I grabbed my pistol and bravely opened the door, calling out the customary "Who's there?" No answer. From halfway up the stairs two big shining eyes were blinking at me. Gradually, my sight becoming accustomed to the darkness, I recognized that the intruder was an owl, apparently with one of its wings injured. Seeking shelter from the cold, it had found its way into the house and was hopping up the stairs. Though it refused my offered hospitality, I felt it was a good omen to have this bird—not a "bird of evil" but one that was sacred to Pallas Athena, the ancient Goddess of Wisdom—pay me a visit on this Christmas night. With renewed enthusiasm I went back to my desk and managed, in a few hours, to clear up a difficult problem that had been puzzling me for weeks.

In due time I obtained my doctor's degree from the philosophical faculty, and when the thesis had been published (in those days the candidate had to bear the cost of printing) the reviews in the philological journals were favorable and one verdict pleased me especially: "His Latinity is simple and faultless."

Feeling that some relaxation was now due me, I went to Paris for a course in French literature and History of Art at the Sorbonne. The need for frugality prevented me from tasting the gayeties of that beautiful city, but frequent visits to the Louvre and other galleries, and an occasional theater made my sojourn there a pleasant one, and I went home to Hamburg with the intention of seeking an instructorship in a German university.

Early in 1895 Baron Heinrich von Schroeder, whose two brothers had been schoolmates of mine at the Wilhelm Gymnasium, came to Hamburg. He had married the daughter of Mervyn Donohue, the San Francisco banker, and wanted a tutor for his son, Heini, one who was familiar with the methods of the German gymnasium and who would be willing to go with him to California for at least a year. The job was offered to me and I eagerly accepted, for all through my student days it had been my dream that some day I might visit America.

In the spring of that year we sailed for New York. Little did I think, when the shores of Germany disappeared from view, that instead of *"Auf Wiedersehn"* I was saying "Good-by."

OLD CHINATOWN

I N 1895 the New York skyline was not the thing of moun-
tainous and bewildering beauty it is today. Yet sailing into
the harbor was an exciting adventure. The moment the ship
pointed its nose into the channel the air seemed filled with that
electric vitality which is so peculiarly New York. The city had not
then spread its mammoth hands over the whole of the island, and
its population was not larger than in some of the European capitals. But it had an overpowering quality. The summer heat was
breathless and my impressions of the few days we stopped there
en route to San Francisco remain a dim but feverish fantasy of
hurrying, nervous crowds, clanging trolleys, cigar-store Indians,
glittering lights, and in the hotels brass cuspidors and the buzz of
innumerable electric fans.

*Chapter
Three*

31

On the seven days' journey across the continent I was in a
state of constant wonder at the rich and incredible distances—the
expanse of the corn and wheat fields, the sweep of prairie and
desert; the broad swift flow of the rivers; the height and immensity
of the mountain ranges; and at last the deep fertility of the California hills and valleys. To one who had come from a civilization
which had been centuries in the making, the pace of the American
epic was only short of a miracle.

San Francisco found its way straight to my heart. For here
was a city with a flavor all its own. The von Schroeders had rented
a furnished house on Sutter Street near Van Ness Avenue. As
soon as I had unpacked I went for a long walk, up hill and down
and up again, until the whole glamorous panorama was spread out
before me. The approach through vestibule of cliff and mountain-
side; the golden stretch of the dunes; the Bay, misted by the silver
fog, or captured by the softly incandescent blue of a clear sky; the
full-rigged barkentines and the many little ships, always coming

and going, their sails bellying in the stiff breeze; the long curve of the waterfront with its rows of liners and sailing vessels from all ports of the world, tied up at their berths or lying at anchorage in the stream; the spicy tang of the sea and of cargoes piled high on the quays; Fishermen's Wharf and its rainbow fleet; the deep-throated songs of the Italian fishermen as they mended their nets; Telegraph Hill, where the fishermen's shacks clung like swallows' nests to the sides of the cliff—against the background of the variant sky they created a mural of such beauty that during the fifteen years I was there my eyes never tired of it.

The city itself with its agglomerate architecture—part French, part Spanish, part Italian, part mid-Victorian, and wholly San Franciscan—might have been accused of ugliness. Looked down upon from a hilltop, it held a strange enchantment. The San Francisco fog has never been sufficiently glorified. It has neither the impenetrable yellow murkiness of the London variety nor the heavy stifling sootiness of the mist that rolls in on New York across the Hudson. The fogs are pure sea water condensed by the clean hot breath of the interior valleys and blown across the peninsula by the trade winds. They come in, not an enveloping blanket but a luminous drift, conferring a magic patina on the most common-place structures, giving them an air of age and mystery.

Like all good tourists I had a Baedeker. A sentence saying, "It is not advisable to visit the Chinese quarter unless one is accompanied by a guide," intrigued me. There is a vagabond streak in me which balks at caution. As soon as I could make myself free, I was on my way to Chinatown, where I was to go again and again, for it was this bit of the Orient set down in the heart of a Western metropolis that was to swing my destiny into new and unforeseen channels.

A small city within a city, it occupied only eight blocks which ran in fours up Grant Avenue and Stockton Street from California Street. Yet within it throbbed the pulse of China.

The painted balconies were hung with windbells and flow-ered lanterns. Brocades and embroideries, bronzes and porcelains, carvings of jade and ivory, of coral and rose crystal, decorated the shop-windows. The wall-spaces between were bright with scarlet bulletins and gilt signs inscribed in the picturesque Chinese characters. Shuffling along in single file were the dark-clad silent figures of the men, their faces strange, inscrutable. Children in gay silken costume thronged the sidewalks and doorways. From the windows in the "Street of the Sing-song Girls," bright eyes peered out from under brighter headdresses.

In the dark alleys and courtyards rickety staircases led up to tenement hovels where the derelicts of the underworld found cover. The most sinister of these was the "Devil's Kitchen," an evil-smelling courtyard where drug addicts and suspicious characters of all sorts cooked on charcoal burners the scraps of food they had picked up in the streets, and came out only at night to squat on doorsills or to pursue their insidious ways. There was the "Street of the Gamblers" with its rows of sliding solid iron doors to be clanked swiftly shut at the approach of the police or the threat of battle with a rival concessionaire. The smell of the place—it was a mixture of the scent of sandalwood and exotic herbs from the drugstores, the sickly sweetness of opium smoke, the fumes of incense and roast pork, and the pungent odors from the sausages and raw meat hanging in the "Street of the Butchers." And in the air there was always the sound of temple gongs, the clashing of cymbals and the shrill notes of an orchestra. It was something for me to write home about.

When I looked for pictures to illustrate my letters, there were none to be had except a few inadequate crudely colored postal cards. I tried to make some sketches. As soon as I got out my sketchbook the men, women and children scampered in a panic into doorways or down into cellars. Finding it impossible to get pictures in this way, I decided to try to take some photographs. Up to that time I had never used a camera and knew nothing about photography.

A fortnight after our arrival in San Francisco, the family moved across the Bay to spend the rest of the summer at the Hotel

San Rafael, a fashionable resort of which Baron von Schroeder was the proprietor. Before going I bought several books on photography with the idea of using my leisure to learn something about it.

My days were occupied with tutoring, which gave me little time to myself. Heini was diligent and easy to teach if one knew how to handle him. That he had not been doing so well in his studies had been due to an error in judgment on the part of his former tutor. He loved horses, and, as a punishment for neglecting his books, his mount had been taken away from him. Through my suggestion it was returned to him. Every day he and I went riding together up into the hills while I coached him in the intricacies of Latin and French irregular verbs. Finding lessons no longer a bore, he went ahead rapidly.

Life at the hotel was pleasant but not exciting, and when I could manage an afternoon or evening off, I went to San Francisco where I wandered around, in Chinatown or on Telegraph Hill, beginning to look at things from a photographic view, although I had not yet bought a camera.

The early fall was passed at the von Schroeders' ranchos in San Luis Obispo County. One, the Nacimiento, was a cattle ranch, which spread in an area of fifty thousand acres over hill and valley and mountain range—an extent vaster than many a principality in Germany. The Eagle Ranch, where the family resided, was smaller, but it was large enough to seem boundless to me, with its sweep of orchard and meadow disappearing over the horizon of the rolling terrain. It was beautiful country and my pupil and I went out daily for long rides, often stopping under some great oak for an hour or two of study or pistol practice.

In the meantime I acquired a knowledge of the rudiments of a camera. Now I set out to buy one. It had to be small enough to carry in my pocket, as I had learned that the inhabitants of Chinatown had a deep-seated superstition about having their pictures taken. To them the camera was a "black devil box" in which all the evils of the earth were bottled up, ready to pounce upon

SAN FRANCISCO CHINATOWN:
IN HOLIDAY ATTIRE
STREET OF THE BALCONIES

STREET OF THE GAMBLERS

A STREET CROSSING

them. Not only did the grown people run from it, but the older boys and girls had been trained to gather up their little sisters and brothers at the sight of one and to run into cellars or up the stairways. So I chose a small camera with a Zeiss lens.

Lenses, plates and films were then about twenty times slower than those of today, which enable the modern photographer to obtain perfect snapshots under almost any light condition. For my first experiment I could scarcely have chosen a more difficult subject. The alleys and courtyards were so narrow that the light found its way through them for only an hour or two at midday. In order to get any pictures at all I had to hide in doorways or peer out from an angle of a building at some street corner. But I went bravely ahead.

On the top floor of the house the von Schroeders had taken, a former occupant had fixed up a small closet as a dark-room. It was there I developed my first roll of films. The result was somewhat discouraging. The pictures were either underexposed or not accurately focused, and the moving figures were just a blur caught at the wrong moment. Still it was a thrill to see the images appearing in the dim red light of the attic closet. And one of the pictures came out with such an unusual effect of light and shadow that fifteen years later I considered it worthy of a place in my book, *Pictures of Old Chinatown* (Kennerley, 1913), which, with Will Irwin's text, is the only record ever made of that vanished "Canton of the West."

Then it was that my Chinatown adventure began. Again and again I went there until I became a familiar figure on its streets. Many days I stood for hours at a corner or sat in some wretched courtyard, immobile and apparently disinterested, as I waited, eager and alert, for the sun to filter through the shadows or for some picturesque group or character to appear—a smoker to squat with his pipe, or a group of children in holiday attire.

In time I got to know a number of the most picturesque characters in the quarter. Some of them were denizens of the dark who seldom came out into the light of day. One was a miserable skeleton who had been smoking opium for many years. He practically lived on it. The use of opium had not then been officially forbidden, and no effort was made to keep it under cover. The old man's only source of income was the few nickels given him by the guides who brought tourists to his shack to see a smoker in action. His only friend was a cat, who sat on his chest purring contentedly as it inhaled the fumes from his pipe. A woman sightseer reported him to the Society for the Prevention of Cruelty to Animals. The cat was taken to the animals' refuge where, refusing to eat, it almost died of starvation. Another woman who had been in the tourist group, indignant at the attitude of her companion, had followed up the case. When she found out what had happened, she appealed to the higher authorities. The cat was returned to its master where, snoozing peacefully on his chest, it lived happily ever after.

Some years after the fire I was visiting San Francisco and I wanted to see what the new Chinatown was like. I had never had the services of a guide, but now out of sheer curiosity I engaged one. After we had gone through the shops and walked around a few blocks, he took me to the basement of one of the new buildings. I had not let him know that I had been in Chinatown before. With an air of mystery he said, "If we are fortunate you will see a rare sight—a Chinaman smoking opium." Rapping on the door, he said some words which were supposed to be Chinese. From the other side of it a woman's voice called out, "Is that you, Jim?" When he had said that it was, the door was opened by a slovenly half-Chinese woman in American clothes.

Lying in the corner on a heap of rags was my old friend, looking more than ever like a mummy. For a few moments he paid no attention to me, but went on quietly preparing the opium for his pipe. Suddenly he looked up and a smile spread over his emaciated face. "Hello, Doc," he chirped in his high, thin voice. "Long time no see, how you been?"

Another friend was San Lung, who sat day and night at the corner of Stockton and Clay Streets, so long as there was promise

ARISTOCRATS OF CHINATOWN

PIGTAIL PARADE

A BUSY DAY

of a tourist invasion, telling fortunes. He had a cylindrical box which his clients shook with a circular motion until one of the sticks it contained slipped out. These sticks were painted with Chinese ideographs, the meanings of which he interpreted from a moldy old book. He, too, was parched and cadaverous, but he had a merry twinkle in his eye and an ever-present grin on his toothless mouth. His was a wise humor, and he brought it frequently to bear upon his prophecies when he wanted to give them a personal touch. As parting encouragement he would announce in shrill key, "By-'n'-by you catchee plenty money—maybe." To an elderly maiden or voluminous dowager his augury would be, "By-'n'-by you catchee plenty chillen—maybe."

It was rumored that he had acquired a sizeable bank roll. One day when I strolled by, his chair was vacant. In front of his stand were two policemen who asked me what I wanted.

When I replied that I wanted to see San Lung, they pointed to the doorway. "Well, you can see him all right. He's in there." Going in, I found San Lung lying on a bench with a bullet hole in his head.

"Just another of those high-binder wars—three chinks killed," was the policeman's laconic explanation. The "high-binders" were the "killers" of the tongs, secret organizations which controlled the gambling and slave-girl rackets. The wars were started by the infringement of territorial rights, gambling debts or the abduction of concubines, and they involved just such complicated stories of intrigue and passion as are to be found in the annals of all civilization. The question of why they were called "high-binders" has never been answered, but it was generally conceded that the origin of the term lay in the assassin's custom of binding his hair tightly around the top of his head under his hat so that the police could not catch him by the pigtail.

The "Street of the Gamblers" and the "Devil's Kitchen" furnished some of my most interesting pictures. Chief of Police Biggy, in going through a number of them, recognized two desperate criminals. "You'll get into trouble if they find out that you took their photographs," he said. "They even dare to raise a rumpus when we take them."

Only once in my many ramblings was I in danger. An English photographer whom I had met said he would like to take some night pictures of the "Devil's Kitchen." Had I been alone I would have had no fear, but going there in this instance involved a responsibility, and I asked the Chief to detail a detective to accompany us. We managed to get in without attracting attention as it was pitch dark in the court. But when the flashlight went off like a pistol shot, on the balconies and rushing down the stairways came a shouting, threatening mob. Several shots were fired. "You'd better run for your lives," said the detective, taking us by the arm. Needless to say we beat a hasty retreat.

My excursions to Chinatown were not, however, confined entirely to the darker spots. Often my camera was focused on the temple, or Joss House, with its finely wrought gilt carvings dimmed by the smoke of incense, the grotesque divinities of pewter, bronze or porcelain, and the blackened chimney into the mouth of which all papers with Chinese lettering—scraps, posters, handbills, newspapers—were daily consigned by the official paper-gatherer lest they should be defiled by alien feet. A goad to my collector's instinct was the pawnbrokers' and other small shops where discoveries were to be made. Two of my rarest pieces of archaic jade were found in just such places.

The theater, too, had its fascination for me. It made no difference that I could not understand the language; the significance and the artistry of the pantomime were enough to arouse the enthusiasm of the most blasé spectator. The building itself was a study in ways Chinese. In it were housed all the strata of life to be found in the district. Above the theater, on the second story, lived the manager and stage director. The first floor underground was the home of the "number two" employees. In the Chinese social code actors belonged in the lower strata. Accordingly they were relegated to the second floor underground. On the third flight down were the opium dens where the smokers in various stages drew their dreams from the long pipes. It was this retreat which was immortalized by Frank Norris in his story, *The Third Circle*.

Sometimes one of the big merchants would ask me into his sanctum where he would show me his treasures—a delicately carved crystal, a rare jade, or a peach blow vase. Occasionally I was invited to a festival dinner, where the men sat at table in silken robes and did the eating and drinking while the women, in gorgeous coats and pantaloons and jewelled headdresses, sat behind them, content if their lords and masters regaled them with an occasional tidbit or a sip of tea. These dinners were epicurean events, for the upper class Chinese are gourmets, and the cooks are artists. The ducks were fed on special diets and killed at a particular time. The vegetables were all sorts of strange delicacies—bamboo shoots, sprouted beans, lotus stems for salad, mushrooms—prepared so as to bring out their finest flavors. Tea was brewed from specially processed leaves picked in the bud. The true virtue of these feasts was their absence of grease, so that no matter how many courses there were, one left the table without the feeling that one had eaten too much.

A challenging member of the community was Donaldina Cameron, for many years the head of the Chinese Presbyterian Mission, and a truly noble and courageous woman. At the risk of her life, which was often threatened, she had rescued many girls from the toils of the slave-traffic. Among the Chinese, daughters were not looked upon with favor except as potential concubines to be sold for a price, or as possible bearers of sons. It was not unusual for them to be sold into slavery between the ages of four and ten, to be resold by their owners when they were fourteen, either as concubines or sing-song girls. I got to know Miss Cameron quite well, and she let me come to the Mission to take pictures of her protégées—lovely little creatures poetically named Tea Rose, Apple Blossom, Plum Blossom. Miss Cameron was not a tight-lipped reformer who wished to make the world over into a monotone. She had respect and admiration for the art and literature of China and she saw that the girls she had taken under her wing were educated in its tradition. When I first went to the Mission the walls were decorated with commonplace lithographs and posters. After I became more at home I told her I thought it was too bad that her pupils, who knew something of the value of their native fine sculpture and painting, were learning nothing of what the art of the Occident had to give them. She had the same thought, but there was no money with which to do something about it. Through the generosity of two or three of the San Francisco art dealers I secured some good photographs and reproductions in color of old masters. The girls were delighted and they had Tea Rose write me a letter which I have kept for the poetry of its style and sentiment.

As I went on making pictures of Chinatown I had better and better results. I began to see that somehow I had evolved something quite different from the ordinary scenic photographs to be found in the shops. The picture I had wanted to catch sometimes formed only a small part of the exposed film. In order to make enlargements, I joined the California Camera Club which had the necessary facilities. At its next annual exhibition I contributed a series of these enlarged pictures, the only ones of Chinatown in the collection. Favorable comment encouraged me to venture into a more exacting phase, one that had been tempting me for some time.

One morning in San Rafael I had been standing in the corridor which ran through the hotel. On each side of it was a row of chairs where the financiers and businessmen sat reading their papers while they waited for the bus that was to take them to the station. Suddenly in the door at one end came a goddess swinging a tennis racket. Her hair was a cloud of flame. Her skin was like a rose petal. With head erect she moved her perfectly molded figure with a free and easy grace. As she walked along between the rows of chairs not one man so much as glanced at her. "What kind of men are these?" I asked myself. "Are they made of stone that they do not at least look up?" It did not take me long to realize that there was some reason for their casualness. Everywhere one went,

one saw these fine-featured, valiant young women, with their extraordinary coloring and their radiant spirit. Theirs surely was a
beauty to be recorded. But when one saw photographs of them
the radiance and the spirit were missing.

There must be some way, I thought, of taking their pictures
so that they would be more than a mere surface record and would
have more relation to life and to art than the stiffly posed photographs that gave the effect of masks behind which the soul of the
subject was lost. Perhaps, I thought, if they were photographed in
the unobtrusive manner which had worked so well with my shy
and unsuspecting Chinese subjects, if they were not allowed to become self-conscious by artificial posing, if they could be kept from
knowing the exact moment the exposure was being made—then
something more of their spirit might be brought out by the
camera.

The Camera Club had a portrait studio with a skylight, and
a good camera especially adapted to portraiture. I had a certain
timidity about experimenting with any of the lovely young creatures I knew. I would first see what I could do by taking pictures of
men. Count Artsimovitch, the Imperial Russian Consul General,
Baron Alexander von Schroeder, my pupil's uncle, and Fred Hall,
the Turkish Consul, offered themselves as my first subjects. They
came to the club studio where we talked casually while I adjusted
the camera, never letting them know just when I was taking their
pictures. The results were an agreeable surprise to both them and
myself and I was again inspired to more ambitious efforts.

Among my friends was a young miniature painter, Mira Edgerly, who besides being a gifted artist had great beauty and intelligence. Sure that I had started something new in photography, she
not only posed for me but gave me many valuable suggestions on
arrangement and composition. Gertrude Stein in her *Autobiography of Alice B. Toklas* says of Miss Edgerly, who had been responsible for her meeting John Lane in London: "She was a very
tall, very beautiful, very brilliant young woman. Arnold Genthe
had made innumerable photographs of her, mostly with a cat."

My next subject was Alma de Bretteville, now the widow of Adolph Spreckels, of the sugar family. She came with Miss Edgerly, who had just painted a charming miniature of her. She was only fifteen and of a classic loveliness. Even then she showed the beginning of an interest in various phases of art, an interest manifested years later in her gift to the city of a collection of Rodin's important sculptures and a beautiful museum in which to house them.

Further experiments made me wonder if my ideas on portrait photography were really different from those of the professional. Perhaps they too had arrived at the same methods. To find out, I had my picture taken at one of the popular studios. Alas! The old muscle-bound traditions still prevailed. I was told to sit up straight. The operator turned my head from one side to the other until the pose suited him.

"Now hold it," he exclaimed, placing my head in a cast-iron vise. By the time he emerged from under the focusing cloth whatever might have been left of a natural expression had vanished.

"Steady as a rock now," he called out as he made the exposure. It is scarcely necessary to add that the pictures were without life and expression.

If this was the way photographs were taken in the best professional studios, then, I thought, maybe there is something in what my friends say—perhaps I have developed something of my own, something worth while.

The art arbiter of San Francisco at that time was Mr. Vickery, the founder of Vickery, Atkins and Torrey, an art firm that has been a far-reaching influence in the development of taste and appreciation in the West. I took the portraits I had made to Mr. Vickery and asked him to criticize them.

He looked them over carefully. "They are very interesting indeed," he said. "But what are they? Mezzotints?"

"No, they are photographs."

"They certainly don't look it," was his response. "Who took them?"

"I did."

"I can't believe it," he said.

Up to that time I had had no criticism from a professional photographer. Now I took my pictures to the man with the most fashionable clientele in the city. When he had gone rapidly through them he said, "Well, they may be art, but you'll never be able to sell them. Take it from me, I've been in business here for twenty years and I know what I am talking about." Within a year he was saying to his clients, "What kind of pictures do you want? Carbons or Platinum? Or perhaps you want that new Genthe style. I can do that, too."

Toward the end of 1897 Heini von Schroeder was ready for his examinations at the gymnasium in Germany and I had to decide what I was going to do. I could have returned to Germany where I had teaching offers from several universities. But my imagination had been captured by this alien land, with its beauty, its energy and its freedom of thought and action. My inmost desire to be an artist had never really left me. My friends among the artists had been generous in their praise of my drawings and watercolors, which I knew, however, to be mediocre, and had no hope that the slight talent they showed might lead to anything worth while. In the camera I saw a new and exciting art medium—one by which I could interpret life after my own manner in terms of light and shade.

If my mother had lived I would perhaps have had no thought but that of returning home. She had died the previous year. A few days after her death I had received the news of the death of my brother Hugo. While he was still a student in the gymnasium, he had accepted an offer from an exporting firm in Hamburg to go to Mozambique. From there he was sent first to Central and then to British East Africa. Learning to speak several African dialects and knowing the land and the way of its people, he had gone into business for himself. On his excursions into the jungle after ivory, he had become a skilful hunter of big game. In response to a request from the men of the district he had gone out after a rogue elephant which was raising havoc in the villages and on the farms. As Hugo was about to shoot, his rifle jammed. The elephant trampled him.

My other brother, Siegfried, had signed a contract with the *Cologne Gazette*. His assignments might carry him to any part of the world. There no longer were family ties to bind me to Germany. Still there was a feeling that one of us, perhaps, should uphold the Genthe teaching tradition. It was a problem to be solved only by much thinking.

It is a habit of mine, when troubled in thought, to go for a long walk. One late afternoon I found myself at the top of Russian Hill. Around me ran the full circle of what I would be giving up if I were to leave San Francisco, a city I had grown to love and where I had made so many fine friendships. I began to see clearly that teaching would never bring me the happiness I wanted. It was here I belonged, in this new country which had broadened my horizons, opened my eyes to a new conception of life and shown me a way to satisfy my desire for beauty. Having absorbed something of the American spirit of independence, I made my decision according to my own lights. I took the first step on my career as a portrait photographer. I started in search of a studio.

MY FIRST STUDIO

ON Sutter Street, opposite the old University Club, I had often noticed a photographer's studio, a simple two-story wooden building with a large skylight. A sign announced "Banquets, Weddings, Machinery, etc. Taken at Short Notice." Climbing the gas-lit stairway I asked to see the proprietor, Mr. George Knight. While I was waiting I looked around. The studio, which did not seem to be in use, was a fair-sized room of good proportions with excellent light. I asked Mr. Knight if he would rent it. He said he had never thought about it, but since most of his work was done on the outside, he did not see why not. The rent agreed upon was twenty-five dollars a month. I knew it would answer my purpose, at least for a beginning. Furniture, quite in the Japanese manner, was distinguished by its absence. After I had moved in a few chairs and covered the walls with burlap and put up a few prints, the room looked quite attractive. A partition in the hall provided a dressing room. In the rear a small compartment with running water was transformed into a dark-room. After moving in my photographic equipment, I sent out cards to the friends I had made while I was with the von Schroeders.

I was determined to show people a new kind of photography: there would be no stilted poses; as a matter of fact, no poses at all. I would try to take my sitters unawares, at a moment when they would not realize that the camera was ready. I would show them prints in which a uniform sharpness would be avoided and emphasis laid on portraying a person's character instead of making a commonplace record of clothes and a photographic mask.

Within a few days Mrs. W. H. Crocker, the wife of the banker, came to be photographed with her three children. The informality of the grouping, resulting in a charming portrait of a gracious young mother and her children, pleased her, so that the following week she brought her sister, Princess Poniatowski, and her sister-in-law, Mrs. Charles B. Alexander, who were visiting her. Her influence did not stop with the members of her family. With the pride of a discoverer, she went about gathering up her friends in her carriage and depositing them at the door of my studio. It was due to Mrs. Crocker more than to anyone else that my reputation was so quickly established at the outset of my career. For more than thirty years her interest in my work continued. On her last visit to New York a year or so before her death, she brought her daughter-in-law to sit for a portrait.

There was Mrs. Joseph S. Tobin, who several times drove the eighteen miles from San Mateo bringing her friends to my studio; and Mrs. Rudolph Spreckels and her sisters, the numerous Joliffe girls. Mrs. Will Tevis, the daughter of Governor Pacheco, was not as slender as she wished to be and she was delighted with a full-length portrait in which through judicious arrangement of shadows, she was made to appear quite svelte. A number of her friends whose figures had the same tendencies as hers, among them Mrs. Mizner, the mother of "The Many Mizners," and her daughter, Mrs. Horace B. Chase, came to have me make similar pictures of them. Mrs. Philip Lilienthal was another friend in my early days as a photographer. Through the picture I made of her with her children, many more names were added to my list of clients.

With so many women of means and position using their prestige in my behalf, it was not surprising that my photographs became the fashion. Before a year had passed, I had acquired a large clientele. Often people had to wait outside in carriages, or sit on the stairs, since I had no reception room. They seemed to prefer the stairs, something of a novelty for them, and often the narrow stairway took on the atmosphere of a fashionable tea party, minus the tea.

I believe that my success was due, more than to any other element, to the rare beauty of some of my subjects. The most ambitious photographer could not have had more inspiring subjects.

If I were to do justice to the long roster of beauties who sat for my camera during those first years it would become a catalogue. But I must mention at least a few: the lovely Genevieve Goad and Elise Clarke; Lillian Geyer, now Mrs. William Timken—she was then a very young girl and had that ethereal loveliness one sometimes finds in a Greuze portrait; Mary Belle Gwin, petite and piquant, with olive skin and sparkling brown eyes, now the wife of Kenneth Kingsbury, president of the Standard Oil Company of California. And there were the two beautiful Maries, cousins, Marie Wells and Marie Oge. They came to my studio together and the result of the many pictures I made of them was the beginning of a delightful and lasting friendship. Frequently on Sundays Truxton Beale (who afterwards married Miss Oge) would join us on an excursion to the beach, where, provided with a luncheon and some French and Spanish books, we would spend the day by the sea, reading aloud to the girls. After her marriage, when Marie Beale had become a leading figure in Washington society, she devoted a great deal of time and study to the early history of Central and South America, particularly the Mayan and Aztec civilizations. Several years ago she spent a year flying into the remote districts of these southern countries, writing, on her return, a scholarly and entertaining book, *A Flight into America's Past*. When my photographs of Greece were on exhibition in Washington, Mrs. Beale invited me to a luncheon to meet some of her diplomatic friends and presented me with a copy of her book, on the flyleaf of which she had written, "To a friend of my youth."

Some military notables found their way to my studio, among them General Joe Wheeler, the famous cavalry commander who had distinguished himself in the Spanish-American War, and General William R. Shafter, who was in charge of the army in Cuba in 1898. These two men presented a strange contrast indeed. General Wheeler was of small stature, thin and wiry. General Shafter was of enormous size and of almost Falstaffian proportion; it was difficult to picture him mounting a horse.

The first theatrical star to come to my studio was Nance

O'Neil. She had unusual versatility, her repertoire including such diverging rôles as Nancy Sykes, Meg Merrilies, Camille and Magda. At that time she was under the domination of her manager, McKee Rankin, a veritable tyrant, but he made her act. One of my pictures of her was used for a three-sheet poster, the first one ever made in monotone from a photograph. Rankin complained that it proved the most expensive poster he had used, as in many towns people would soak it off the walls at night to keep for a souvenir.

Henry Miller, upon seeing the poster of Nance O'Neil, had me make some photographs of him in his famous rôle of Sydney Carton in the *Tale of Two Cities.* The photograph was always one of his favorites. The only copy of it in existence today hangs in the New York office of his son Gilbert. Henry Miller was a great actor and an even more remarkable director. He inspired his artists to give their best to each rôle, no matter how insignificant the part might appear. During the twenty-five years of our friendship, I made a great number of pictures of him, and I shall always be grateful for his helpful, constructive criticisms. In his company there was a young Canadian actress who was destined to become one of the leading figures of the American stage, Margaret Anglin. I photographed her in the rôle of Ophelia, and later on in the various parts in the Oscar Wilde plays which she and Henry Miller did so delightfully. The greatest achievements of her career were the brilliant performances in later years of the classic Greek plays *Antigone, Electra,* and *Medea* which she first gave in the Greek Theatre at Berkeley, California. She had a nobility of speech and gesture seldom equaled on the American stage.

It was through Margaret Anglin that Maxine Elliott came to my studio. I was glad she had brought her English bull pup along. She was so interested in him that she forgot all about the camera and I was able to get some good front view pictures of her. Most of her published photographs had been profiles. She was, without doubt, one of the most beautiful women of the stage at that time. She had, like Julia Marlowe, the perfect bone structure so essential to the permanence of beauty.

CHINESE MERCHANT WITH BODYGUARD

JACK LONDON

FRANK NORRIS

GEORGE STERLING SINCLAIR LEWIS

Of my photographs made in those early days the first ones that were reproduced in a magazine were not portraits, but some snapshots I had taken of the "Cliff Dwellers" of Telegraph Hill. My long friendship with John O'Hara Cosgrave dates from that time. He was the editor of *The Wave,* a brilliant illustrated weekly, concerned with society, art and literature. Someone had told him about those pictures and he asked me to bring them to his office. "I have to confess that I've never noticed how picturesque these dilapidated houses on the edge of Telegraph Hill are. It takes a blooming foreigner like you to show us the beauties of our own city." He then said he would like to use the pictures in his magazine and would send one of his staff to get the material for a story to go with them. The following day a striking, aristocratic young man came to see me. He was tall, with piercing, deep-set eyes and iron-gray hair. We had a pleasant chat and when the pictures appeared the following week the accompanying article was signed "Frank Norris." Norris wrote many editorials and a series of brilliant short stories for *The Wave*. His last contribution was the novel, *Moran of the Lady Letty,* which Cosgrave ran serially. The untimely death of Frank Norris—he was only thirty-two—was an irreparable loss to American literature. Frank's brother Charles, and his wife Kathleen, whom I knew when she was working for the *San Francisco Call,* have been good friends of mine ever since those early days.

Another writer whose genius Cosgrave nurtured was Jack London. One of his stories had been published in *The Overland Monthly,* but it was the series in *The Wave* that first attracted the notice of the critics. Cosgrave had given him a note to me, which read, "Please make a picture of bearer. He has written a rattling good story for *The Wave* and I feel sure he will be heard from in the future." I made many pictures of London during the following years, and as a token of his appreciation he gave me copies of every one of his books, inscribing some lines on the flyleaf of each. Sometimes just a word, like "Friendship's Grip." In *Tales of the Fish Patrol* he wrote, "San Francisco Bay used to be my stamping ground and all that I utilized in this book is mine by first hand. I was once 'Prince of the Oyster Beds.' " His four-act play, *Theft,* published six years before his death, had these lines, "Dear Genthe: My last latest. Honest I'll be good and not write so many in the future."

When Frank Norris left for New York his place on *The Wave* had been taken by Will Irwin. Will's brother Wallace was induced by Cosgrave to join the staff of *The Wave,* which now included Gelett Burgess, James Hopper, Ambrose Bierce, and Juliet Wilbur Tompkins.

Edwin Markham, who had risen to sudden fame by his poem, *The Man with the Hoe,* came to be photographed for *The Wave.* Even at that time (1899) he bore a striking resemblance to the portraits of Longfellow, and the picture I made of him, while he was reciting, brought out some of that resemblance. I recall his note of thanks which began: "I stand transformed by your wonder-working camera."

To Cosgrave I am indebted also for having arranged for me to take Paderewski's portrait. When the famous pianist appeared at the studio he said he could give me only ten minutes. I promised not to keep him longer. In some way we got talking about Oriental art in which he was particularly interested. Suddenly he looked at his watch: "We have used up all the time. I shall have to leave at once," he declared. When I told him that I had made a number of pictures while we were talking he said, "I don't believe you took a single one." One of these photographs became his favorite portrait. He used it for many years. It is the same that is reproduced in the Encyclopaedia Britannica under the article on Photography.

On another visit to San Francisco, he asked me if I would take him and Mme. Paderewska to the Chinese Theatre, knowing that I was well acquainted with Chinatown. As non-Chinese visitors we had to sit on the stage directly behind the orchestra. After a quarter of an hour, Mme. Paderewska said, "I think a little of this goes a long way. Let's leave." The maestro would not hear of it. "No, no, wait," he exclaimed. "This music is exceedingly interesting. There is an almost Wagnerian character to it. Each rôle has a definite motif of its own. You will see, before the General enters his arrival is indicated by his individual rhythm. It's the same with the heroine, the villain and the others."

Up to this time Chinese music had been nothing to me but a din of unrelated dissonances. I was beginning now to know better.

My hours of work in those days were long and often exhausting, as I had no one to help me and I did all my own developing and printing, besides constantly experimenting. Hundreds of plates were discarded when they did not show the vital spontaneous quality I deemed so essential. I wanted my portraits not only to look alive and natural; they had to have, aside from being honest character studies, a definite pictorial quality which would give them an added interest. That there was a place for this kind of photography was proved to me by the generous response of the public.

Payments were then made in gold, and I used to deposit the money in a box which I kept in a corner of my studio. One day I found that I had three thousand dollars in twenty-dollar gold pieces. It was more money than I had ever dreamed of possessing. Box in hand I went to the Union Trust Company and opened my first bank account.

My clientele continued to increase, and with such rapidity that I could no longer do all the work myself. As my bank account grew in the same proportion, I felt justified in branching out. I bravely took a long lease on a three-story house on the corner of Sutter and Jones Streets, where I added a fourth story with skylight for my studio. Until then I had had little time for relaxation. Now with an ideal place to live and work in and with success stepping easily through my doorway, a series of vivid and unforgettable chapters were opened to me.

SAN FRANCISCO

IN the nineties San Francisco had retained much of the color and prodigality of the days of forty-nine, pleasantly tempered by the native culture which had come to California out of Spain. The French and Italians who had planted the orchards and vineyards in the valleys and on the hillsides beyond the Bay had taught her how to eat and how to live. The strong Anglo-Saxon element had given her poise and sophistication.

One of her aspects that most impressed me was the general well-being of the crowds. One seldom saw the hungry or unkempt. Human wreckage was, of course, to be encountered along the waterfront, on the Barbary Coast, or in Chinatown, but there was little of the kind of misery that comes from real want. On Nob Hill, on California Street above Powell Street, the mining and railroad millionaires—the Huntingtons, the Floods, the Crockers, the Townes and the Stanfords—had their palaces. A block further down was the beginning of Chinatown—a Canton colony of ten thousand. The Palace Hotel on Market Street was the pivot around which the gay life of the city revolved. In the large court the carriages of the rich and fashionable were always coming or going, carrying the ladies and their escorts back and forth from tea or luncheon in the Palm Garden or the Ball Room. At the bar many spectacular figures would congregate: men who had made their money in mining, grain, or timber; politicians in frock coats and Stetson hats who had come here to spend their money. There were such eccentrics as "Emperor Norton" who had crowned himself as Czar of the city and went about in silk hat, cutaway coat and white boutonnière. Every afternoon "White Hat McCarthy," jaunty in fawn-colored suit and white topper, drove his pacer down Market Street in a racing cart, drawing up in the court to find victims for his tips on the races.

Living with the von Schroeders had given me an opportunity to meet a number of the men and women who played an important part in the social life of San Francisco. One of the most prominent figures, who for a great many years was a real leader, was Mrs. Eleanor Martin, an aunt of Baroness von Schroeder. Through her father, who had been governor, she had inherited considerable wealth. Her keen zest for living never permitted her to be idle. She was a lavish hostess and her dinner parties were never a bore. Sometimes, even if her family disapproved of this form of humor, she would take an ironic pleasure in gathering about her those who were either at sword's point with one another or socially uncongenial. Up to the last, when she had reached the remarkable age of one hundred years, she enjoyed taking an active part in social activities, and continued to be the gracious hostess in her home. Sitting at the head of the table, beautifully coiffed and gowned, with a collar of pearls and diamonds about her throat, she presented an amazing figure. If she felt like talking, she did so; if listening were too great an effort, she took a little nap. At the end of the dinner, she would bid her guests good-night, and on the arm of her son, Downey Harvey, the unconquerable old lady, head high and shoulders straight, would walk up the broad staircase to her rooms.

An entirely different kind of leadership was that of Ned Greenway, who for quarter of a century was the virtual dictator of the younger set. He came of a Southern family, but his chief distinction lay in the fact that he was a generous host and an agent for a French champagne. The fate of a débutante, no matter what her background, depended on her being included in the invitation list of the "Greenway Dances." Unless her name was on that list she remained an outsider. The opening of the social season was marked by a dinner and dance given by Greenway on his birthday in his own honor, and the débutantes invited to this event would hold a preferred standing.

Outside of this inner social circle there was a gay Bohemian element, a group of writers and artists, whose playgrounds were the many French, Italian, and Spanish restaurants, and who did not care if they belonged to this or that social set. Coppa's, which has figured in several of the novels written around the life of San Francisco, was the favorite meeting place.

The city's markets provided a variety of food unknown in these days of tea-rooms and dairy lunches. Wild game in season—teal ducks and canvas backs, quail and venison—could be had in the open market and fresh vegetables and fruit were plentiful. And within the reach of the most impecunious artist was a five-course dinner including a bottle of native wine, all for fifty cents. If one had no money one could eat at Coppa's anyway. He was generous with credit, knowing that when better days came the debt would be paid. And there was space on the walls which a painter could decorate in payment for food and drink. This privilege was extended to both visiting and local talent. A frieze of black cats running clear around the top of the walls was painted at various intervals by Martinez, about whom I will have more to say later on.

Song and laughter and good talk ran on at Coppa's, and a visitor ceased to be a stranger once he had entered the door. It was there that we had the much publicized dinner where Isabelle Fraser, the Cholly Francisco of the *San Francisco Examiner,* was crowned Queen of Bohemia. My recollection of it is somewhat hazy, but I have a faint picture of Gelett Burgess, who was then editing *The Lark,* sitting at the end of the table pouring libations into an enormous loving-cup to toast our exalted guest of honor. Other faces I see dimly are those of Porter Garnett, Will Irwin, Maizie Griswold, now Mrs. Edwin Emerson, and George Sterling. Here my memory fades, to come clear again when we were making our way homeward. On Montgomery Street we heard the distant notes of the Salvation Army band which was having its midnight rally somewhere on the Barbary Coast. Nothing would do but that we should have a Salvation Army of our own. Up and down Montgomery Street we marched in file—stopping at various intervals while the men knelt in a circle singing "Hallelujah, I'm a bum," the women in chorus chanting, "Oh, why don't you work as other men do?" to which came the answer, "How'n hell can we work when there's no work to do?"

Two policemen, coming from opposite directions, met at a corner.

"What's all this rumpus? Why don't you send them on their way?" one asked the other whose beat it was.

"Sure," was the reply, "what's the harm? They're only a bunch of crazy artists."

The free-lunch counters in the saloons, many of them truly palatial, were more like buffet luncheons. And here a complete meal with a glass of beer or port was at one's disposal for the large sum of five cents. On the counter were piles of crisp French bread, platters of cold meats and cracked crab, and different kinds of cheese, to all of which a man was free to help himself.

The large French restaurants, such as the Poodle Dog, Marchand's, the Pup and Delmonico's, were the peers of any of the famous eating places of the old world and they were arranged to cater to their patrons in diverse ways. On the ground floor was the general dining room where on Sunday evenings all of San Francisco, so to speak, came for their family dinners. On the second floor were the private dining rooms and banquet rooms. And on the third and fourth were the suites for impatient and clandestine lovers. Delmonico's had an entrance into a court where the cabs could drive in under cover and deposit their fares at the door of an elevator without danger of detection.

It was at Delmonico's that one of the most memorable dinners of my recollection was held. During the days of the Imperial Russian Empire, a certain Grand Duke passed through San Francisco on his way around the world. Grand Dukes, being something more than they are today, the keys of the city were his to command, and society did its lavish best with receptions, dinners and balls. When he had been there about a week, Count Artsimovitch, the Consul General, came to see me, greatly agitated. "I'm in an awful fix," he said. "His Imperial Highness is bored to death with all this formal entertaining. On account of my official position I can't give him the kind of party he wants. I'm wondering if you can help me out."

"What you want," said I, "is an intimate and not very large dinner without speeches, one where the guests will be clever men and beautiful women."

"Exactly."

It could be arranged, I told him, and I would help out on the condition that he would leave it entirely in my hands. He was to give me a list of the men he would like to have invited. We would go over it together and eliminate whoever might not fit into the spirit of the occasion. The selection of the ladies was left to me. I don't think I have ever seen twelve such beautiful women at one time as those who were gathered about the table that night. Some of them were from the theater, others were just gay young things to whom I had explained that they need only be charming and entertaining. By way of innovation—and it was startling—the most glamorous of the city's demimondaines had been included. No one knew anything of her background, but it was obviously an aristocratic one. She had the face and figure of an empress, and the poise and manner of one as well.

Her place at table was beside the Grand Duke. He was enchanted with her. From that evening until he left, the secret service men and his aides had a hard time trying to keep track of him. To be with her he broke official and social engagements. He went about freely with her in public. When it was time for him to leave for home, he begged her to go with him. "I will make you the most talked about woman in Russia."

"Thank you," she tossed back at him with a gay laugh. "I'm quite talked about enough here, and I adore San Francisco."

Before leaving he had me make a life-size enlargement of the portrait I had taken of her.

The climax to this romance occurred at a luncheon given at Newport in his honor, before his return to Russia. He made a little farewell speech. "It is with deep regret," he said, "that I must leave a country of such marvelous hospitality. I would not do so if my duty did not make it imperative. I have been enchanted by the beauty of the American women—it is beyond anything I have ever dreamed of." Raising his glass he continued, "Now I wish to propose a toast . . . to the most beautiful woman I have met in your country." More than one of the beautiful ladies present hoped that she was being referred to. He continued, "She shall be nameless. Even if she were not many miles away, she would not have been included in this gathering. I ask you all to drink her health." The story of his infatuation had traveled ahead of him across the continent. But a request from a Grand Duke was a command. And so it was that these ladies of unquestioned virtue and secure social position raised their glasses and drank to the star of a forbidden world.

A
Toast

58

THE BOHEMIAN CLUB

THE best that a man could have in those days in San Francisco, if he were to enter into its life, was membership in the Bohemian Club, a favor that was mine for many years. A club like the Bohemian could not have developed anywhere else, certainly not without that genial spirit which gave color to San Francisco's personality. It started from small beginnings in 1872 when San Francisco was still an outpost, removed by time and distance from the artistic advantages of the larger and older cities of the American East. A group of men of education and travel met to discuss the possibility of creating these benefits for themselves, and having a good time of it as well. They founded a club which was to be Bohemian in the best sense of the word— a place where kindred spirits could get together for the purpose of fostering talent and putting care to rout with conviviality. The first members included Charles Warren Stoddard, Clay Greene, General W. H. L. Barnes, Frank Unger, Joseph Grismer, George T. Bromley, William Greer Harrison, Raphael Weill, Horace G. Platt and General Lucius H. Foote. Not hampered by any tradition, the club made its own pattern. Its dedication to the "Burial of Care" demanded something more from its members than financial or social prestige. They had to have either talent or appreciation, and as a gentle reminder that it was not to be used for business contacts and that shop-talk was taboo, the club took for its motto the subtle injunction, "Weaving spiders come not here," and for its monitor that wise old bird, the owl.

With its atmosphere of cordiality, it became the rendezvous of wits, bon vivants and celebrities—writers, painters, sculptors, musicians, men of the theater, and those who occupied high places in government and finance. The dinners in honor of visitors became known for their originality. Every autumn there was an art exhibition to which the public was invited. It gave a real impetus to the cultural life of the community.

The beginnings of the annual midsummer "jinks" were week-end outings held in different parts of the Russian River country. In 1880 the ritual of the burning in effigy of man's enemy, care, was inaugurated, and from then on there was a planned program which grew from year to year. It was in 1900, due chiefly to the efforts of Vanderlyn Stow, then vice-president of the club, and of James D. Phelan, that the Bohemian Club succeeded in acquiring one of the few virgin redwood forests that the lumberman's axe had not despoiled. It was an ideal setting for the Grove plays which were to become such an important part of the club's activities—gigantic ancient trees that were there in their youth when Phidias fashioned his sculptures for the Parthenon, a vast natural stage on the far side of the Grove, a backdrop of cliff, hung with fern and tree and undergrowth. Such inspiring surroundings were bound to result in the creation of a new and significant beauty.

Just a year after I had joined the club, Charles K. Field, who later became editor of *Sunset Magazine,* wrote the first complete original drama produced in the Grove, entitled *The Man in the Forest.* It was based on an Indian legend which told of the despair of the tribes because of the havoc of a long drought. The crops were ruined, the animals were dying and a council was held to discover a way to propitiate the gods. Suddenly from the top of a mountain, over cliff and rocks and through the trees, came a runner bearing the tidings that the white man had been captured, an omen that the anger of the gods had been appeased. The part of the runner was taken by Robert Aitken, the sculptor, who had a magnificent physique. A trail had been cleared for him, but he had so completely assumed his part that he ignored the trail, and rushing in wild leaps over rocks and brush, made such a dramatic entrance that today when old Bohemians get together it is spoken of as a glorious memory.

This was the beginning of the annual Grove play to which

invitations are now so eagerly sought each year by eminent men all over the country. The high spot for all time—and few Bohemians would dispute it as such—was Will Irwin's classic *Hamadryads,* produced under Porter Garnett at the "jinks" in 1904. In poetic and lucid prose the pagan myth of the indwelling spirit of the trees was brought to life in the manner of the Greek dramatists, the players actually creating the illusion of hamadryads springing to life out of the very heart of the redwood trees. The lighting was under the direction of Edward Duffy. Away ahead of his time, he was a master of light, and many of his effects of over thirty years ago now find their counterparts in the mechanics of the modern theater. Such was the spell cast by the text of the play, the acting, the lighting and the cathedral forest, that it was as if a long lost dream had been given reality. The only disappointment was that Will Irwin could not be there to witness his triumph. He had been called to a job on the *New York Sun* and spent his evenings reporting a murder case.

The charm of life at the Grove lay not alone in the surroundings but in the fellowship. We were, in effect, one large family in whose circle there was neither gloom, pretense nor taking offense. And the boy that is at the heart of every man had his outlet. We wore our old clothes, roughed it in the open, poked fun at one another. The hoaxes at the campfire and the stunts were often ruthless in their satire, but they were taken in good part by the victims and with hilarity by the perpetrators.

Many are the profiles that come back to me through the vista of the redwoods. Nat Goodwin and Dave Warfield telling their stories at the campfire. David Bispham singing the *Two Grenadiers.* Bill Hopkins, MacKenzie Gordon and Charles Dickman, in costume and make-up, rendering Neapolitan folksongs to the strum of mandolin and guitar. Charles Warren Stoddard, the gentle poet, surrounded by an audience eager for his vivid word-pictures of a California that was fast disappearing. "Uncle George" Bromley, at eighty and beyond, as young at heart as the youngest of us, acting High Priest at the "Burning of Care." Raphael Weill, in cap and apron, gathering his friends about him to enjoy his favorite French recipes prepared by himself in his inimitable way.

And there was unforgettable Joe Redding. He had a scintillating wit and a deep, resonant voice. It was always a treat to listen to him, no matter what the subject of his conversation might be, but his erudition never interfered with his taking part in some of our most frivolous activities. For one of the Friday night entertainments he had written what was announced by the president as a German *lied*. Sung in the grand manner by David Bispham, with full respect to accent and inflection, it sounded absolutely like German though it was entirely written in English, but with such a selection of words that its vowel sounds and consonants were convincingly German.

A remembered silhouette is that of Ambrose Bierce with his derby hat—the only one ever seen at the Grove. One night when nearly everyone had retired, Bierce, Jack London, George Sterling and I sat late around the campfire talking. Our subject was some deep cosmic problem, and our discussion was punctuated by frequent libations. With each one our observations grew more profound, even if none of us quite knew what we were talking about. The only other person to be seen was MacKenzie Gordon, the tenor, who was giving a demonstration of his chest expansion, his great pride, by valiantly trying to blow out the campfire. As dawn came up, Bierce, his derby changing angles with alarming rapidity, remembered that he was staying on the other side of the Russian River with his brother who would be alarmed, upon awakening, not to find him in his bed. It was still dark in the forest and Sterling insisted that the clubby thing to do was to see Bierce home. So we started out, Sterling leading the way with a lantern. We had gone about a hundred yards or so when he stumbled against a root of a tree which sat him down on top of the lantern and put out the light, but we managed to grope our way over the bridge, landing Bierce safely within the door of his brother's home.

Willis Polk, gone now as have so many of those I have mentioned, was another who contributed merrily to the encampment.

Incidentally, it was chiefly to his genius and vision as an architect that the Panama-Pacific Exposition owed its beauty and the city of San Francisco its Civic Center, one of the finest groups of municipal architecture to be found anywhere. Willis was a great joker and loved to put people in their place. One summer it happened that several New York bankers were guests of William H. Crocker at the jinks. Willis, who was also staying at his camp, said to him, "Will, I want you to do me a favor. It won't cost you a cent. When we are ready to leave here to take the train I want you to give the impression that you are acting as my valet. It will impress your important friends and may help me when I go East."

Crocker thought it would be amusing to cooperate. Monday morning when the guests were waiting to go to the train, Willis took out his watch and looking at it said, "Will, don't you think it's about time for you to pack my bags?"

The surprise registered on the faces of the visiting financiers grew to consternation when Crocker, who was California's most important banker, not only packed the bags but lugged them to the station and put them on the train.

"Now," said Willis, "they'll think I'm somebody to be ordering Will Crocker around. And when I go to New York they'll be eager to entertain me and give me a good time."

Scarcely a man of note who came to San Francisco failed to be introduced into "Bohemia," and the parties given for visiting celebrities were not the least of its happy achievements.

At the dinner in honor of Mascagni, when he came to direct the orchestra for his operas, Dick Hotaling made the presentation speech. His manner was lofty and his Italian impressive. Charles Webb Howard, who was president of the Spring Valley Water Company and an ardent disciple of things cultural, irritated at the asides of some of those at the table, admonished them to be quiet. Cupping his ear, he leaned forward, whispering, "This is magnificent and I don't want to miss a word of it. The man's Italian is perfect." The speech was composed entirely of the stage directions for *Cavalleria Rusticana.*

Just as it was finished the door opened and Charles Dickman, who had a gift for impersonations, came in dressed as the maestro. He was followed by twenty of our musicians dressed in red gowns, who marched around the table, playing the intermezzo in perfect harmony and with all its swelling cadences and crescendos on "kazoos"—a glorified adaptation of paper over combs. Mascagni roared with laughter. Taking his place at the piano he played the whole thing through, insisting that the musicians sing along with him as he played.

At the time that Samuel Hopkins Adams was on the staff of McClure, Phillips and Company, the publishers, he came West on a "drumming trip." Some of the members, including Robert Aitken, George Sterling, Xavier Martinez, Charlie Field, Porter Garnett, Maynard Dixon, Gelett Burgess, Jack London, Will and Wallace Irwin, and I, decided to give him a party.

The day before the party Adams asked Will Irwin whether it was to be a formal dinner. "You tenderfoot," laughed Will. "Don't you know we don't dress out here?"

We asked a girl, of whom he was seeing a good deal, to help us carry out a joke we had planned. According to our instructions she said to him, "They just want to make you feel uncomfortable. They always wear dinner togs."

Arriving at the club in his tuxedo, Adams was ushered into the red room where he found us all in cowboy costumes, chaps and sombreros, and two guns apiece in our belts. The guns were, of course, loaded with blank cartridges.

As he entered the door we gave his feet a two-gun salute, shouting in chorus, "Dance, critter, dance." Maynard Dixon, throwing a noose over his shoulders, caught it at the waist and strung him up to the chandelier, as the writers in a circle beneath handed him a sheaf of manuscripts at the point of a revolver. "Now you'll read these, you son of a gun, and like 'em."

The sound of the shots brought the police.

"What's going on here?" demanded the officer, forcing his way in.

"Oh," replied the steward, who was a Swede, "yust a little yinks."

The last time I was in San Francisco—it was in August, 1926—I was the guest of Will Crocker at his camp in the Grove. Many changes had taken place. There was little of the old roughing it in the open. Many of the canvas tents had been replaced by substantial cabins with running hot and cold water, electrical equipment and "all the comforts of home." Professionals from Hollywood were becoming as important on the program as home talent. But the spirit of Bohemia had not changed. The spirit that sprang straight out of the heart of the forest will endure as long as the redwoods are there to hold it.

BOHEMIAN FRIENDS

IT was among the writers and artists of the Bohemian Club that I found my most congenial friends. One of the writers to whom I felt attracted from the first was Porter Garnett, then a contributor to *The Lark*. He was a man of sensitive taste and a great stickler for purity of form. He was responsible for the production of several of the Grove plays and wrote a history of them. In recent years his work with the Laboratory Press of the Carnegie Institute is particularly noteworthy.

My friendship with Will Irwin, begun in the early Bohemian days, has lasted through all my San Francisco and New York years. It is the same with Robert Aitken, who during his early California years showed only traces of the genius that was to be responsible for his magnificent later achievements. The man who created the pediment sculptures of the Supreme Court building in Washington and the frieze of the Fine Arts Building in Columbus is one of the foremost sculptors of our time.

Another great sculptor of quite a different mold was Arthur Putnam, whose career was only too brief. He had an extraordinary genius for modeling animals in motion, particularly the puma, the California lion, and his bronzes gave a complete feeling of their grace and power. Rodin, who saw some examples of his work in Mrs. Adolph Spreckels' apartment in Paris, said that he considered Putnam one of the greatest animal sculptors. The disintegration of his talent, when he was still young, was one of the tragedies of the art world. He was in his thirties when he began to be troubled with severe headaches which made it impossible for him to work for months at a time. The doctors diagnosed the cause as a clot on the brain. They insisted on an operation. When after some weeks he was permitted to leave the hospital and return home, his wife asked me to have dinner with them on the evening of his home-coming. I noticed that he was lame, but thought it was only weakness from the shock of the operation. Always an erratic talker, he seemed no more so than usual. After dinner as we sat before the fire he asked his wife for pencil and paper. "They wouldn't let me have them at the hospital," he said, "and I want to see if I can still draw." He drew a slinking puma—the thing he knew and understood better than anyone else. When his wife and I saw the drawing, it was all we could do to hide our horror. It looked like the caricature of a dachshund.

Holding it at arm's length he looked at it critically, and wholly unconscious of its grotesque appearance, said with a hearty laugh, "I guess the old boy is all right."

In operating, the surgeon had found it necessary to remove a small layer of the brain tissue surrounding the clot. Putnam lost not only his sense of proportion in his art but in his attitudes, and he was to be a partial paralytic for the rest of his life. He lived for a number of years during which he made a desperate struggle to recover. It was futile. He had done only a comparatively small amount of work. A complete collection of his bronzes was brought together by Mrs. Adolph Spreckels, and is housed in the Museum of the Palace of the Legion of Honor in Golden Gate Park.

Haig Patigian, who for several years was president of the Bohemian Club, is a distinguished sculptor responsible for many public monuments and other sculptural work, mostly in California. He has remained faithful to San Francisco.

The dean of the painters was dear old William Keith. Scotch by birth, he had come to San Francisco in 1869, after having studied several years abroad. He was a great admirer and friend of George Inness, whose influence is strongly noticeable in his work. The California landscape was an inspiration to him and he brought to his canvases an indefinable charm which gained him recognition as an important American artist.

Xavier Martinez, or "Marty" as he was known to all of us, was a pupil of Whistler. He was a gifted Mexican with an unusual sense of color, and if he could have been persuaded to go to New

York, he would have been universally known. When William Chase saw one of his paintings in my studio in New York, he was startled. "Who painted this?" he asked. When he was told, he exclaimed, "Why don't we know this man's work? He is a great artist. Tell me more about him."

Marty was the most colorful figure of the Bohemian artists. With a shock of black hair, and eyes like great beads of jet, he dressed like the painters in the Latin Quarter—in corduroys, and always wore a bright crimson flowing tie, no matter what the time of day. When we were going to Del Monte for the first exhibition of the paintings of California artists, we had quite a time prevailing upon him to get some dinner clothes, for which he paid his tailor with a painting. He appeared at the preview wearing his tuxedo, but with the inevitable red flowing tie. "It makes a good spot," he chuckled. Every Sunday he kept open house in his home at the top of Berkeley Hills, where there was always a big caldron of spaghetti or chili con carne on the stove and plenty of red wine to drink it down with. Hot arguments on any subject which came into our minds were the order of the day, and I have a picture in my mind of Jack London sitting at one end of the table, intense and questioning, and Marty at the other, gesticulating with a chicken bone. His wife had the poetic beauty of Rossetti's "Blessed Damozel," and he was jealous of her. A well-known writer who was his frequent guest had expressed his admiration for Mrs. Martinez too fervently. Marty took an intense dislike to him. One day at table we were startled by shots in the garden. Going out to see what had happened, we found Marty shooting at a piece of paper tacked to a tree. "I am going to keel that son of a beech," he shouted, but there never was a killing.

A true Bohemian in every sense of the word was Charles Rollo Peters, the father of the actor. He had an extra flair for capturing on his canvases the elusive, poetical effects of moonlight. His home near Monterey, with its spacious studio and garden, lent itself admirably to his talents as a host and his guests went away with something to remember with pleasure.

Once when I was spending the week-end as his guest, he came to my room quite upset. "I don't know what to do," he declared. "The sheriff has been to my studio and put his seal on every piece of furniture in it. I have over fifty people coming to a party to-night. I'll be disgraced."

After some thought I asked if the sheriff was a friend of his. "We're the best of friends," he replied. "He said that he felt badly at having to do such a thing, but he could not put it off any longer."

"Then why not make it a party in his honor?" I asked. "It will please him and amuse your guests. The Carmelites and the Bohemians will probably guess the truth. The others will never suspect, but will think the seals are just a stunt." He took my suggestion and the party was a huge success.

Mrs. Bowditch Morton, a close friend of Mrs. Peters', got some of her wealthy acquaintances to buy five of Peters' moonlight canvases. The check ran into the thousands.

"Now," said Peters, after paying his most urgent creditors, "I'm going to have something I've wanted for a long time. I'm going to have a lake." Immediately twenty men were set to work, at the foot of the hill, digging. In due time the lake was finished. "Now," said Peters again, "I'm going to have a Venetian Night to inaugurate it."

Invitations were sent out and gladly accepted. Gondolas, borrowed from the lagoon at Del Monte, were lying peacefully at anchor on the blue water of the lake. The famous Italian trio from the Bohemian Club was coming down with their costumes and guitars to sing the boat-songs. The tables for the refreshments were set out under trees hung with lanterns.

The morning of the party I was in my room—Peters had asked me to stay at the house to help with the preparations—when he burst in. "Something terrible has happened," he shouted. "The damn lake has dried up."

Somewhere there had been a subterranean leak. All that was left of the lake was a glistening mud-flat. When his disappointment had toned down, I was able to persuade him that the fiesta was not dependent for its success upon the lake. The garden was at its finest. There would be a moon. And after the guests were warmed up, they would not care whether there was a lake or not.

The party went on with the gondolas parked in the mud, the trio singing Venetian boat-songs at its edge, and everyone having such a good time that the water was not missed.

That night late, after the guests had departed, I went looking for Peters. He was standing by a tree gazing at the ruins of his long-cherished dream. "You know," he said, "the moon makes a better reflection on the mud than it did on the water."

When Charley Peters left us, he took with him something that has gone, never, I fear, to return. He was a true Bohemian of a forgotten school of life—one that is to be found now only in the pages of Du Maurier or Henri Murger.

CARMEL-BY-THE-SEA

A FEW miles from Monterey, running in a semi-circle on Carmel Bay, was a peninsula of pine forest, cypressed beach and rolling hill country, which, in 1902, was yet untouched by invasion. Frank Powers, an attorney, the brother-in-law of Ernest Thompson Seton, saw it as a perfect setting for a colony of writers, painters and kindred spirits. Concentrating his resources, he acquired the whole peninsula and founded there the village of Carmel-by-the-Sea, put up a small hotel, and cut up the land into forest lots, which he sold on long time, easy payments. Providing further for extensions and for help in erecting the cottage studios, he made it possible for artists and writers to have homes where they could work, away from the interruptions of city life.

One of the first to take advantage of the opportunity was George Sterling. Shortly after, I followed, building the kind of a bungalow I had always wanted to have. I drew up the plans myself. The sloping roof, following the lines of the distant hills, was shadowed by two great pine trees, the largest in Carmel, and was supported by four large redwood trunks, with the bark left on. A wide porch looked out on the sea. The spacious studio and living-room, thirty by sixty feet, with a high ceiling and two skylights, was built entirely of redwood, the rafters being, not box beams but solid redwood. My particular pride was the fireplace which was large enough to take four-foot logs. And there was a cellar—the only one in Carmel—solidly built of cement. The bungalow still exists, but all I own of it now are the color plates which I made of it thirty years ago.

The next to come was Mary Austin, then the MacGowan Cookes, Jimmie Hopper and the Perry Newberrys. Hartley Manners came there to write plays. There, too, for their summer vacations came professors from Stanford University and the University of California. This was the beginning of the Carmel Art Colony.

It was a studious group but a jovial one. Week days were devoted to work, week-ends to play. And the time I spent there over a period of nearly ten years remains a bright spot in my memory.

My particular cronies were George Sterling and Jack London. The latter had no home there—he lived on his ranch in Glendale—but put in many weeks as the guest of Sterling.

London did considerable writing at Carmel, for he liked to be near Sterling who was his best critic. They would write all day in adjoining rooms and in the evening would go over each other's

work. Jack London in those days rarely gave a manuscript its final typing until he had submitted the drafts to Sterling, who had an eagle eye for careless writing or the misuse of words.

It was an odd circumstance that this mutual assistance sprang from the same root—a preoccupation with the dictionary. Jack London, when he was just a youngster earning a living by picking up odd jobs about the wharves of San Francisco, would spend his free hours poring over the grimy pages of a tattered dictionary which he had found in the back room of a saloon. Sterling, as he naïvely told me, had spent a whole year going through the Standard dictionary, making a list of words that would give color to his poetry. He had an enormous vocabulary of polysyllables derived from the Greek or Latin. London was ruthless with his blue pencil. If there were an image or expression that he thought confusing, he would persuade Sterling to change it. Some of Sterling's poems —the simpler ones—have a beauty that has hardly been surpassed by any other American poet. That was Ambrose Bierce's verdict.

Jack London had a poignantly sensitive face. His eyes were those of a dreamer, and there was almost a feminine wistfulness about him. Yet at the same time he gave the feeling of a terrific and unconquerable physical force. When he built his boat, *The Snark,* which he had designed himself for his trip to the South Seas, some of the naval officers at the Bohemian Club insisted that it was not seaworthy. "He won't get as far as Hawaii," said a commander. "If he strikes the tail end of a typhoon, that boat will go down to the bottom like a flash."

"The boat may go down," said I, "but Jack London never will." That was the impression he gave one.

He had a great respect for Mary Austin's mind and for her achievements. But he could not refrain sometimes from poking fun at her.

George Sterling often gave abalone or mussel parties on the beach on Sunday afternoons. He and Jimmie Hopper would dive under the deep water by the cliffs and pry the abalones from the rocks. The abalones would then have to undergo an hour's pounding with stones—we all took a hand at it—and after another hour or two of parboiling they would be cut into steaks and broiled on a grill over the open fire. At one of these Mary appeared, as she often did, in the beaded leather costume and long braids of an Indian princess. George Sterling, who was proud of his classic contours, had climbed to the top of the cliff in his bathing trunks. Somewhere or other he had procured a trident and he was standing silhouetted against the sky while Jimmie Hopper was taking his picture. This was too frivolous for Mary who was gazing at the setting sun. Standing on the beach with outspread arms, she began something which sounded like an incantation, but which turned out to be a quotation from Browning.

" 'Tis a Cyclopean blacksmith," chanted Mary, "striking frenzied sparks from the anvil of the horizon."

London was standing with fork in hand, having just disposed of an abalone steak. Taking a look around which included both Mary and the horizon, he exclaimed, "Hell! I say this sunset has guts!"

Mary Austin was proud of her psychic power. After an evening at Sterling's, where several of us had sat long listening to a heated argument between Mary and Jack—he was not sure of the hidden mysteries Mary claimed to have solved—I took advantage of a sudden calm to suggest that it was time to be going. Mary's house was in the same direction as mine and I offered to see her home, asking Sterling for a lantern, as the woods were dark and there were no paths to follow.

At the mention of a lantern Mary was highly incensed. "Don't you know," she asked severely, "that I can see in the dark? All you have to do is to take my hand and let me lead you."

With some misgivings on my part, we started out. All went well until we were in the thick of the woods. Then there was a sudden lurch as Mary's head collided with a pine tree. She fell, but before I could move she was on her feet again. "Come along now," she said as if nothing had happened. "I tell you, we don't need a light." Hand-in-hand we stumbled over roots and into trees until a sympathetic Providence landed us right side up on the road. Her little idiosyncrasies did not prevent her from being a real person and a true genius. She had about her a kind of majesty, and when one got beyond her forbidding surface, there were warmth, loyalty and a genuine humor.

At a later period in the Carmel days, there came to the colony a tall, gangling young man in his early twenties. He had a head of unmanageable red hair and a freckled face and a pair of remarkable blue eyes, the pupils of which were darted with light. He and I would often walk together through the woods, indulging in philosophical discussions, sometimes lapsing into German, while we both knew that, more than with philosophical problems, our thoughts were concerned with the lovely Helen Cooke to whom we were both devoted. Some years later she married Harry Leon Wilson. The young man was Sinclair Lewis, and if anyone had told me then that he would be the first American to be awarded the Nobel prize for literature, I should not have been particularly surprised.

Aside from the inspiration it was to poets and painters, Carmel deserves the credit of the beginning of the little theater movement in this country. There every summer in the Forest Theater, plays of dramatists, past and present, were given intelligent production. If among the actors there were no Julia Marlowes or Edward Sotherns, at least the lines were given sympathetic reading and a real interest in good drama was aroused.

It was inevitable that such a place as Carmel, which offered such a variety of superbly beautiful scenery, would in time become too popular and attract a class of people out of touch with those for whom it originally had been intended. But there are things immune to the hand of man. The unique beauty and charm of Carmel will never cease to be an inspiration to painters and writers.

STARS OF THE OPERA

BRIGHT stars that radiated their light in my studio every
spring for several years prior to 1906 were the members
of the Maurice Grau Opera Company who came to sing
in San Francisco after their season in New York and Chicago. Often I stood in the wings through a performance, visiting
in their dressing rooms between acts, and it was sometimes my
pleasure to call upon them in their hotels or to dine out with
them, so that I knew them not only for their peerless gifts and
the great artists that they were but for their engaging qualities
as human beings.

It was on a Sunday morning that I made my first pictures
of Melba. She came costumed as Marguerite, and the two hours
she gave to my camera were more an operatic concert than a sitting. She was in very good humor and between pictures she
walked up and down singing snatches from the opera.

A few days later I met her manager. "Do you realize," he
asked me, "that Madame Melba sang about two thousand dollars'
worth at your studio?"

At one of Mrs. Benjamin Guinness' famous Sunday evenings
at 8 Washington Square, just after I had come to New York, I
found Melba sitting by herself in a chair by the door of the
drawing room. "I'm so glad to see you," she said. "I want to talk
to you. Let's go into the other room where there are not so many
people."

When we were seated she told me that Sarah Bernhardt had
sent a young singer with a letter to Mrs. Guinness. "Now she's
going to sing," said Melba, "and I have been asked to give an
opinion. It places me in an awkward position, as I can't bear
to hurt a young girl who is trying to get started and yet I'm not
going to say anything I don't feel."

The girl began to sing and I suggested that we return to the drawing room. "No," said Melba, "we'll stay right here. Then if I don't like her voice I won't have to come out and say so."

The girl had a small voice and it was badly placed. In a few minutes another singer was heard. Immediately Melba was interested. "That," said she, "is a real voice."

When the song was finished she went in and spoke to the young woman who had been singing. It was Marguerite Namara, who was just at the beginning of her career. "You have an extraordinary voice, my dear," was Melba's encouraging comment, "but you have certain faults in tone production that must be remedied. I'm going back to London in a few days. If you come over there look me up and I will be glad to give you some lessons—and I don't say that to many."

Some years after this I was in the reception room of my studio in New York, with my back to the door. Quickly, hands were put over my eyes and someone asked, "Who is it?"

"It sounds like Madame Melba, but it can't be, because she is not in town."

"Turn around," she said. "She is here. And she wants you to make some pictures of her."

It was winter, and it was cold. As she did not want to come out again on account of her voice, I took my camera to her apartment at the Plaza Hotel. After I had made a number of photographs, she said, "I think we both deserve a reward." Going to the telephone she ordered two "Cocktails Melba," which incidentally were Bacardis. When I got up to go she said, "Sit still. You deserve something special." She sat down at the piano, playing the accompaniment as she sang an aria from *La Bohème*.

Her voice had a quality which I can describe only as celestial, so clear and rich and true were its tones. "Tell me," I said, "I've known you for many years—"

"Now don't tell anyone how many," she interrupted.

"What is your secret?" I went on. "How have you been able to retain the freshness and purity of your voice?"

"One reason," she replied, "is that I have never permitted myself to let it out to its full range. No matter what the temptation to do otherwise, I have always kept a reserve fund to draw on, and that is the wisdom I try to impress upon my pupils. In America there are a number of young singers with truly beautiful voices, but I fear what is going to happen to them. They are so ambitious to show what they can do that they let their voices out on every occasion. If they continue this they'll be through in a few years."

The aristocrat of the company was Emma Eames. In addition to her splendid voice she had beauty and style and stature, which made of her a glorious Aïda. Julian Story, the sculptor, to whom she was then married, had designed a gorgeous costume for her. The picture I made of her was on my table one day when Gadski and her husband, Dr. Tauscher, came in. He looked at it and said, "Humph! She thinks she can sing *Aïda!*"

Weeks later, it was Gadski's turn to sing *Aïda* and she had me make some pictures. Gadski, of course, had the voice, but in style and manner she lacked the glamour and verve that distinguished Emma Eames' rendition.

Gadski's picture was on my table one afternoon when Eames dropped in with Dr. Hugh Tevis, who was an old friend of hers. He looked at it, remarking, "Humph! She thinks she can sing *Aïda!*"

With her lovely figure Emma Eames made an enchanting Marguerite, another one of her popular rôles. She was in her early forties when she decided to retire from the operatic stage. There was a rumor that the reason of her retirement was her marriage to the singer, De Gogorza, who had said that one artist in a family was enough.

About a year ago, I found a distinguished elderly lady waiting in my studio. She looked at me in a way that indicated she expected me to recognize her. When I failed to do so, she said,

"Well, I don't blame you. It is over thirty years since you have seen me, but I still have that charming portrait you made of me when I was with the Grau Opera Company. I am Emma Eames. And before I go back to Paris I want you to make the last picture that I shall ever have."

I found her to be much milder than the Emma Eames I had known. Evidently she read my thoughts, for she said, "I'm a nicer person than I used to be. Life has taught me many valuable lessons."

Emma Calvé and Fritzi Scheff supplied the temperament for the Grau Opera Company. They both had a tendency to explode at unexpected moments, bringing consternation to all within their radius. Fritzi was the youngest of the company, and its darling. A fascinating little imp, she had a devilish sense of humor and a temper to which the same adjective could well be applied. At a rehearsal of *Carmen* in which Calvé was to sing the lead and Fritzi was to appear with her for the first time as Micaela, Fritzi came on the stage in a fury. "I'm not going on," she announced with several stamps of her dainty little feet. "I'm not going to rehearse, and I'm not going to sing." It was some time before Grau could discover what was the matter. Finally when she had found her breath Fritzi said, "I just saw the posters outside. They have my name as Miss Scheff. I'm not Miss Scheff—I'm Fritzi Scheff."

Grau's efforts to make peace were unavailing. Scotti tried to reason with her, but she flounced off the stage crying out, "I won't sing. I just won't and that's all there is about it." Edouard de Reszke was the peacemaker. In the wings he put his arm around her. "You poor little child," he said. "What is the matter with you? What difference does it make whether the posters call you Miss Scheff or Fritzi? The public knows you as Fritzi and that is all you need to care about." She stamped and fumed a while longer, but when De Reszke began to laugh at her she had to see the funny side of it, and she was subdued.

The following night Fritzi's singing of Micaela brought down the house. In the third act an enthusiastic young girl threw her some violets from a box. Behind the scenes, and having seen Calvé in action, I said to myself, "That is the last time Fritzi will sing Micaela with Calvé." Sure enough. When the curtain was rung down on the last act, Calvé marched off the stage with fire in her eye and went in search of Maurice Grau. The next time she sang in *Carmen,* and for the rest of the season, there was another Micaela.

Capricious as Calvé was, she had at the same time a remarkable presence of mind in emergencies. At a benefit concert one summer she was singing an aria from *Carmen.* It was rather a hot day, and as she started to take a high note, no sound came. A momentary look of terror spread over her face. Then putting her hand to her throat she said with a smile, *"Il fait vraiment trop chaud pour chanter,"* and she walked off the stage. It was something that only a great artist and a great personality could get away with.

There is no moment so terrifying to a prima donna as when she realizes that she cannot reach the note she wants. It may be but a second before she is able to continue, but the silence that accompanies is terrific. I was present once when this happened to Emma Eames. She was singing *Aïda* and suddenly she could not finish a phrase. She hesitated, then went on to the next one. At the close of the scene she came up to me in the wings. The tears were streaming down her cheeks.

"I'm ruined," she sobbed.

In the next act, before she had a chance to utter a sound, she was greeted with an applause that told her of the affection in which she was held by her audience. The rest of the evening she sang magnificently, never in better voice.

Edouard de Reszke, with his enormous frame, his goatee and long frock coat, was an imposing figure. He looked as if he might have been a bank president or the president of France. His most important rôle, and the one he sang the best, was Hans Sachs in *Die Meistersinger.* I had been listening to him at a rehearsal and his German was distressing to my ears. Off stage, he said to me, "What a terrible language yours is!"

"It certainly is the way you pronounce it," was my reply.

He said that he had given much time and study to it, but for some reason or other he had never been able to master it. My professorial instinct impelled me to offer my help. Every evening before dinner for two weeks he came to me in the library of the Bohemian Club, which was deserted at that hour. In starting out I suggested that our phonetic exercises would be less wearing under the mellowing influence of Rhine wine. So each evening we started out with a bottle of good Rüdesheimer. The morning after the next performance of *Die Meistersinger* the critics were unanimous in their praise of Mr. de Reszke's German which they said was distinguished by the clarity of its enunciation. However, he still persisted every time he saw me that German was a "terrible language." "But," he added, "your music is divine."

David Bispham's great rôle was not Wotan, which was the public's favorite, but his Beckmesser in *Die Meistersinger*. His trick, one that Caruso also had, of whispering asides, was often upsetting to the singers about him.

Scotti, who had a deep appreciation of things Oriental, often went to Chinatown with me, where I introduced him to my Chinese friends. He became very much interested in the study of Chinese character and manners. He had no inkling then that what he was learning would be of value to him years later in Franco Leoni's *L'Oracolo,* an opera based on Chester Bailey Fernald's Chinatown play, *The Cat and the Cherub.* Scotti's rôle was that of Chin Fen, the sinister proprietor of an opium den, and the critics in reviewing it spoke of the authority of his impersonation, for which he gave credit to his rambles in San Francisco's Chinese quarter. It was this opera which he selected for his farewell performance in New York.

It is scarcely necessary for me to say that Schumann-Heink was, to everyone, a grand and noble person. I remember her best as Ortrud in *Lohengrin,* a rôle which lent itself so admirably to her deep, rich notes and her dramatic power. And one of my most inspiring photographic experiences was taking her picture in the purple robe embroidered with a silver dragon which a German artist had designed for her.

At one of her concerts in New York not long ago she came on the stage attired in a fashionable afternoon gown and the latest French model in the way of a hat. I said to the friend who was with me, "I'll bet that hat won't stay on very long."

The accompanist started the prelude. Schumann-Heink gave her head an uncomfortable jerk, and seizing the hat in both hands she slapped it down on the piano. "Ach," she exclaimed, "they want me to be shtylish."

It was Maurice Grau who brought Constant Coquelin and Sarah Bernhardt to San Francisco, where they played together in *L'Aiglon* and *Cyrano de Bergerac* for the first time. Not even Paris had been so honored. Madame Godchaux, who gave French lessons to the débutantes of the city, and who was an old friend of Coquelin, asked me if I would be with him backstage, as he could not speak English. I was, of course, delighted to grant her request. He came sometimes to my studio and when he saw the portraits I had made of other artists of the stage he wanted me to make some of him as Cyrano, stipulating that I must do so at the theater as it took him two hours to build up that prodigious nose. The picture had to be done by flashlight, a process which was not permitted by the management. With Coquelin's connivance I managed to smuggle in the necessary equipment. Flashlights were not silent then as they are now, and when I set mine off, it was a terrific explosion and the stage was filled with smoke. Immediately the firemen were on the scene and the manager, a pompous Englishman, with them.

"Did you take a flashlight?" he said in a fury. When I answered that I had, he shouted, "Well, who in hell gave you the permission?"

"I deed," spoke up Monsieur Coquelin in one of his few

English sentences. "I gave ze au-tor-i-zation." The manager retired in chagrin.

Coquelin understood Sarah's vagaries and could always restore her to equilibrium when she had been taking a flight in temperament. One matinée, in the balcony scene of *Cyrano,* when Sarah, as Roxane, stepped out into the moonlight, there was no moonlight. The man in charge of the lighting had not timed himself properly. For two or three seconds Sarah was left in darkness. Absorbed in her part as she was, to her those seconds were endless. When the curtain went down she ordered the culprit brought before her. He was a great husky creature who knew not one word of French. But Sarah's voice and manner left little doubt in his mind as to what she was saying.

"Out of my sight!" she ended up dramatically. He slunk away like a whipped, overgrown puppy. Sarah, turning to Coquelin who had been watching her with an amused smile, threw her arms around his neck. *"Ah, mon pauvre ami!"* she exclaimed. *"Quel pays! Quel pays!"* A few soothing words from him and she went blithely on with her part.

To have seen Bernhardt and Coquelin together in *L'Aiglon* and *Cyrano de Bergerac* was to have witnessed the culmination of art in the theater. Sarah I was to see many times, but never with a leading man like Coquelin. In *L'Aiglon* his part as the old sergeant was not a great one, but he made it so with his illuminating genius. And to *Les Précieuses Ridicules* he brought such humor and gusto that he made one fully realize the eternal vitality of Molière's satire.

EARTHQUAKE AND FIRE

ONE of the great social events of the opera season in the spring of 1906 was the joint appearance of Enrico Caruso and Olive Fremstad in *Carmen*. A large and enthusiastic audience filled the house for this gala occasion. It was the night of April 17th. After a quiet supper party with some friends, I walked home and went to bed with the music of *Carmen* still singing in my ears. It seemed as if I had scarcely been asleep when I was awakened by a terrifying sound—the Chinese porcelains that I had been collecting in the last years had crashed to the floor. (My interest in Chinese porcelains ever since then has been purely platonic.) The whole house was creaking and shaking, the chandelier was swinging like a pendulum, and I felt as if I were on a ship tossed about by a rough sea. "This can't go on much longer," I said to myself. "When a house shakes like this, the ceiling is bound to collapse. As soon as the plaster begins to fall, I'll cover my head and accept what comes."

An ominous quiet followed. I was about to get up when I found Hamada, my Japanese servant, standing beside me. An earthquake was, of course, no new experience for him, but now he looked thoroughly frightened and was as pale as a Japanese can be. "Master," he said, "very bad earthquake—many days nothing to eat—I go, yes." Before I could say anything he was on his way downstairs. I looked at the clock; the time was a quarter past five. I looked out of the window and saw a number of men and women, half-dressed, rushing to the middle of the street for safety. Pushing his way through them, with a sack of flour over his shoulder and carrying a basket of provisions, was Hamada.

I went to the top floor to see what had happened to my studio. The chimney had fallen through the roof, most of the book shelves had collapsed and the books were buried under mounds of plaster from the wall and ceiling. A sixteenth-century wood sculpture of Buddha had landed right side up and stood unharmed and inscrutable in the midst of the debris—"serene, indifferent of fate."

The earth continued to indulge in periodic tremors, though less violently. I started to get dressed and decided that the most suitable "earthquake attire" would be my khaki riding things— I was to live in them for weeks.

The streets presented a weird appearance, mothers and children in their nightgowns, men in pajamas and dinner coats, women scantily dressed with evening wraps hastily thrown over them. Many ludicrous sights met the eye: an old lady carrying a large bird cage with four kittens inside, while the original occupant, the parrot, perched on her hand; a man tenderly holding a pot of calla lilies, muttering to himself; a scrub woman, in one hand a new broom and in the other a large black hat with ostrich plumes; a man in an old-fashioned nightshirt and swallow tails, being startled when a friendly policeman spoke to him, "Say, Mister, I guess you better put on some pants." . . . But there was no hysteria, no signs of real terror or despair. Nor did buildings show an alarming evidence of destruction; here and there parts of damaged walls had fallen into the streets, and most chimneys had collapsed. At Delmonico's, the front of one of the rooms on the third floor had fallen into the street. A chair with some clothes had been carried with it. The distressed owner called out to a passing workman, "Do you want to make $20?" "Sure," he replied, "what is it?" "See that suit there? I want you to bring it up to me here." Just then another shock occurred. "Ah, you better come and get it yourself."

After wandering about for a while, I went to the house of some dear friends of mine, Milton and Mabel Bremer (she is now married to my old friend Bertram Alanson). I found them calmly sitting on the front steps. The one thing that Mabel was apparently most anxious to save was a pair of evening slippers—a purchase of the day before—which she thrust into my large coat pockets. But it did not save them. I left them at my studio when I returned there later and they were burned with all my possessions.

We decided that it would be a good idea to have some breakfast and went to the St. Francis Hotel which had not been damaged. When we arrived we saw that we were not the only ones who had had the brilliant idea of breakfasting there. The lobby and the dining room were crowded. Near the entrance we saw Enrico Caruso with a fur coat over his pajamas, smoking a cigarette and muttering, " 'Ell of a place! 'Ell of a place!" He had been through many earthquakes in his native Italy but this one was too much for him. It appeared that when he was awakened by the shock, he had tried his vocal cords without success. " 'Ell of a place! I never come back here." And he never did.

Inside the hotel, people in all kinds of attire from evening clothes to nightgowns went milling about. There was no gas or electricity, but somehow hot coffee was available which, with bread and butter and fruit, made a satisfying breakfast. When I asked the waiter for a check he announced with a wave of his hand, "No charge today, sir. Everyone is welcome as long as things hold out."

After seeing my friends home, I went back to my studio to get a camera. The one thought uppermost in my mind was not to bring some of my possessions to a place of safety but to make photographs of the scenes I had been witnessing, the effects of the earthquake and the beginning of the conflagration that had started in various parts of the city. I found that my hand cameras had been so damaged by the falling plaster as to be rendered useless. I went to Montgomery Street to the shop of George Kahn, my dealer, and asked him to lend me a camera. "Take anything you want. This place is going to burn up anyway." I selected the best small camera, a 3A Kodak Special. I stuffed my pockets with films and started out. It was only then that I began to realize the extent of the disaster which had befallen the city. The fire had started simultaneously in many different places when the housewives had attempted to get breakfast for their families, not realizing what a menace the ruined chimneys were. All along the skyline as far as eye could see, clouds of smoke and flames were bursting forth. The work of the fire department was badly hampered, as the water mains had burst.

By this time the city had been put under martial law with General Funston in supreme command. He decided to check the progress of the conflagration by dynamiting a block in advance of the fire in order to create a breach over which the flames could not leap. All day and night the detonations resounded in one's ears and yet the fire continued to make headway. By noon the whole town was in flight. Thousands were moving toward the ferry hoping to get across the bay to Oakland or Alameda. On all streets leading to Golden Gate Park, there was a steady stream of men, women and children. Since all wagons or automobiles had been commandeered by the military authorities, only makeshift vehicles were available. Baby carriages and toy wagons, carts constructed out of boxes and wheels, were used to transport groceries, kitchen utensils, clothes and blankets; trunks mounted on roller skates or even without them were being dragged along by ropes. No one who witnessed these scenes can ever forget the rumbling noise of the trunks drawn along the sidewalks—a sound to which the detonations of the blasting furnished a fitting contrapuntal accompaniment.

Farther out on Geary and Sutter Streets, men and women cooked on improvised stoves on the sidewalks and as the crowds passed they called out invitations to stop for a rest and a cup of coffee. Up on the hill the wealthy were taking strangers into their homes, regardless of any risk they were running. I recall the picture of Henry J. Crocker laughing heartily as he carried the pails of water from the faucet in his garden to a little iron stove, probably one of his children's toys, set up by the curb in front of his red stone mansion.

I have often wondered, thinking back, what it is in the mind of the individual that so often makes him feel himself immune to the disaster that may be going on all around him. So many whom I met during the day seemed completely unconscious that the fire which was spreading through the city was bound to overtake their own homes and possessions. I know that this was so with me. All morning and through the early afternoon I wandered from one end of the city to the other, taking pictures without a thought that my studio was in danger.

As I was passing the home of some friends on Van Ness Avenue, they were on the porch and called out, "Come in and have a drink." While we were raising our glasses, there occurred another shock. Everyone but my hostess and I ran outside. "Let us finish anyway," she said.

"Sure," I said, giving her as a toast the line from Horace, "And even if the whole world should collapse, he will stand fearless among the falling ruins."

On my way to the Bohemian Club I met Charles K. Field. "You dummy," he said. "What are you doing here? Don't you know that your house is going to be blown up?" This was the first time I had thought of such a possibility. Turning back I hurried up Sutter Street to find a militiaman guarding the entrance of my studio.

"You can't get in here," he said, handling his rifle in an unpleasant manner.

"But it's my home," I said.

"I don't care whether it is or not. Orders are to clear all houses in the block. If you don't do as I say, I shoot, see?"

There were rumors that some of the militia, drunk with liquor and power, had been shooting people. I did not want to argue with him, but I did want to get inside, with the hope that I might save a few of my things.

"How about a little drink?" I asked.

"Well, all right," he replied eagerly.

In my cellar I had been keeping a precious bottle—Johannisberger Schloss 1868, which I had brought from the Bremer Rathskeller in 1904—reserving it for a special occasion worthy of it. There had been several gay events that might have justified its consumption, but now there was no doubt about it. The special occasion had arrived. I knew that to my unwelcome guest it would mean nothing, so I brought out for him a bottle of whiskey and while he poured himself drink after drink, I sipped the wine, if not with the leisurely enjoyment that it called for, at least getting some of its exquisite flavor without having to gulp it down with barbarous haste. When my militia friend had absorbed enough of his bottle, he pushed me through the door saying, "Now you have got to get out of here or I'll have to shoot you, see?"

From a safe distance I watched with others the dynamiting of the block of our homes. There was no expression of despair. ("Well, there it goes!" "That's that!" being the only comments heard.) That night I slept in Golden Gate Park together with thousands of others who were in the same plight. The crowd there suggested more a camping out than refugees from a disaster in which they had lost their homes and all their material possessions. A cheerful spirit seemed to prevail throughout and whatever one had was gladly shared.

The fire raged all the next day and well into the morning after, when it was stopped at Van Ness Avenue, which was wide enough to break the spread of the flames. Ten square miles lay devastated with hardly a building intact. In some parts of the city dynamiting continued and the crash of toppling walls could still be heard.

The day of the earthquake, a committee of outstanding citizens met with the mayor and the military authorities and it was unanimously voted that the mayor be empowered to draw checks for any amount for the relief of the sufferers—the committee guaranteeing the payment. The relief measures were carried out with remarkable efficiency. All vehicles and foodstuffs were commandeered for the public good. No food was sold in the shops. Rich and poor had to stand in line at the relief stations to receive their daily rations. On Market Street, rough tables and benches had been put up for the length of several blocks to accommodate the hundreds of people for whom food was being provided. In the military reservation, the Presidio, a city of tents had sprung up affording a shelter for thousands of homeless. In the public squares likewise, tents and shelter of a more substantial form were put up, the occupants readily adapting themselves to this new mode of housekeeping. Some of these shacks were marked "Excelsior Hotel," "The Ritz," "The Little St. Francis," "New Palace Hotel," etc.

In the houses no cooking was permitted; it had to be done on stoves put up on the sidewalks. Water was rationed to be used only for drinking and cooking purposes. Not more than one lamp or candle was permitted in each home. It had to be out by eight o'clock and those who had no business to attend to were obliged to stay indoors. Military patrols on all streets saw that these rules were carried out, and over a period of many weeks of this mode of improvised living, there was not a complaint of neglect or an instance of wrongdoing.

During the day, piling bricks became the enforced pastime of pedestrians. Any man walking through the burned district was likely to be stopped by a soldier or marine and ordered to do his share. Several times while I was out taking pictures, I was put to work.

Rebuilding started while the ruins were still smoking. On top of a heap of collapsed walls, a sign would announce, "On this site will be erected a six-story office building to be ready for occupancy in the Fall." An entertaining illustration of the indomitable spirit of San Francisco was furnished by Mattias (whose restaurant was almost as popular as Coppa's). Having been very prosperous he had decided to take a long vacation and visit his relatives in Spain. He closed his establishment, placing a sign on the door: "Gone to Spain. Will be back in six months." He had been gone only a few weeks when he received a cable from his brother: "Everything lost. Come back at once." When he returned, he found not a house standing in the district where his restaurant had been. Undismayed, he put up a large sign: "Gone to Hell. Will be back in three months." And he was. His was the first building completed in that neighborhood. I recall that Professor Morse Stephens of the University of California made a delightful dedication speech at the opening of the restaurant.

In the Frank Cowderys' home on Maple Street and later on in the Octavia Street home of Dr. Millicent Cosgrave (whose friendship throughout these years has meant so much to me) I had found a haven of rest. For several weeks I did not concern myself with any thought of the future. I blithely continued to take photographs. Of the pictures I had made during the fire, there are several, I believe, that will be of lasting interest. There is particularly the one scene that I recorded the morning of the first day of the fire (on Sacramento Street, looking toward the Bay) which shows, in a pictorially effective composition, the results of the earthquake, the beginning of the fire and the attitude of the people. On the right is a house, the front of which had collapsed into the street. The occupants are sitting on chairs calmly watching the approach of the fire. Groups of people are standing in the street, motionless, gazing at the clouds of smoke. When the fire crept up close, they would just move up a block. It is hard to believe that such a scene actually occurred in the way the photograph represents it. Several people upon seeing it have exclaimed, "Oh, is that a still from a Cecil De Mille picture?" To which the answer has been, "No, the director of this scene was the Lord himself." A few months ago an interview about my work—I had told the story of that fire picture—appeared in a New York paper with the headline, "His pictures posed by the Lord, says photographer."

The ruins of Nob Hill became a rich field for my camera. All that remained standing of the Towne residence on California Street was the marble columned entrance. The picture I made of it by moonlight brought out its classic beauty. Charles K. Field found the title for it, "Portals of the Past," by which the portico

SAN FRANCISCO: APRIL 18th, 1906

STEPS THAT LEAD TO NOWHERE (AFTER THE FIRE)

SARAH BERNHARDT AS PHÈDRE IN THE GREEK THEATRE OF BERKELEY (1906)

MARGARET ANGLIN AS ELECTRA

is known today. It has been removed to Golden Gate Park where in a setting of cypresses it remains a noble monument to a noble past. Charles Rollo Peters made a large painting of it, using my photograph, for the Bohemian Club, and for once the photographer was given credit by a painter. Over his signature on the canvas he inscribed, "With thanks to Arnold Genthe."

On the other side of California Street, in front of the Huntington home, were two marble lions, the traditional commonplace guardians of a home of wealth. The terrific heat of the flames had broken off parts of the stone here and there, simplifying and ennobling their form, as a great sculptor might have done. Of another house all that remained were some chimneys and a foreground of steps. Beyond them was devastation with only the lights of the Mission District visible in the distance. It was another scene that had to be taken by moonlight so as to bring out its full significance. I called the picture "Steps That Lead to Nowhere."

The attitude of calmness of which I have spoken, the apparent indifference of the people who had lost everything, was perhaps not so much a proof of stoic philosophy that accepts whatever fate brings. I rather believe that the shock of the disaster had completely numbed our sensibilities. I know from my own experience that it was many weeks before I could feel sure that my mind reacted and functioned in a normal manner. If I had shown any sense, I might easily have saved some of the things I valued most—family papers, letters and photographs of my parents and brothers, books written by my closest relatives, and of course my more important negatives, which I could have carried away in a suitcase. As it was, practically everything I possessed had gone up in smoke.

To make my loss more complete, it happened that less than two years before, all my family possessions, including my brother Siegfried's, had been brought to San Francisco from Hamburg: the library of over three thousand volumes, some two hundred of which had been written by members of my family in the last century, several pieces of furniture designed by my architect grandfather, family portraits painted by Gruson in the eighteenth century.

Since the death of my brother Siegfried, no family ties had remained to hold me in Germany. As a correspondent for the *Cologne Gazette* he had traveled all over the world, his last assignment being Morocco, where he had been sent during the Buhamara rebellion at the beginning of 1903. He had lived in Fez for a year and was ready to return to Germany, where I had planned to join him. We were to start out together on a several months' expedition to Persia. His trunks were all packed and he was to leave Fez the next day. That afternoon he went out for his daily ride, though he had frequently been warned against these solitary excursions on account of the unrest of the tribes. Not far from the outskirts of the city, he was killed by bandits, who were merely after his fine Arab stallion.

I went to Germany in the summer of 1904—I have never been back since—and had all his belongings shipped to my house in San Francisco. As I needed more space, I had added to my studio the top floor of the adjoining house which was on the level with the studio floor, and there in rooms filled with furniture, books and paintings that I treasured, I had created for myself a background and an atmosphere which gave me peace and happiness. Now all this had gone up in smoke and with it all evidence of the work I had done since the beginning of my career. The thousands of negatives which I had made during that time were now but chunks of molten, iridescent glass, fused together in fantastic forms. Everything I possessed was destroyed except my enthusiasm for work. However, I still had my bungalow at Carmel and, more important, my old negatives of Chinatown. The latter were saved in a curious manner. Before returning to New York, Will Irwin had come to my studio, and looking through my Chinatown pictures remarked, "You really ought not to keep these plates and films here. Some day the whole city will burn up. There'll never be another Chinatown like this one, and you have its only picture record." I heeded his warning, giving all the negatives into the keeping of a friend who had put them into his vault. They were not damaged in the fire.

Among the many telegrams I received was one from Edward Sothern and Julia Marlowe. "Now that you have lost everything," it read, "you should come to New York. We will see that you find a fully equipped studio waiting for you, so that you can start work without delay." It was heartening and consoling to have this fine proof of real friendship. The temptation was great, but I was not willing to leave San Francisco then. I wanted to stay, to see the new city which would rise out of the ruins. I felt that my place was there. I had something to contribute, even if only in a small measure, to the rebuilding of the city. I started my search for a new studio. It would take years before the business section would be rebuilt. No one knew exactly just where the new center of the city was to be. Location was unimportant. On Clay Street, not far from the gates of the Presidio, I discovered a picturesque one-story cottage. In its small garden was a fine old scrub-oak, and I believe it was this and not so much the house that made me decide to take a five-year lease. My friends encouraged me. "Don't worry about being so far out. We'll come anyway, no matter where you are. The chief thing is for you to have a place that you like and where you feel you can work." And so I started to make a few structural changes and to get together the necessary equipment that would enable me to continue my work as a portrait photographer.

SARAH BERNHARDT

A FORTNIGHT after the fateful April 18th, Sarah Bernhardt came West to give a performance of Racine's *Phèdre* at the Greek Theatre in Berkeley. As hotel accommodations were uncertain she made her home in her private car in Oakland. Ashton Stevens of the *San Francisco Examiner* and I were the "reception committee." She asked us to have luncheon with her in her car and take her on a trip through the ruins. Conveyances were at a premium. She refused to consider an automobile. Finally we managed to find an old "sea-going" hack, and we started out, her doctor joining us.

In scattered places fires were still smoldering, and there was some dynamiting where the firemen were razing dangerous walls and chimneys. Her reactions to the devastation were such that by the time we reached the Palace Hotel where she was to have stayed, it was apparent that she had taken the catastrophe to herself. Ordering the driver to stop, she stood up, tears streaming down her face. Heaving with sobs and with arms extended, in her golden voice she delivered an apostrophe to the city that had been, the city that next to Paris was the "darling of her heart." Looking at her there in the clear sunlight, I thought her tragically old and I wondered how she was ever going to create the illusion of Phèdre on the stage of an open-air theater.

On our way back she wanted to send a cablegram to her son, Maurice. As it was expedient to word it in English, she wrote it out in French and asked me to translate it. "Have just completed a tour through the ruins of this once so beautiful city. Sights are indescribable. In many sections the fire is still burning, walls collapsing dangerously near us. Thank God I'm safe." The truth was that at no time were we within a quarter of a mile of the danger zone, which was under heavy military guard and no one was allowed inside. But such was the power of the divine Sarah's imagination that she projected herself, not as a mere spectator but as a sufferer into the very heart of the disaster. Often, years later when I saw her, she would talk about it, and what she really had seen was colorless by comparison with what she claimed to have been through. Once, in New York, when I was calling on her at her apartment in the Hotel Marie Antoinette and there were other visitors, she said, "Do tell them, dear Doctor, how you saved my life when that wall collapsed. It was terrible."

Whatever doubt I had that this great actress would not be able to look the part of Phèdre was dispelled the next afternoon in Berkeley. Young, vital and magnificent, she gave one of the great performances of her life. When it was over, I went backstage as I had promised. She was excitedly walking up and down, her hands to her head. "I never have played Phèdre like this," she exclaimed, "and what an audience! Never has there been one like it. Never have I been so stirred. How marvelous to think they could come here to me today, after all they have been through, and respond with such sympathy and appreciation. They felt that I had something to give to make them forget the loss of their material possessions."

After San Francisco she played two or three night stands in other cities in California, from where she was to go on tour in Mexico and South America. Anxious to see the pictures I had taken during our memorable tour through the ruins, she asked me to bring the proofs to her in San José. When I arrived at her apartment in the Hotel St. James, I was received by her doctor who was in a state of great agitation. "What are we going to do?" he asked me. Taking a clipping from his pocket, he went on, "Madame is so upset by this that she refuses to go on. We tried to keep it from her, but she insisted upon seeing the paper. She says it is the end, that she will never act again."

The criticism, as I remember it, said that her golden voice had grown tinny and that the great Bernhardt had become a tottering old woman who had to hold on to the furniture for support.

"When you go in," said the doctor, "do your best to divert her mind. We have not been able to do anything. And we must leave at five o'clock this afternoon."

When I entered she was sitting up in bed, and although she said nothing to me about the review, I could see that she was depressed. Looking at the pictures, she was immediately interested and began to recall incidents of the fire and quake which had taken place only in her mind. "Now," she said after half an hour or so, "tell me something about Mexico. I wish you would write down the names of some of the places where the train will stop and their amusing pronunciations." When I came to Chihuahua she exclaimed, "Oh, yes. That is where they have those charming little dogs!" Calling out to her secretary in the next room, she said, "Make a note when we come to this place that you must get me one of those darling dogs."

Her doctor told me, months later, that when they got to Chihuahua, where the train stopped for half an hour, the men who were usually on hand with dogs to sell to travelers were not around. The secretary had been dispatched to the town to find one, but the twenty-five dollars he was asked for it was too much for his French thrift. Instead he bought a little mongrel from an old man on a street corner, took it to a barber and had it shaved. Sarah was delighted! *Le pauvre petit mignon. Comme il est adorable.* Her enthusiasm, however, lasted but a few days, and by the time the bristles were becoming apparent, she had abandoned her new pet and was off shooting alligators.

I knew Sarah Bernhardt over a period of years, and her vitality was always amazing to me. She never wanted to rest for fear she would miss something. Once, after I had watched her through a tiring rehearsal, she insisted upon fencing for half an hour with her doctor. Then she lay down on a couch in her dressing room and read over the manuscript of a play someone had sent her. While she was reading she dropped her bracelet. I hastened to pick it up. She stopped me. "But you must be tired," I said.

"Don't bother about me," was her reply. "I'm never tired. To tell you the truth, I'm convinced I will never die unless someone kills me."

Her granddaughter, whom I met later, told me that in 1915 when Sarah had her leg amputated in Bordeaux, she went gaily in her wheel-chair to the operating room, and turning to her weeping relatives said, "Keep your heads up. Don't worry, I'll be all right."

Daniel Frohman tells, as an illustration of her indestructible humor, of a telegram she sent after the operation to some Barnum-like showman at the Panama-Pacific Exposition in San Francisco, who had cabled an offer of $100,000 if she would exhibit her leg. It contained just two words—"Which one?"

In September of the following year she made her sixth American tour, lasting until April, 1917, when she was operated on in New York for a kidney infection. She had a sudden sinking spell, and word was sent to her friends to come and see her for the last time. I was among those who responded. The women could not keep back their tears, and even the men were visibly affected. "Don't weep, my friends," Sarah said. "I shall not die until France is victorious."

During her convalescence she was taken to Spring Lake, New Jersey, where she refused to stay. "Get me out of here," she ordered. "The place is dead. I want to be at some place where I can see life." Removed to the Hotel Nassau in Long Beach, she would sit for hours at a corner window armed with a large telescope, watching the amorous couples on the beach. "You know, my friend," she said to me, "the things I see here are quite incredible. I've never seen anything like it in France."

It was after this illness that Bernhardt went on her last tour, doing a one-act play and a scene from *Camille*. I saw her a day or so before she sailed for France. She was still the divine Sarah, the unconquered.

The letter in which she thanked me for my San Francisco fire pictures is characteristic of her fine spirit:

Mon cher Monsieur Arnold Genthe:

Je vous remercie de vos si jolies et si douloureuses photographies. Vous aussi vous avez tout perdu dans l'horrible catastrophe; mais votre jeunesse, votre courage sont des biens qui vous restent.

Partez à nouveau, recommencez. La vie s'ouvre devant vous, la fortune vous tire le bras. Allez, courage, mon jeune ami. Je sens, je devine, que tout va être beau pour vous. C'est le souhait de

SARAH BERNHARDT.

1906

A Gracious Letter

103

OLD FRIENDS AND NEW

WHEN a notice was published in the papers that I had opened my new studio on Clay Street, Hamada, my Japanese servant who had so ignobly deserted me on the morning of the earthquake, appeared on the scene carrying in his hands a bronze incense burner and an ancient Japanese sword. "I found these in place where studio was. Yes, I come back." No apologies, no explanation about where he had been, but since with all his Japanese peculiarities he was a good servant, I took him back. He stayed with me until I left for New York in the summer of 1911. When I told him that it would not be feasible to take him there with me, he declared, "I will be photographer. Please give me lens of your camera. Many people will like to be photographed by your lens."

He belonged to a distinguished family, and as so many well-born young men of his race were in the habit of doing, he had gone into service as the easiest way of learning the language and customs of America and perhaps pick up some information here and there that might be of use to his government. In his Japanese clothes—incidentally I believe that the costume of a Japanese gentleman is one of the most aristocratic and comfortable attires a man can wear—Hamada truly looked like the son of a samurai, which he was. One day during the visit of the Japanese training squadron he came to me and with some embarrassment said, "Master, I have favor to ask. Tomorrow Japanese captain come at eleven o'clock. Must not know I am servant." "Well, what do you want me to do?" I asked. He replied, "I like captain to think I own studio." "So you want me to act as butler?" "Yes, Master, please." It amused me to do as he wished. Promptly at eleven the next morning the Japanese captain arrived in full dress uniform and I opened the door and ushered him into the studio where Hamada ceremoniously received him, and remained in conference with him for an hour.

My new studio proved a success from the very start. The fact that it was so far away from its old location did not prevent my old friends and new patrons from seeking me out. There was an added element of interest to attract them. I had been making a number of color photographs, portraits as well as landscapes, with a recently perfected process that enabled the photographer to obtain with an ordinary camera, on one plate and with one brief exposure (followed by a very simple method of development), a glass transparency that recorded the colors of nature with astounding fidelity. In 1905 the Lumière brothers of Lyon had invented the Autochrome process, which even in the hands of an inexperienced worker would yield a color positive of great beauty. Of course it was only a transparency that had to be viewed by transmitted light; it was not possible to make prints on paper. But now for the first time, the photographer had at last the means of recording color, of making a color composition, in the way his eyes saw it.

My first trials with this medium were made at Carmel where the cypresses and rocks of Point Lobos, the always varying sunsets and the intriguing shadows of the sand dunes offered a rich field for color experiments. I gradually made myself familiar with the intricacies and uncertainties of the process, and I now was ready to turn my attention to making color portraits. Again it was my good fortune to have before my camera a number of beautiful young women who were ideal subjects and whose color qualities were an inspiration for my new experiments.

There was Olympia Goldaracena, of Spanish descent, whose beauty was as extraordinary as her name. She had the most glorious auburn hair with actually purple shadows, deep-set dark eyes and a flawless skin. An entirely different type was Goldah Charmack, dark complexioned, her finely chiseled features framed in a mass of jet black hair. Virgilia Bogue, chosen as the Queen of

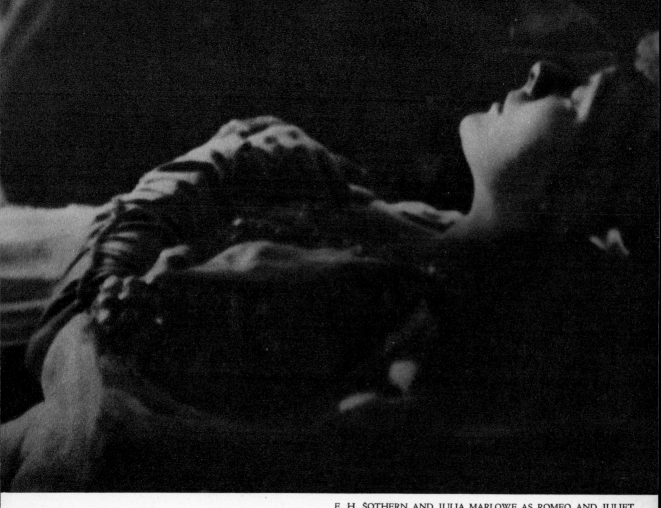

E. H. SOTHERN AND JULIA MARLOWE AS ROMEO AND JULIET

GERTRUDE ATHERTON

MARY AUSTIN

MINNIE MADDERN FISKE AS BECKY SHARP

MRS. PATRICK CAMPBELL

the first Portolá Fiesta, was sent to me by Gertrude Atherton who considered her the typical California girl. Marie Louise Black and Elyse Schultz were photographed in Japanese costumes. The Herrin girls, Alice and Katherine, were photographed in my garden with their faithful collie. Their parents always were afraid that I would elope with one of them, though they did not know which one. One of the most beautiful girls of the younger set and the toast of the season was Enid Gregg. She had not only a rare beauty but talent and a sparkling intellect as well. Hers was the kind of loveliness that would have delighted a Romney. Alice Cowdery and her sister Ina, called "Rimsky" by her friends, with their exquisite coloring, were responsible for a number of successful pictures. And there was little Marian Owen with her extraordinary blue eyes and chestnut-colored hair. She had come to me with a letter from Dr. Cosgrave, asking me to try to find some work for her, since her family had lost everything in the fire. I was looking for someone to help me in the studio and she fitted very nicely. Today, under the pen name of Frances Marion, she is one of Hollywood's most successful scenario writers, and a novelist and short story writer besides.

Some of my best color portraits made in those years were the ones I did of Minnie Maddern Fiske as Becky Sharp, of whom I had made many other photographs (as Hedda Gabler and as Rebecca West in *Rosmersholm*) in the preceding years.

Mrs. Fiske came to me through her young cousin and traveling companion, Emily Stevens, who was soon to become a star of the stage herself. It was the beginning of a true friendship, one that lasted until her death. Mrs. Fiske insisted that I call her Cousin Minnie, and to her I was Ginky, a nickname invented by her cousin. I often was her escort in the few hours of leisure she permitted herself away from her work. She never knew what it was to have a real rest. When she was not playing on Broadway or on tour, she was reading manuscripts or getting ready for a new rôle. The long runs that were so irksome to some actresses were never so to her. Once when I asked her if she didn't find it tedious having to play the same part over and over, night after night, she said:

"No. It's never the same. You get a reaction from the audience that makes you change an inflection or a gesture. A part is always new to me, even if I play it a hundred times."

She was strangely sensitive to the character and mood of her audience. After the theater, when she and Emily Stevens and I went to supper together, she would say, "Do you remember that line in the second act that usually gets a laugh? I wonder why it didn't get over tonight?" Or between acts, if I were behind the scenes, she would point out some particular person. "Do you see that man in the third row? I wish he were not here. He is an antagonistic and disturbing influence." She expected me to be out in front every night, no matter how often I had seen the play. By the time I had sat through two or three performances, I knew it almost by heart and could do a little cheating.

Her sympathy and kindness to young actresses was truly splendid. A young English girl who had studied at the Sargent School of Acting came to me with a letter. Her mother had died, the girl with whom she had been living had escaped with all her belongings, and she was almost without funds. She was very anxious to get in Mrs. Fiske's company. When I told Cousin Minnie about her she said, "I have no place for her, I'm afraid." But when I had explained the girl's situation she said, "Very well, I will write in a line for her and she can have twenty-five dollars a week." I remember that line to this day. My friend Julia would come often to rehearse it with me. But at the opening night, she was so nervous that nobody in the audience could hear that the girl with the beautiful red hair was saying, "So this is a picture of the dear departed one."

One Sunday evening in San Francisco, Mrs. Fiske said she would like to have dinner at one of "those queer places" and see a variety show. I took her to Mattias' Mexican restaurant, quite forgetting that the walls there were covered with pictures of bull-fights, and that her one interest outside of her work was her campaign against cruelty to animals. In an effort to save the evening, I told her of a bullfight I had attended in Spain given for the benefit of the Society for Prevention of Cruelty to Animals. She was horrified, but her sense of humor prevailed and after a dinner of enchiladas, frijoles and some good wine, we went merrily on to a variety show, where we sat in a booth opposite the stage. There were cakewalks, a shuffle dance and some songs. Then out came a young and very pretty girl from Morocco. Although she was doing the *danse de ventre,* she brought no suggestion of vulgarity to it. Not once did she glance at her audience.

"Do you know," Mrs. Fiske said, "that girl has real charm. I'd like to talk with her."

When I spoke to the proprietor, a most unprepossessing individual, he said, "She is my niece—well, not exactly my niece. This is her first appearance since coming from Marakesh." The girl spoke no English and, as Mrs. Fiske spoke no French, I did the interpreting. It was a lovely picture to see this great artist, sitting in those sordid surroundings, gently questioning an obscure girl about her life and her ambitions. It seemed she wanted to be a great dancer. She had heard of the opportunities in America and accepted the first offer made her, not knowing what she was getting into. And she listened eagerly to the advice which Mrs. Fiske so sincerely gave her.

I never knew Mrs. Fiske to be anything but gentle and courteous, and yet there were many who found her difficult. On one of her visits she called me on the telephone, explaining that Gertrude Atherton had written a play for her which they were to talk over the next day at luncheon. "Everyone says that she is so difficult, and I am wondering, since you know her so well, if you would come along." I said I would be delighted. Soon the bell rang again. This time it was Gertrude Atherton. "I have written a play for Mrs. Fiske," she said, "and tomorrow we are going to have luncheon together and talk it over. Everyone says she is so difficult and I am wondering, since you know her so well, if you would come along." I said I would be delighted. And the next day there I was at the St. Francis Hotel between these two Royal Bengal tigers as they sat facing each other at the table. However, with the help of some delectable sand-dab and a bottle of Chablis all difficulties were smoothed over. The play was produced on the road in Canada with Mrs. Fiske in the leading rôle, but for some reason or other it never got to Broadway. A glimpse into the mind of an author: Mrs. Atherton told me that when she started to write the play she knew little about the construction of a drama, but had acquired a feeling of how to go about it by several successive readings of Ibsen's *Rosmersholm.*

We had many good times together, Cousin Minnie, Emily Stevens and I. Often, when the play was over, we would be joined by the Ashton Stevenses and drive out to the beach, stopping at the Cliff House or the Casino for supper. Then we would drive back through Golden Gate Park and Mrs. Fiske and Emily would sing for my special benefit my pet aversion, "Darling, I am growing old, Silver threads among the gold." One night as we went rolling along through the fog, we were stopped by a policeman at the beach entrance to the park, five miles from the city. He put his head in the door and said, "I'm wondering if you'd be so kind as to give my girl friend here a lift." "Indeed," said Mrs. Fiske, "we'll be glad to, if she doesn't mind sitting with the driver." And all the way in Mrs. Fiske worried about the "poor girl" and how terrible it would have been, if she had been forced to walk alone all that distance in the dark through the fog.

Another time, when she was staying in Oakland with the first Mrs. Jack London, who was her cousin, we had been to supper and had to hurry in order to catch the last ferry boat. We were at the top of the hill when our cab broke down. No other conveyance was in sight. There was nothing to do but walk. Arm in arm we trotted down hill and were in sight of the ferry, when the clock told us that we had three minutes to spare. We started to run and suddenly in front of us we saw the figure of a man sprawled across the sidewalk. "Cousin Minnie," I said, "we'll have to jump." And without changing our course or slowing up we jumped clear over the unconscious body and got to the ferry just in time to get through the gates.

A most diverting afternoon was one when she was compelled to write an interview with herself. A dramatic critic had made an appointment for an interview which was scheduled to be run in the following Sunday's paper, and the deadline for it was Thursday evening. That morning his wife called up in a frenzy. Her husband had been out all night and was not in a condition to either appear or write his story. It was decided that I should go to the office of the newspaper, look through the files and set down certain characteristic phrases which the critic frequently used, and with the help of my notes and suggestions Mrs. Fiske would ask and answer her own questions and write her own personality sketch. It was Friday before the critic returned to the realm of reason. His first thought was about the interview. "Well," he said to his wife, "I guess my job is gone."

"Why?" she asked.

"On account of the Fiske interview."

"But you wrote it, don't you remember, and I took it myself to the office," she said. When the Sunday paper came, there was the interview written in his best manner. "My God!" he said. "I must have been stewed. I have no recollection whatever of writing this thing. But it's pretty good."

Of the many stars of the theater whom I have known, Minnie Maddern Fiske was the only one who cared nothing about her personal appearance. She had little if any vanity and frankly admitted that she had no taste for clothes and was not interested in them. Emily Stevens and I often teased her about her hats. One day she appeared with a gorgeous looking affair trimmed with American Beauty roses. "Now, Ginky," she said, "I hope that at last I have a hat that you will like. You ought to, for I paid $45 for it."

She had no love for music. It did not mean anything to her; concerts and the opera left her unmoved. Once in New York, a mutual friend, Alice Kauser, the playbroker, suggested that we take

Mrs. Fiske to hear *Tristan und Isolde,* believing that the divine music of this greatest of Wagner's operas could not fail to stir her. We were mistaken. Mrs. Fiske did not even listen, but kept on talking, to the annoyance of the people near us. There were indignant sounds of "shhh" all around us. This is probably the only time that Mrs. Fiske was ever hissed.

It was this great artist's incapacity for idleness that wore her out before her time. I have a letter from her written during her last months. "At last," it read, "I have found a place in the country such as I have always wanted." To me these lines had a subtle pathos, for she did not live to enjoy the home to which she had looked for so long.

Some months before her death she dropped in at my studio in New York. "I'm so tired," she said. "I'm always tired these days. Do let me rest a while here." She lay down on the couch and slept for three hours. It was the last time I saw her.

When I first knew Emily Stevens—she was only fifteen then—she had not shown any stage ambition, though as Mrs. Fiske's constant companion she lived in the world of the theater. One day a member of the company who played a minor rôle was taken ill and Emily was coached in the part. She acquitted herself so well that from time to time she was given small rôles. That was the beginning of one of the most brilliant stage careers of an American actress. Though for quite a while she played only small parts and was not considered an actress of any particular promise, occasionally a reporter interviewed her. Once, when asked if she was related to Mrs. Fiske, her answer was, "Yes, she's my cousin. She's also an actress." Her success in New York was sensational. She is probably best remembered for Louis Anspacher's brilliant play, *The Unchastened Woman,* which, thanks to Emily's scintillating performance, kept running for several seasons. Her supper parties in her studio on Sixty-seventh Street were a gathering of the most brilliant men and women in the theater world, and of writers and artists. She was one of the few women I have known who was able to keep up with Alexander Woollcott's wit.

Julia Marlowe and Edward Sothern, whom I had known for many years, were the subjects of my first really ambitious venture in color photography. In the garden of my cottage studio, I took them in a number of scenes from *Macbeth*. The weathered boards of my kitchen annex looked like the gray walls of Glamis Castle and were a good background for the colorful costumes. I made plates of both of them on the throne, of Sothern as Macbeth alone, and a whole series in fifteen different poses of Marlowe as Lady Macbeth in the sleep-walking scene, which formed a frieze that might have been taken from a motion picture.

Some years before I had taken some photographs in black and white of the death scene in *Romeo and Juliet*. When the catafalque had been put up in all its completeness by the men from the theater, it filled the whole floor space. Fortunately I had a little foyer which permitted me to set my camera at the right angle. The pictures created a moving dramatic effect with Sothern kneeling over the bier and looking at Marlowe's profile of rare and perfect purity. I had also taken her profile alone as Juliet, which she referred to as the most beautiful picture ever taken of anyone. It has been interesting to me to compare her profile as it is today with what it was then. Two years ago she was asked by a new magazine, *Fashion Art,* to have some photographs taken in her Molyneux gowns for its first issue. She was willing to do so, but stipulated that nobody but Arnold Genthe should take the pictures. When she came in I also took a portrait of her in exactly the same pose as the one I had done of her thirty years before. The Juliet profile has youth and a certain lyric beauty. The other is that of a head modeled by life, that greatest sculptor of all. Those who see the two photographs side by side invariably remark, "How marvelous, that she should have retained her contours over so many years." And I always reply, "Yes, it is remarkable as a proof that good bone structure and the right attitude toward life are more important than beauty doctors."

Many times Peter Robertson, the dramatic critic on the *San Francisco Chronicle,* and I would have supper with Sothern and

Marlowe at the St. Francis Hotel and eagerly listen to their revealing and exciting comments on the Shakespearean drama. One evening when Julia Marlowe was not there, Sothern got out his copy of *Romeo and Juliet* in which Romeo's text was all marked up with mysterious little signs and symbols. "Those," he said, "are Julia's annotations. She went over every bit of the part with me, marking the inflections and cadences. Whatever praise I may receive for my rendition of the part belongs to her." A unique admission for an actor.

In 1911 they were making their home in New York, on the top floor of an old house on Madison Avenue, and they had invited me for dinner. When I was about to leave, Sothern left the room for a moment. While he was gone Miss Marlowe said, "I want to give you a little book of poems Edward wrote to me. Don't let him see it, because he's very shy about them."

As I was putting the book in my pocket he returned. "What have you given him?" he asked.

"Never you mind," she laughed, and turning to me she said, "Now don't tell him. Hurry up," as she pushed me gaily through the door.

Sothern was so modest that he did not want anyone to see the poems, but they had definite charm. At rehearsals, I must say, he was not so meek. He was a real general, insisting that his orders be carried out and with slight patience if they were misunderstood or neglected.

The music of Marlowe's voice, once heard, was never forgotten. It was not God-given, but the reward of conscientious study and practice. She told me that she had begun training it when she was very young, learning how to modulate it and at the same time project it so that it would lose none of its timbre and cadence. Recently some friends of mine who had returned from a Mediterranean cruise told me that they were visiting the Museum in Cairo when they heard a woman's voice in the next room.

"That is Julia Marlowe," said the wife. "There isn't another voice like it in the world."

ULIA MARLOWE AS JULIET

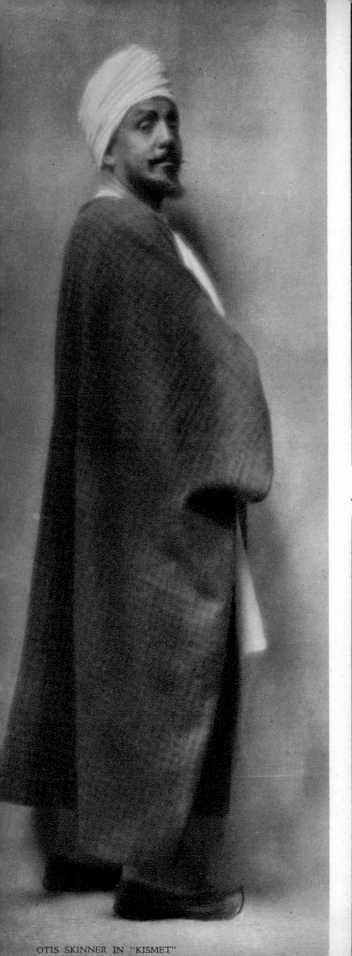

OTIS SKINNER IN "KISMET"

DAVID BELASCO

WALTER HAMPDEN AS HAMLET

"Don't be absurd," said her husband. "How could it be Julia Marlowe?"

But it was Julia Marlowe who now has a house in Cairo where she spends her winters. I recently sent to her all the color plates I had made of her and Sothern. She had looked through them at my studio after her husband's death and had asked me to send her the whole collection.

Another great artist of the stage, whose voice will always remain a melody in the ears, is Mrs. Pat Campbell. She made several visits to San Francisco and each time she came to have her picture taken. I photographed her as Mrs. Tanqueray, in Bernard Shaw's *Pygmalion,* and as Electra. In 1902, which was when I first met her, she invited me to have tea with her. When I arrived and started to sit down, she gave an agonizing shriek. To my embarrassment I discovered that I had been about to make a cushion of Pinky-Panky-Poo, a rather horrid little Belgian griffon which the Leopold who was then King of Belgium had given her.

At the height of her career Mrs. Campbell had a radiant and imperious beauty. When she came to have her picture taken as Electra, she brought Miss Agnes Tobin (Dick Tobin's sister) and Mrs. Francis Carolan (Harriet Pullman of Chicago, now Mrs. Arthur Schermerhorn) who carried her admiration of Mrs. Pat to the extreme of imitating her in speech and posture and dress. The sitting began in the morning and lasted well beyond noon.

"I think it would be fun to have lunch here," said Mrs. Campbell.

It was Hamada's day off and I was not prepared to offer my hospitality.

"I'll tell you what," she said, turning to Mrs. Carolan. "You go out and get us some sandwiches and cheese and olives—and don't forget a bottle of Rhine wine." Mrs. Carolan went meekly forth to carry out the orders, and I am sure it was the first time she had known what it was to step across the doorsill of a delicatessen shop, even if she was conveyed there in her limousine.

Mrs. Pat then insisted that I take a picture of the luncheon party which she wanted to send to Hugo von Hoffmansthal, whose version of *Electra* she was presenting. It is his son, by the way, who is now the husband of Alice Astor.

Alvin Langdon Coburn, the English photographer, told me when he was visiting San Francisco that he was very anxious to make a picture of Mrs. Campbell. He said that Bernard Shaw, of whom he had made a great variety of portraits, had given him a letter of introduction which he couldn't possibly deliver. The letter read: "Dear Stella, My friend Alvin Langdon Coburn has just made a splendid photograph of me in the nude. He wishes to do the same by you."

It was years before I saw her again. At a luncheon given by the Walter Rosens in New York—I did not know Mrs. Campbell was in America—I heard her voice. As I turned around she rushed up to me with outstretched arms and exclaimed, "Oh, it is good to see you. You haven't changed a bit." Then standing back she said, with a gesture signifying rotundity, "But look at *me*. Isn't it terrible?"

She had taken on some weight, but she still was beautiful. We talked over old days and she asked me to tea at her hotel. As a surprise I prepared a portfolio of all the pictures I had ever made of her. When she had looked at them, she called to her niece who was in another room, "Stella, come and look at these. Aren't they beautiful? And they are all me. And look at me now."

In 1908 I had my long-hoped-for trip to Japan. For six months I wandered with my camera all over the islands, visiting many districts remote from the tourist routes, spending several weeks on the island of Yezo (Hokkaido) among the Ainu. Of this journey and of others I shall tell in another chapter.

It was after my return from Japan that Lloyd Osbourne, the son of Mrs. Robert Louis Stevenson, asked me if I would come to his home to look at some Japanese books which had belonged to his stepfather. They were the complete set of Hokusai's famous

Mangwa—the fourteen sketchbooks he had published for the benefit of his pupils. While I was explaining their significance to Osbourne, the heavy door of his study opened. It was not opened by a hand but by the kick of a foot. The foot was followed by an elderly lady attired in a Mother Hubbard wrapper. It was Mrs. Stevenson.

She said, "You have come at an opportune moment. Today I received a letter from John Singer Sargent asking me for a photograph of the two paintings he made of my husband."

She brought out a canvas that showed Stevenson walking in his library with one hand on his hip and the other holding a cigarette. In the background was a doorway through which one got a glimpse of a figure sitting on a sofa.

Pointing to it Mrs. Stevenson said, "That blotch of color is supposed to be me."

When I asked to see the other portrait she answered in a somewhat evasive manner that she did not have it.

"But where is it?" I questioned.

"Well, if you must know," she replied, "it wasn't a portrait. It was a vile caricature and I destroyed it."

From then up to the time I left San Francisco we were good friends, and I often visited her there and in Santa Barbara. When she had her house in Santa Barbara remodeled, she drew her own plans. The architect whom she had consulted said they were absolutely impractical. She engaged a local builder who proved they were practical. When the architect saw the completed house he came to see her. "I must apologize," he said. "You certainly know more about remodeling houses than I do."

It was here that I listened to her read some passages from her Samoan diary. In speaking of a missionary whom she particularly disliked she had written, "May the dogs eat his bones."

I took a number of pictures of her, and on the day that the proofs were ready, learning that it was her birthday, I sent some flowers along with them. In the next morning's mail I received her card on which she had written:

"Like a god from fair Olympus, thou
With grace and beauty me endow;
And then to make the deed complete
You lay sweet blossoms at my feet."

The color plates that I had made in San Francisco, portraits and landscapes, had created quite a stir and I was urged to arrange an exhibition. In the spring of 1911 at the Vickery Galleries on Sutter Street, they were on view for two weeks. This was, I believe, the first exhibition in America of color photographs. Among the many portraits were, of course, the stage celebrities who had sat for me, including David Belasco and portraits of my Bohemian friends. Society was represented by Miss Jennie Crocker, Mrs. Phoebe Hearst, Enid Gregg and several of the beautiful débutantes, whom I had photographed in a variety of colorful costumes. There were also a number of the scenes I had done at Carmel: poppy and lupin fields, cypresses and cliffs of Point Lobos, a rainbow reflected in the wet sand of the beach at low tide, and a whole series of sunsets.

The exhibition created a real sensation and the public as well as the press were generous in their praise.

On a hurried trip East to arrange the transfer of my Hegel manuscript to the library of Harvard, I had met a number of artists and editors to whom my work was known. They all urged me to come to New York. My old San Francisco friends who now lived in New York, Will Irwin, Jack Cosgrave, Robert Aitken, and others, were equally insistent. So were the Sotherns and Mrs. Fiske. Heretofore I had closed my mind to such suggestions. I felt I belonged to San Francisco. I loved the city not only for its beauty and its spirit but for its generosity and the opportunities it had given me. I had a clientele that left nothing to wish for and friends whom it would be difficult to say good-by to. I knew that I could go on leading a delightful, comfortable existence, but I was beginning to feel that I had gone as far as I could go there. When I looked at my artist friends I realized that whatever ambition I might have would likewise gradually diminish. Life had taught me that progress grows only out of change and struggle. I made

PRESIDENT THEODORE ROOSEVELT

ARTURO TOSCANINI

GERHART HAUPTMANN

JOSEPH PENNELL

IGNACE PADEREWSKI

up my mind to leave San Francisco, difficult though it would be, and come to New York.

None of my friends believed me at first, but in true San Francisco manner they made my announced departure the motive for a number of farewell parties, one of which was a dinner given by the Bohemian Club. I was presented with an etching by Will Sparks on which all the Bohemians present at the dinner signed their names. A number of amusing caricatures painted by Maynard Dixon, Haig Patigian and Robert Aitken added to the gaiety of the evening.

I had arranged my trip to New York so that I would have at least one week in the Grand Canyon. I had been there in 1904, prepared to take a number of pictures. I did not take any. "It is useless," I had said. "Unless it can be done in color it would be a desecration." Now I planned to make some color plates.

In the deep gorges of the canyon there was rich picture material. One day I went down to the bottom on foot, and after most of my plates had been used up I started back on the seven-mile climb to the top, when I was caught in a terrific thunderstorm. It was not just one thunderstorm but a convention of them. As there was no place to seek shelter, all I could do was to trudge on carrying my camera which seemed to be getting heavier every minute. When I got to the rim of the canyon, the storm had subsided, and there before me, descending into the purple depths, was the most magnificent rainbow I have ever beheld. I had just two plates left. Quickly I set up my camera. It was still drizzling and I had nothing to protect the lens from moisture, since my hat had blown off in the storm. Glancing around I saw a forest ranger on horseback to whom I signaled. He came cantering up. "What's the trouble?" he asked.

"I want to make a photograph of this rainbow," I said. "Would you be kind enough to hold your sombrero over the lens?"

Silently he did as I requested. When I had finished he gave me a doubtful look, asking, "Can you really take a picture of a rainbow?"

"I think I have," was my reply.

He said he would like to see it, and I took his name and address, promising that perhaps I could send it to him. The following spring, Stuart Benson, then art editor of *Collier's*, reproduced it in the Easter number.

I sent the ranger, who had been my friend in need, a copy of the magazine. He thanked me in a letter, written not according to the rules of a correspondence school but in his own vernacular. It began: "Say," and went on, "You sure are O.K. The picture of that rainbow is a pippin. I thought you was joshing me."

*Picture
of a
Rainbow*

120

PRESIDENTS AND FINANCIERS

WHEN I arrived in New York, though I stayed at the old Brevoort Hotel—far from the noise of Broadway—the terrific tempo and rush of the city's life, the haste and hurry of the people, bewildered me. I wondered if they really knew what they were running after. In the clubs to which I had cards I found an atmosphere different from that of the Bohemian Club. My friends were all out of town and the other members seemed too busy to talk to a strange visitor. I was to realize later that this attitude is not due to any lack of cordiality. Bohemian warmth and friendliness cannot blossom forth spontaneously in the terrific rush and pressure of New York life.

My old San Francisco friends, especially Will Irwin and Jack Cosgrave, when they returned to town, were unsparing in their efforts to put me in touch with people who might be of use to me. My chief concern, of course, was to find a suitable studio. In the old Thorley Building at the corner of Fifth Avenue and Forty-sixth Street, the top floor had been used as a photographer's studio. The location, space and arrangement were quite ideal for my purpose, yet the rental seemed to be much more than I could possibly afford. I looked at many other places, but having seen what I really wanted, they failed to satisfy me. If one is to inspire faith in others, one must have confidence in one's self. Thorley, the florist, who was the landlord, was not encouraging.

"You won't last a year," he said. "A photographer had the place for six months and he had to give it up because he could not make a go of it." But I was not to be deterred. I had made up my mind and was determined to make the experiment, no matter what the result might be. I was to have no reason to regret my decision.

As soon as I was settled Will Irwin took me on the round of the editorial offices. John Phillips, the editor of the *American Magazine,* was very much interested in color photography. When he saw some of my plates he asked me if I thought they could be reproduced in a magazine. "I don't think," he said, "that it has ever been done. But it should be possible."

I told him that it depended upon the engraver. "I know," said I, "that the Beck Engraving Company of Philadelphia can reproduce them."

Mr. Phillips followed my suggestion and in 1912 an article about me by Will Irwin and a series of my color photographs—Sothern and Marlowe in *Macbeth,* Mrs. Fiske as Becky Sharp, a portrait of an unknown beauty in a yellow gown—were run in color in the *American Magazine.* This was the first time in America that any magazine of large circulation had direct reproductions of color photographs. *Collier's,* as I have already told, was the next to do so with the rainbow picture. Other plates I had made elsewhere were also reproduced. George Barr Baker, the editor of *Delineator,* used several. One appeared on the cover of the *Forum* and one on the cover of *Town and Country.*

In the spring of that year I held in my studio an exhibition of my California autochromes which was a novelty for New York.

One of the most interested visitors was Dr. Alexis Carrel. He came originally from Lyon, where the autochrome was invented. The Lumière brothers were his friends, and it was at Dr. Carrel's suggestion that one of them visited New York that year, and I had some pleasant and profitable talks with him. The portrait I made of Dr. Carrel was the first that I did in my new studio. He liked the picture so much that he brought his wife, of whom no successful photograph had ever been made. Only a short time ago Dr. Carrel spoke of the charming pictures I had made of his wife, without her even realizing that she was being photographed.

Another who became a client through attending my exhibition was John Patterson, the founder and president of the Dayton

Cash Register Company. Mr. Patterson was always eager to be the first to use a new invention or an improvement on an old one. He commissioned me to take a series of pictures in color of his plant, the factory, and the vegetable gardens of his workers, to each of whom he had given a little plot of land for cultivation.

It was evening when I arrived in Dayton and I was greeted at the station by Mr. Lee Olwell who had written me to bring my riding togs.

It seems that Mr. Patterson, who loved horses and went riding every day, summer and winter, seldom employed a man in a position for important work unless he was a good horseman. "A man," he said, "who cannot control a horse is not fit to direct men."

My week in Dayton was a pleasant one. Through it came the friendship of Mr. Thomas J. Watson, then vice-president of the company. Today he is president of the International Business Machines Corporation in New York. He was as fond of horses as I was, and every morning we went out together for an hour or two. Since then I have had the pleasure of being a guest at his estate in New Jersey and have made many photographs of his wife and children. In the tranquillity of his home and the mutual devotion of its members, I have found what is to me the ideal American family.

Another visitor to my exhibition was Miss Belle Da Costa Greene, the director of the Morgan Library, through whom I was asked to make a series of color plates of its treasures. This was not the library that has since been made accessible to the public, but the private sanctum of Mr. J. P. Morgan the elder. Without exaggeration it could be called the most beautiful room in America. Everything in it was a world famous masterpiece. Neither in color nor arrangement was there a discordant note. The rich red of the Florentine walls, the old furniture, the rare books, the fine antique marble mantel, created a perfect environment for the old masters.

I took pictures of many of the paintings—among them Ghirlandaio's masterpiece of Giovanna Tornabuoni, a Botticelli Madonna and the portrait of a man by Castagno. Working in that room was a privilege indeed. During the long exposure of the plates I was permitted to go into the vault where the rare and precious manuscripts were kept and to study those in which I was particularly interested. This of itself would have been ample compensation to me.

Mr. Morgan was so pleased with results of my work that he had me make a number of duplicates which, mounted in Morocco cases, he gave to some of his friends, including George F. Baker and Thomas Fortune Ryan, as Christmas cards. Later on when I met Mr. Ryan he said to me, "I have been wanting to thank you for making it possible for me to own Mr. Morgan's Ghirlandaio. I keep the plate in my desk at the office and when things go wrong I take it out and, looking at it, my equilibrium is restored."

Sometimes, when I was taking the pictures, Mr. Morgan would stop to talk with me. He was one of the most compelling personalities I have encountered. His eyes were like those of an eagle, and when he spoke, they made one completely oblivious to anything else that might be going on around one. His manner was somewhat abrupt and even brusque in its straightforwardness. But under the surface there was a great kindliness. To me he seemed like a hardy and unconquerable old sea-captain. His attitude toward his pictures was ingenuous and yet direct. He was, I think, as much attracted by the subject of a canvas as by its artistic merit. He had a profound piety—he read the Bible every day—and his collection of paintings and sculptures were mostly religious in nature.

In the room was a portrait of him by Baca Flor, the Peruvian painter. As a work of art it was indifferent—the artist had a habit of making lavish use of bitumen, putting it on in layers so thick that in hot weather the canvas actually sweated. Like his portrait of Joseph D. Choate, it was an excellent likeness, as it had caught the eagle look in the eyes. I took a photograph of the head alone. Someone had told Mr. Morgan that I had a way of making pictures of people when they were not aware of it, and when I showed him this one, he said, "When did you catch me like that? I suppose they would recognize it on Wall Street."

In preparing for the Christmas celebration in the home on Madison Avenue, Miss Anne Morgan had asked Elizabeth Marbury to arrange a program which would please children of all ages —seven to seventy. Miss Marbury, having seen my color plates, had the idea that, since everyone likes to look at pictures, it would be a novel entertainment to have me put on a stereopticon "picture book."

The plates I had taken were four times the size of lantern slides and there was no projection lantern which could be used with them. Besides they could not stand the intense heat from the brilliant light. I had to devise a lantern that would be large enough and with a cooling contrivance to filter the light so that they would not be marred. This was the first time that such plates were projected.

They were shown on a large screen and included pictures of the California scenery, of the Arizona desert, the rainbow taken in the Grand Canyon and, of course, those I had made in the Morgan library. For the last of all I had reserved a surprise for Mr. Morgan. He had a favorite and favored Pekinese that was never out of his presence when he was in the house. In the financial conferences which took place in the library, Chang always sat with his master or lay on the floor at his feet. (A pity that Chang could not have written *his* memoirs.) One afternoon when such a parley was going on, I had Chang kidnapped and brought into the garden where I took his picture. At the end of the Christmas program Mr. Morgan said to me, "That rainbow and the California scenes were charming, of course, but the best of all was Chang."

The homey atmosphere of the entire evening was a reflection of that simplicity which is ever the mark of true greatness. The presents, displayed on tables in the living room, were just such gifts as might be exchanged in any well-bred American family of moderate means. And Mr. Morgan was in an appreciative and affectionate mood. It all gave quite a different impression from the austere and unbending autocrat which has been handed down by some of his biographers.

Three Presidents of the United States—Theodore Roosevelt, William H. Taft and Woodrow Wilson—came into my sphere, or perhaps I should say I had a glance into theirs.

A prelude to my actual meeting with Mr. Roosevelt was in the Yosemite Valley, where he was making the trip in the company of John Muir. Some friends and I were on a camping trip and with a packtrain we were taking the steep narrow trail leading up to Little Yosemite. I was riding ahead, when about three hundred yards up the trail a man on horseback dismounted and stood to one side. At closer view I saw it was Theodore Roosevelt. When I got to him I took off my hat and said, "I am sorry, Mr. President, that we put you to so much trouble."

"Quite all right," he replied with a wide smile. "I must follow the mountain rules. Where are you going?"

"To the Little Yosemite."

"That's where I'm coming from. Had a bully time," he said.

It seemed a strange procedure for the President of the United States to be riding alone in a mountain wilderness. Five minutes later we met two forest rangers. We told them of our meeting. "We're his bodyguard," they said, "but he didn't want to be bothered with us. He is going to meet John Muir, the man who knows the name of every flower, tree and shrub in the Reservation."

We returned to the floor of the Valley the day the President was leaving. The Park Commissioners, wishing to do something in his honor, had planned to illuminate the waterfalls. Hearing of it in advance he sent out the ukase, "No nature faking—*please*."

As he was about to ride out, the guests and the people who lived there gathered to wave good-by. At the edge of the crowd was a little boy who called out to him as he passed, "Hello, Teddy."

Mr. Roosevelt turned his horse around and, cantering back,

PRESIDENT WILLIAM HOWARD TAFT

A. W. MELLON

SENATOR ROBERT LaFOLLETTE, SR.

PRESIDENT WOODROW WILSON

JOHN D. ROCKEFELLER, SR. (1918)

said, "You little rascal. Hasn't anyone taught you to have respect for your President?" The child was petrified.

Six months or so later I was walking on Pennsylvania Avenue in Washington one Sunday when I saw the President and his daughter, Alice, coming toward me. As is my habit, I was holding my hat in my hand and I put it on so that I could salute properly.

As he passed me he smiled, calling out, "How's the Yosemite?"

After he had left the White House I was commissioned to go to Oyster Bay to take his portrait. I was told to be there at eight o'clock in the morning. As I wished to get him outdoors, I was there a little ahead of time and had my camera all set. Promptly at eight o'clock he came out of the house in his riding clothes. "I'm sorry," he said, "but I can give you only ten minutes. I have an important meeting with a delegation that was to come tomorrow, but it will be here today instead."

In the hope of engaging his interest so that he would give me more time I spoke of his *African Game Trails,* telling him what a relief it was to find an explorer's book so well illustrated with good photographs.

"I didn't take them," he said with a wide smile. "I realized that I was too busy and too old to learn how to use a camera, so I had my son Kermit take some lessons in photography." One of the photographs is of a herd of elephants, the most successful one taken up to that time of this difficult subject.

The talk then drifted to American painting. "Why is it," he asked, "that our young artists think they have to go to France and paint Brittany fishermen? Why don't they stay at home and paint Michigan lumbermen? They're just as picturesque and they're Americans." A truly Rooseveltian remark.

Mr. Taft was my introduction to the White House. He was genial but busy. As I entered his office he said, "I can give you but five minutes. Do you think you can get me while I'm reading my letters?" It was not easy to take him in the way I wanted because of his enormous bulk. Upon leaving, I was asked to bring him the proofs when they were ready—which I did. Looking at them he gave a jolly laugh, as he exclaimed, "My! You have succeeded in making me look almost slender."

In the summer of 1913, Percy Mackaye's bird masque, *Sanctuary*, was produced out of doors in Cornish, New Hampshire, at the dedication of the Bird Sanctuary. President Wilson and his family were making their home close by at the Winston Churchill estate which was the summer White House that year. Eleanor Wilson played the lead and behind the scenes Margaret Wilson sang the song of the Hermit Thrush. I made color photographs at the rehearsal of all the participants. Eleanor Wilson said she hoped while I was in Cornish I might make a portrait of her father. "He has never," she said, "had a really good picture."

The next week I received an invitation for luncheon from Mrs. Wilson and was asked to bring my camera with me. Upon my arrival I noticed there seemed to be some commotion in the household.

Eleanor told me: "There has been a slight accident. A window flew open, striking Father on the forehead. It is nothing serious, but there is a bruise and there can be no photographs."

The President, however, came to the table accompanied by his physician, Dr. Cary T. Grayson. The President himself proceeded to say grace and, when the conversation had started, I remarked that this charming custom reminded me of the days of my youth in Hamburg, as my mother always said grace before the meal. I added that it brought to memory an experience of mine some years before in the Arizona desert.

Mr. Wilson asked me to relate it. So I told him of the time Frederick Munson, the lecturer, and I had started on a trip to the Navajo reservation one day to make photographs. Our supply wagon failed to appear as expected, and all we had to eat for several days was what we had brought with us in our saddle bags—the traditional desert food—canned tomatoes, sardines and crackers. The diet was getting on our nerves when we had a visitor. Introducing himself as a missionary who was living eight miles away, he said, "My wife and I heard you were here, and, not having had guests for a long time, we would like to have you ride over to-morrow and have dinner with us."

Upon his departure Munson and I executed a dance at the prospect of a real meal at a table. The next day we arrived at the corrugated iron shack of the missionary promptly at noon. We were cordially received and through the door leading into the other room we could see the table set with a white cloth. As we entered the dining room, there before us, arranged on a platter in the pattern of a star, were sardines and tomatoes, with a side dish of crackers. Before we had a chance to recover, the minister intoned, "Once more, O Lord, thy bountiful table is spread before us. . . ."

As I finished the story there was a moment's silence as everyone looked at the President. He smiled. "That 'once more' certainly was a joke on you, wasn't it?"

Several days later Dr. Grayson told me: "You had us all worried there for a second. The President is very religious and he will not tolerate anything which might be characterized, even in the lightest way, as ridicule of a sacred subject. But he liked your story and has repeated it several times when there have been guests."

In November that year, Mrs. Wilson invited me to the wedding of Jessica and Francis Sayre, asking me to come to Washington two days in advance as she wanted me to take some pictures in color of her daughter and the bridesmaids, which she would give to her husband at Christmas. The day of the rehearsal the President was in a high mood and when he came down the stairs with Jessica on his arm, he gave a little imitation of a cakewalk.

The wedding took place in the afternoon. After the ceremony there was a buffet luncheon and two large bowls of an innocuous punch of which the main ingredient was Mr. Bryan's favorite beverage—grape juice. The Diplomatic Corps was there, in all its gold braid and decorations. I happened to be at the buffet as the French Ambassador came up. He took one sip of the punch, and a look of horror came over his face. *"Quelle saleté!"* he said to the Belgian Minister who responded in kind. To Europeans it was, of course, unthinkable that on such an occasion there was no wine.

While I was there that week I made a picture of the White House gardens just before sunset, when the building was reflected in the waters of the fountain. Shortly afterwards I showed it to Mr. and Mrs. Wilson and they said simultaneously, "I didn't realize the White House was as beautiful as that."

"Where did you take it from?" asked the President.

We walked around together and I pointed out the place. Mrs. Wilson told me afterwards that whenever her husband personally conducted friends through the grounds he always stopped at this spot to ask, "Doesn't that make rather a nice picture?"

The first Mrs. Wilson took a real interest in art and had quite a gift for painting, having done some creditable landscapes. She was a gentle and gracious hostess. I have sometimes wondered if she was not happier as the wife of the Princeton professor than when, as First Lady, the quiet tenor of her life was broken into by the exacting duties of the White House chatelaine.

The portrait of Woodrow Wilson which I was to have taken that summer at Cornish was not made until November, 1916, when the second Mrs. Wilson sent for me to bring my camera to the White House. The President received me in their private sitting room. "I suppose," he said, "that you expect me to tell you that you can have but ten minutes. But I know the kind of work you like to do and I'm not going to hurry you." We went into his study where we talked for half an hour or more and in my pictures I succeeded in getting something of the real Woodrow Wilson—not the reserved university professor, but the thinker and genial philosopher that he was to those who were privileged to know him at his leisure. The photographs pleased him and his family. I am very proud of the letter I received about them from Helen Woodrow Bones, the President's cousin, who acted as his private secretary.

BILLIE BURKE

MARY PICKFORD

ELISSA LANDI

KATHLEEN NORRIS

EDNA
ST. VINCENT
MILLAY

The White House
Washington

November 15, 1916.

My dear Dr. Genthe:—

The President and Mrs. Wilson ask me to thank you most heartily in their name for the stunning photographs of the former. Mrs. Wilson and all the rest of the President's family are delighted with the success of your effort to get a picture of him such as no one else has been able to get; he is not an easy person to put on paper or canvas, and those of us who know him best, are not easily satisfied. Your pictures of him are wonderful.

Very sincerely yours,

Helen Woodrow Bones.

The pictures were to have been used for campaign purposes. But his political friends did not like them and they were not reproduced in the press.

One of my most treasured possessions is a copy of President Wilson's historic address delivered at the joint session of the two Houses of Congress, April 2, 1917, which he had privately printed and bound in green morocco. He sent the little volume to me with a personal inscription.

It was Welles Bosworth, the architect, who arranged (in 1917) to have me take Mr. John D. Rockefeller's picture and also the photographs for a book on the gardens of the estate in Pocantico Hills. I found him a sprightly and alert old gentleman, and distinguished in appearance. He was carefully dressed for the sitting and as I was about to focus my lens he suddenly got up to look in a mirror on the wall. "I wanted to see if my hair was all right," he explained as he smoothed it and sat down again, prepared to pose.

He was taking it all very seriously when Mr. Bosworth said, "You look too solemn for your picture, Mr. Rockefeller."

"Well, then," he answered, "suppose you tell me something to make me smile."

Mr. Bosworth, who was on close terms with him and was permitted a liberty, changed his voice to that of a suppliant. "Mr. Rockefeller," he asked, "could you lend me ten dollars?"

The response was a wise and engaging smile which I was able to perpetuate with my camera.

Several times while I was photographing the gardens I was invited to have luncheon with him. His conversation was always fascinating to me. He talked well on a variety of subjects and he had an unusual feeling for words and an enunciation which any public speaker might be proud of. The comments about him that appeared in the newspapers from time to time were highly amusing to him, particularly those about diet, claiming that he subsisted almost entirely on gruel. "The report is current," he said, "that I am not permitted to eat anything. You see that I have had a substantial meal and have enjoyed it." Noticing that I used salt, he warned me, "That is something which you must not do if you wish to have a long life and enjoy good health. Salt hardens the arteries."

After luncheon one day he said that he had a painting he would like to have me see. We went downstairs into the basement and he showed me a large canvas of two boys out of doors. Evidently it had been done by an itinerant painter, one of those who were the founders, I would say, of a certain school of American painting. Mr. Rockefeller asked me what I thought of it. "It has its merits as an honest piece of work," I said. One of the boys had on a strange looking vest, different from any I had ever seen. "What a funny vest!" I said, pointing to it.

A twinkle came into the old gentleman's eyes. "Yes," he said, "my mother made it for me out of a pair of my brother's pants."

Going over the pictures I made of his gardens, he was obviously puzzled. "I don't know whether I like them or not," he said. "They are not clear. I feel when I look at them as if I needed to wipe my glasses. And I don't see why you took only a part of the fountain and only a corner of the tea house."

I explained that what I had tried to do was to bring out the beauty of his place through vistas which would show the relation of the sculptures to their surroundings and with a view to light and shadow.

"Well, maybe," he replied. "But in spite of what Mr. Bosworth and Mr. Sargent say, I am not so sure."

When the book with the views was completed—it was privately printed just for friends of the family—Mr. Bosworth told me that Mr. Rockefeller wished to speak to me. "I wanted you to know," he said, "that I have learned many new beauties of my garden through your pictures." Bosworth, who overheard the remark, said to me, "You may consider this the greatest compliment ever paid to your work."

The relation between the elder Rockefeller and his son is quite an ideal one, based on perfect understanding and devotion. I wish I could illustrate it by an episode which Mr. John D. Rockefeller, Jr., related to us some years ago at the Dutch Treat Club, when he was the guest speaker. The Dutch Treat Club is a famous organization composed of writers, editors, publishers and artists who meet every Tuesday for luncheon, when some prominent artist sings or plays, or a literary celebrity, or a man of distinction in any other field will speak. Mr. Rockefeller's theme was "What It Means to Be a Rich Man's Son." Since the speaker is assured of absolute discretion on the part of his audience—that nothing he says will ever be published—I am not permitted to relate the charming story that he told us that day. I remarked to him afterwards that if, in our day and civilization, we had such a record as the *Book of Filial Piety,* which since the time of Confucius has been a classic illustration of Chinese culture, his talk of that day would have to be included as an example of paternal understanding and filial devotion.

Mr. Andrew Mellon, when he was Secretary of the Treasury, came to my studio with his daughter Ailsa. While I was taking her picture, I hoped he would notice my collection of jades and Chinese sculptures and paintings. But he sat lost in thought. When it came his turn to be photographed, I knew better than to interrupt his mood with conversation. He was the most silent and aloof man I have ever seen—and the most distinguished and aristocratic in appearance. There is a kind of aesthetic nobility about his face seldom found in men of our hurried age. His deep-set and yet penetrating eyes are those of an idealist and dreamer.

Soudbinine, the Russian sculptor, who for ten years made Rodin's marbles, told me that he had a similar experience with Mr. Mellon. Soudbinine's splendid head of Senator Medill McCormick had caused Mrs. McCormick to urge Mr. Mellon to have his head done by the same artist. Soudbinine was sent for.

"I have been prevailed upon by Mrs. McCormick," said Mr. Mellon, "to let you do my head. I will give you ten sittings of an hour each. But I wish to stipulate that if your work should not be to my satisfaction, you are to destroy it without my being under any obligation to you."

"Quite agreeable," replied Soudbinine. "But I also have something to stipulate. If, at the end of the ten sittings, I should not be satisfied with what I have done, I want to have the right to destroy my work without any obligation on my part."

Mr. Mellon looked surprised, but after a moment said, "I suppose that is only fair."

In the course of the ten sittings Mr. Mellon had no conversation whatever with Soudbinine—merely "Good-morning" and "Good-by." When the head was finished, his only comment was to say that he wanted six replicas made of it.

AUCTIONS, ART DEALERS
AND COLLECTORS

FOR one who cannot afford to pay the high prices which a dealer has to ask for art objects of importance and distinction, the auction room offers a field of profitable adventure and the opportunity to acquire, often for very little, things of real value. It is a thrilling game, full of excitement, disappointments and unexpected rewards.

Ever since I came to New York I have been an auction enthusiast. Most of what I own has been bought at auction sales: paintings, sculptures, rare old books, furniture, tapestries, jades, etc. Even the horse I had for over twelve years was bought at an auction. My friends claim that if it were possible to acquire a wife at auction, I would probably not have remained a bachelor.

It is not easy for one unacquainted with auction technique to be a successful buyer. In the first place the mode of bidding is bewildering to the newcomer. Frequently there may not be a sound or a visible gesture from the audience, and yet the auctioneer goes on calling higher bids. It seems that attendants posted on the floor register and call out the bids according to the silent signal given by the interested buyer: the raising of a catalogue, the placing of the hand on the chin or on the ear, may signify "go on" or "stop," according to a prearranged understanding. Any gesture is a dangerous thing to indulge in, since it may have an auction significance, as I found out one afternoon at a sale when I happened to be sitting next to Edward Knoblock, the playwright. As the things we wanted were far down the list, we chatted and he started to tell me of an eighteenth-century English candelabra he had bought the week before.

"It was a big one," he said, "as big as this," measuring the air with his hands.

"Knocked down," called out the auctioneer, "to the gentleman in the third row on the left."

"It seems you've bought something," I said. When we looked in the catalogue, the number proved to be "Ten Turkish pewter cups."

In this instance the result was not disappointing. A fortnight later I saw Knoblock again. "That auction deal wasn't so bad after all," he laughed. "When I took those cups to a jeweler he declared them to be solid silver and the engraved inscription on them turned out to be the name of the Sultan. An expert said that unquestionably they had come from the Imperial household; he bought them from me for fifty times what I paid for them."

Without having had a chance before the sale to study the catalogue and to inspect carefully the object one is interested in, disappointment is liable to follow, as I have often found out to my sorrow. In the auction room distance, it may truly be said, lends enchantment. A Greek Tanagra figurine, which according to the catalogue was of the fourth century B.C., completely deceived me by its graceful lines and beautiful surface. When I examined it at home, I found the name of its Berlin manufacturer engraved under the base. It was such a charming thing that I kept it anyway. In the basement of the Metropolitan Museum there is a whole case filled with Tanagra statuettes which one must not admire with too much enthusiasm. A sign warns you: "All objects in this case are modern reproductions."

Sometimes a reproduction will deceive even the trained eye of experts. In a collection offered for sale at the Anderson Galleries some years ago, a small fifteenth-century French miniature (painted on parchment, according to the catalogue) attracted much attention. A friend of mine who is an authority was very enthusiastic about it, and since his opinion was corroborated by two museum experts, he did not hesitate to bid for it at the sale. Proudly he took it home and showed it to his wife. Though not an expert, she had a peculiar flair. "I don't like it," she said. "It doesn't seem right to me. Let's take it out of the frame and examine it without the glass." They found that it had been done on paper and was marked "Printed in Vienna." It was one of those amazing reproductions made by Dr. Arthur Jaffe, which are so perfect that when the original drawing and the reproduction are put under glass side by side for comparison, it is almost impossible to tell the difference. The miniature was returned to the gallery and the money refunded.

Among my great finds was a portfolio of thirty sketches by Hokusai, which were included in a sale of Japanese prints at the American Art Galleries in 1918. They were small sheets, about four by six inches, illustrating the street life in Yeddo. Apparently nobody of authority had taken the trouble to examine them. They were listed and described as prints. After a careful inspection, I came to the conclusion that they were not prints but original drawings by Hokusai and probably the ones that were exhibited at the Hokusai Memorial Exhibition in Tokio, arranged by Fenollosa and described in his catalogue. I decided to bid for them and I was prepared to go as high as five hundred dollars. The sale took place on a chill and sleety afternoon, ideal for the buyer but fatal for the seller. When the drawings came up, somebody bid ten dollars. In a determined tone of voice I raised it to twenty. There was no other bid, and they were mine.

As I was leaving, a dealer came up to me. "Would you take two hundred dollars for those Hokusai's?" he asked.

I declined as I wanted to study and enjoy them myself.

Within a week he came again, this time offering four hundred dollars.

"Why didn't you bid for them yourself?" I asked.

"I don't know why I didn't," he said, "unless it was because when I saw that you were after them, I thought it would be useless." He explained that his neglect had placed him in an awkward position, as he had had an order for them from one of his big clients who now was furious.

After a fortnight he returned, making a final offer of a thousand dollars. Since by that time I had had the leisure to study them and absorb them—I had also made photographs—I let him have them for the sum he offered. Subsequently I learned that he sold the drawings to his client for three times that amount.

My preference at auctions has always been for things of the Orient. My collection of Japanese prints owed some of its best items to the auction room. I had begun it in San Francisco and had made some valuable additions to it during my journey through Japan in 1908. In New York I found that auction sales offered even greater opportunities—I am speaking of a time twenty years ago—and though I made many mistakes, often accepting as an original impression a print whose flawless condition was solely due to the use of new blocks, new colors, and new paper, I gradually learned how to discriminate and how to discard. When I disposed of my collection at auction (at the Anderson Galleries in 1917), my two thousand prints had been reduced to four hundred. The sale was a great success, but what pleased me more was the praise that my catalogue received. I had prepared it very carefully, with detailed descriptions and references and with many illustrations.

I now proceeded to devote myself more to the greater art of China, especially the paintings, sculptures and jades. The Chinese painter—a philosopher and poet as well as an artist—is not concerned with the realistic presentation of the scene before him, as it appears to the outward eye. His chief aim is to convey with his brush an impression of the spirit back of the realities, to show the insignificance of Man, and the sublimity of Nature.

I have a large landscape (thirteenth century). In the distance are vast mountain ranges. On the river, from under a group of trees in the foreground, is seen a fisherman in his fragile boat, meditating as he waits for the fish to bite. The misty delicacy with which the mountains are indicated conveys a feeling of immensity of space. Though the painting is done entirely in monochrome, the various shades of ink actually give a suggestion of color.

Another auction acquisition is an early Ming painting. In a moonlight-landscape of cliffs, far up on the branch of a pine tree an eagle looks down with contempt into the valley of little men.

HENRI CHARPENTIER

FREDERICK W. GOUDY

CHILDE HASSAM

CAPTAIN EVERETT EDWARDS

JOHN BARRYMORE

GENE TUNNEY

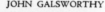

JOHN GALSWORTHY   JOHN McCORMACK

This painting has been an inspiration to several of my musician friends.

It requires many years of study to be able to differentiate the free and inspired brush stroke of a Chinese master from the hesitating brush work of even a good copyist. Often a painting was copied simply as a tribute to a great master and for no other purpose. Frequently at auctions, even when I have sat in the front row, my eye has been deceived by another kind of copy, one that was more or less skilfully done with the deliberate purpose of misleading the buyer. From a distance the composition and colors of the picture might be convincing, but when I took it home, I often found that it had been painted by a clumsy hand on silk that had been doctored to give the appearance of age. I have discarded many of the Chinese paintings which at first I was enthusiastic about. Among the ones which remain on my walls are several that no collection need be ashamed of.

It is equally hazardous to acquire archaic jades at auction, if one has not had the chance to examine them beforehand, especially since of recent years a whole industry of fabrications has sprung up in China. There is a brownish stone found in the Province of Shantung that quite looks like jade, but it has neither its hardness nor texture. I have frequently been deceived, but with each mistake that I made—and had to pay for—I have added to my knowledge.

It is due chiefly to my old friend, A. W. Bahr, the great collector and scholar, that I have learned what to look for and what to avoid. I was fortunate years ago, at a time when authentic collections from China reached the American auction room, to acquire some pieces of ancient ritual jade which are not obtainable on the market today.

There is a magic quality in the smooth surface of jade which for many centuries has felt the touch of sensitive and reverent hands. One has to learn how to "see" jade not only with the eye but with the fingers. I always carry in my pocket a small jade carving (of a cat or a horse), the kind the Chinese call "fingering pieces." My Chinatown friends refer to it as "Him Lucky Stone." Perhaps it brings luck. At any rate, its touch helps one to relax.

In collecting Chinese sculptures, luck has favored me. I have not many, but the few I own have interested museum curators and other experts. My favorites among the pieces I have gathered are some terra-cotta horses' heads (seventh century) done with a simplification of form that has an astonishing modernistic touch, and a Buddhistic memorial stele of the Sui dynasty. It shows Kwan Yin, the Goddess of Mercy, seated upright with her feet crossed, holding in her raised hand a lotus blossom. On the back of the stele are two Bodhisatvas, disciples of Buddha, standing on a double lotus—of a design I have not seen in any other Chinese sculpture.

I have found that to be influenced by remarks of a friend sitting next to one at a sale may be fatal, or not to come to a quick decision may lose one the chance of a lifetime. Just to give one example: When the Metropolitan Museum decided to dispose of the duplicates in the Cesnola collection, a large group of them was sent to the Anderson Galleries and exhibited under the competent supervision of Dr. Karl Freund before the auction sale. Cesnola, an archeologist, had for many years conducted excavations on the island of Cyprus and collected sculptures (chiefly memorial statues) and vases, etc., ranging from early Phoenician and Greek to late Roman periods. They were acquired by the Metropolitan Museum shortly after it was founded. Nothing like them in the way of classic sculptures had ever come into the open market. A week before the sale I had luncheon with Mr. Herbert Fleishacker, the San Francisco banker, who has made so many splendid gifts to his city and to the museum erected in Golden Gate Park by the late publisher, M. H. de Young. Thinking that Mr. Fleishacker might be interested in the Cesnola marbles, I drew his attention to them.

"Oh, I know," he said, "and if I had the time, I would go with you to have a look at them. But I have to leave for Washington on an early afternoon train on important business. Perhaps when I return."

The Cesnola Marbles

140

When I saw him again, he was somewhat downcast. "I saw my friend John Ringling yesterday," he said, "and he was crowing because his museum in Sarasota had gotten ahead of me. He told me that he had bought a large part of the Cesnola collection at that sale you spoke to me about, and he claimed that for seventy-five thousand dollars he had acquired things that were worth a million. I see now that I missed the chance of a lifetime."

Often an ill-considered remark in the catalogue may be a boon to the collector. Among a group of paintings to be sold at the Anderson Galleries some ten years ago was a work of Jan Breughel, the son of Pieter, "The Garden of Eden," which particularly attracted me. It was painted on a wooden panel—not cradled—and parts of the picture were obscured by streaks of dark brown varnish. The description in the catalogue ended with the words "sold as is," indicating that something about it was damaged. Since this is a danger sign to most buyers, I was able to get it with slight competition. Much to my surprise I found the panel in perfect condition, and when the old varnish had been removed (by Frank Harth, who had successfully done similar work for me before), the colors appeared in their original freshness, just as they had been painted by the master three hundred years ago. It now hangs over the fireplace in my studio.

One rainy day I was passing Silo's old auction rooms on Forty-fifth Street in New York. A furniture sale was going on, so I went in to get out of the storm, and sat down next to Mr. Thomas Clark who was waiting to bid on an Inman painting to add to his gallery of American portraits. The sale held little interest for me until a canvas, described in the catalogue as "Portrait of a young girl—Italian school, artist unknown," was put up, when to my amazement I recognized in the girl the figure that is in the lower right-hand corner of the famous Velasquez, "The Weavers" (*Las Hilanderas*), in the Prado Museum in Madrid. It was knocked down to me for very little.

"You must have money to throw away," said Mr. Clark, "buying a thing like that by an unknown artist."

"Perhaps," I replied, "the artist is not as unknown to me as he was to the man who made the catalogue."

Closer scrutiny of the painting proved that the subject was unmistakably the same girl Velasquez had immortalized. The pose, the face, the costume, in detail and color, the same arrangement of the hair—all were the same. Some passages were painted with the superb mastery of a man of genius. Others were obviously done by a crude and unskilled hand. It is my theory that either it was begun by Velasquez as a study for the figure in "The Weavers" and completed by an indifferent pupil, or it was done by the latter at the time when the master was working on the big composition and corrected by him with brilliant brushstrokes.

Herbert Bailey, then editor of the London *Connoisseur,* and Lewis Hind, author of *Days with Velasquez,* who were visiting in New York, saw the picture in my studio. They both agreed that my theory was plausible. Some day a Velasquez authority may "discover" the picture and give it official standing.

In 1926 Dikran Kelekian's auction of his modern French paintings caused much excitement and consternation. Kelekian is a unique figure in the art world. No other dealer has such catholicity of taste and knowledge. His interest ranges from early Egyptian and Assyrian sculptures—incidentally the Assyrian sculptures in the Metropolitan Museum, donated by John D. Rockefeller, Jr., came from Kelekian—Coptic textiles, Chinese paintings, Gothic marbles, Persian potteries and miniatures, Flemish tapestries, to French paintings from the beginning of the nineteenth century to the latest modernists. Since he is concerned more with art than with money values, and has no patience with anything inferior or of doubtful origin, he was not popular with a certain group of dealers, and systematic attempts were made to spread the impression that the French paintings in the Kelekian collection did not represent the artists at their best, though anyone with an eye for quality must have realized that this was untrue. It was a regular conspiracy and the sale was an absolute slaughter. I was able to take away with me a Courbet painting, listed in the catalogue merely as "Portrait of a Man." I believe I have identified it as a portrait of Alfred Bruyas, one of the benefactors of the Museum in Montpellier. Bruyas was an eccentric, sensitive and generous, who encouraged artists, not by buying things they had already painted, but by having them do his likeness. Courbet painted him eight times, Delacroix twice. He was also done by Couture, Cabanel and Glaize and others. The portrait I have was perhaps the last Courbet did of him, as he did not flatter his friend and patron, but accentuated the morbid sensitiveness of the man, giving the features a definite downward tendency. Brilliantly executed, it is a real "painter's canvas."

A recent auction of paintings (at the Rains Galleries) which Marie Sterner (now Mrs. Barnard Lintott) wanted to dispose of, surprised everyone by bringing higher prices at the sale than had been expected. It was merely a proof of the public's realizing that whatever Marie Sterner stamps with her approval and adds to her collection is worthy of serious consideration and good enough for anyone to take a chance on. With her it is not the academic knowledge of a scholarly expert, but rather the unerring eye and uncanny flair for what is really art, which makes her opinion valuable. I have greater confidence in her judgment than in the verdicts of most of our official experts.

I seldom let an opportunity go by to look around in the shops of antiquarians, or even pawnshops, where one may have the chance to discover an object of real value and acquire it without auction competition. One of my favorite hunting grounds for many years has been C. V. Miller's Louis XIV Shop, formerly located in San Francisco, now in New York. I have found many things of merit there, without ever having to regret my purchase. Years ago, in San Francisco, there was displayed in his window a landscape that intrigued me. It was done in the manner of Constable, but did not have a signature or history. All Mr. Miller could tell me was that it had come to him from a collector in Buenos Aires. The painting represented a lock on a river under a stormy sky, with trees shaking in the aftermath of a thunderstorm.

It became mine for a modest sum. Years later in New York, I found in the rare volume of mezzotints made by Lucas, the English engraver, an exact reproduction of my canvas, after Constable's painting, entitled "A Lock on the River Stour."

To experience the thrill of making a discovery, to have one's hunch justified by later findings, to gamble on one's own judgment against the opinion of others, to acquire something one really wants for a fraction of what one would have to pay in a fashionable shop—that to me is a more satisfying source of excitement than the card-table or the roulette wheel can furnish, to say nothing of the stock market.

Ever since I was a boy, wherever I have been, in the old world or the new, much of my leisure has been given to wandering in museums and galleries, or to the study of the various art movements, until the pursuit has become my most satisfying avocation. For the pleasure I have derived from it I must give thanks to two fine old friends of my youth.

Every Saturday afternoon during the long winters for many years I used to go to one or other of the two large museums in Hamburg where I was taught how to look at pictures and to understand them. My teachers were Professor Hans Lichtwark, Director of the Kunsthalle, and Dr. Justus Brinckmann, Curator of the Natural History Museum, who wrote the first comprehensive book in German on Chinese and Japanese art.

Their classes were not the sterile exercises in dates and periods which so many courses of this kind are apt to be. Rather they were voyages of discovery into our sensitiveness to beauty and capacity for appreciation. We learned how to look at pictures, not from the point of view of the instructor but through our own eyes according to our own reactions. In the Kunsthalle there were even then a number of good examples of the masters of the different schools, and Professor Lichtwark had an intelligent way of directing our attention to them. He would not run us from room to room, scattering dry crumbs of information. A painting was something to be taken into the mind until it had left an indelible impression, for its faults as well as its merits. Sometimes we spent an entire afternoon before one picture, looking at it from different angles, and writing down everything we could remember about it with our backs turned. In order to answer his questions we had to ask many of him. We went away from these stimulating discussions eager to learn all that we could about the individual artist, his work and the influences brought to bear upon it.

In the Natural History Museum was one of the first significant collections of Japanese and Chinese painting and sculpture. Some of my happiest days were passed here in the company of Dr. Brinckmann, through whom I had my first glimpse of this phase of Oriental art which was to mean so much in my later life.

My interest was stimulated and I was shown a method of approach toward an intelligent appreciation of an art so difficult for us to understand. After I had obtained my degree, I devoted some months of leisure to the study of the Chinese and Japanese art treasures in the museums of Paris, London and Berlin. When I came to San Francisco, a chance meeting with Professor Ernest Fenollosa, the great Oriental scholar, was responsible for my beginning to collect Japanese prints. As I realized later, they were the best introduction to an understanding of the strange methods and conventions—so perplexing at first to the Western mind—of Japanese as well as Chinese pictorial art.

It was through my studies and interest in things Oriental that I had the privilege of a closer acquaintance with the late Charles L. Freer of Detroit. Besides owning a large group of Whistler paintings and etchings, he had assembled one of the finest collections of Japanese and Chinese art. Before his death, he made a gift of his collection to the nation. It is housed in its own building as a part of the Smithsonian Institution in Washington. I first met Mr. Freer through William H. Truesdale, for many years president of the Lackawanna Railroad. Freer was a strangely silent man, and would feel like talking only in the company of old friends or new

ones with whom he was in accord. At a dinner at the Truesdales',
two of his close friends were present, George F. Baker and Mel-
ville Stone, whom he had known at the beginning of his career.
The only other guests besides myself were Miss Belle Da Costa
Greene and Mitchell Kennerley. Mr. Freer was in an expansive
mood and talked on through the evening, telling us in his fascinating manner some of his experiences. He spoke of the beginnings of his collection. When he was a young man working in an
humble capacity on the railroad, and with no money to spend, he
would pass his spare time looking at the illustrations in magazines,
cutting out those he liked and pasting them in albums. "I made
up my mind then," he said, "that some day I was going to own
some real pictures.

"I still remember," he went on, "what a thrill I got the first
time I walked into an art shop and came out with an etching under
my arm. Soon I began to collect Japanese prints, and I shall never
forget the debt I owe to them for developing my taste for Oriental
art."

The talk then turned to the ways of dealers and he told us of
a fraud so picturesque and so canny that none but Chinese could
have conceived it. On one of his trips to Peking he had let it be
known that he was not going to buy anything from dealers while
he was there. One day a merchant, who was also a trusted friend,
brought him news of some rare bronzes, sculptures and paintings
in a monastery two hundred miles away in the desert. The monastery, in need of money, had decided to sell its treasures, and was
sending them by caravan to Peking. "There is a real chance for
you. I know when the caravan is due. If it can be intercepted, I
can arrange to have you see the things before the dealers, and
you will be able to buy them very reasonably."

On the appointed day Mr. Freer and his friend started out on
their camels for the meeting place some twenty miles outside of
Peking. When they got there, the monastery caravan was waiting
for them. The things were unpacked and inspected and Mr. Freer
bought a number of sculptures and bronzes for what he thought

was a low price. "I was sure," he said, "that for once I had put something over on the dealers."

When he was back in his hotel and had his purchases unpacked in the solitude of his rooms—prepared for the joy which only a collector knows—his enthusiasm collapsed. Under the arm of one of the sculptures he discovered a pricemark of a dealer. Subsequently he learned that the monastery was a myth. The things, while authentic, had been contributed by a group of merchants. The caravan was just a part of the plot. And they had chosen for their ambassador a dealer who they knew had access to Mr. Freer. "Really, though," he said, "I was more amused than angry because of the clever way they had gone about it."

He told us that evening something of Whistler and his wife, who were close friends of his. He said that while Whistler was painting his portrait he was called to Paris on a business conference. Before leaving London he promised the artist that upon his return he would come straight from the train to the studio. After a week's absence he arrived back early one morning and went immediately to keep his promise. The door was opened by the Master himself who insisted that Mr. Freer have breakfast with him and his wife.

While they were waiting Mrs. Whistler came into the room vigorously shaking a bottle. "Mr. Freer," she said, "I have a treat for you. I have just been made a present of some American cocktails. I have never had one, and all I know about them is that they have to be shaken."

"For some minutes," said Mr. Freer, "the dear lady kept on shaking the bottle of un-iced and pre-mixed cocktails, insisting that I must have one before breakfast. Of course I had to take one, as I would not hurt her feelings. I spent several weeks with the Whistlers while my portrait was being painted.

"Do you know," he continued, "that Whistler died in my arms? When it was evident that his end was near, Mrs. Whistler sent for me, and I was sitting on the bed with my arms around his shoulders while he went quietly to sleep, never to wake up."

From time to time, whenever Mr. Freer was in New York, he would send for me to see some of the things he had bought. He would ask my opinion, but if it conflicted with his, he would ignore it. Once when he was staying at the Plaza Hotel, he showed me some paintings he had just acquired through his Chinese dealer, Lee Van Ching. Of one of them he said, "It is undoubtedly an original of the northern Sung school." Very meekly and with some hesitancy I replied, "It looks more like a later copy. The brush strokes haven't the freedom and strength of a great master. Besides some of the colors as well as the silk don't look right."

"Curious," replied Mr. Freer, "that you should have that impression. I did too, at first, but under the magnifying glass I found that the silk was of the period and the colors likewise."

While he was talking Miss Katherine Rhoades, who was well up in such things, came into the room. She expressed some doubts and for the same reasons as I did, but we could not convince him.

From Dr. David Fairchild of the *National Geographic Magazine,* I have the story of how the Freer collection was almost lost to the American government and was saved only by the intercession of his wife, the daughter of Alexander Graham Bell. Mr. Freer, in making known his intention of donating all of his art treasures to the Smithsonian Institution, stipulated that an adequate building be erected to house them. Theodore Roosevelt, who was President at the time, sent a commission, among them Speaker Joseph Cannon and Mr. Bell, to Detroit to report on their value and importance. Not one of the men knew anything about Oriental art or was in any way capable of judging it. Particularly was this true of Mr. Cannon. While he may have been a good politician, anything relating to beauty was far removed from his orbit. I happened to be present when he got out of the stage on a trip to the Yosemite. With his cigar at an angle he glanced up at the Falls. "Huh!" he said. "Is that all? I'm going back tomorrow."

"Nothing there," decided the committee after seeing the Freer collection, "but a lot of pictures and screens, Japs and Chinks, and some paintings on which one can't see anything." Taking their word for it, the President decided the building of a gallery would not be justified.

The evening after their meeting with Mr. Roosevelt, Alexander Bell told his daughter, who was an artist herself and knew values, about the decision. "Father," she said, "what have you done? Do you realize that Mr. Freer has things that can be found nowhere else, not even in the British Museum?"

"Well, I don't know," replied Mr. Bell.

"I should say you *didn't* know," said his daughter. "If we refuse it we will become the laughing stock of Europe. You've just got to go over and see the President and tell him he must come to another decision."

z

Her father went at once to see Mr. Roosevelt. Expert advice was sought. The gift was accepted and an appropriation was made for the building. The Freer Gallery of Art in Washington, under the direction of John Ellerton Lodge, is today one of the most important and beautifully arranged museums in the world. Mr. Lodge is an intelligent, competent and courageous curator. He has not hesitated to "demote" some of the Chinese paintings to their true positions and to give them their correct labels. One, for which Mr. Freer paid thirty thousand dollars, thinking it to be an original work of one of the great masters of the Sung dynasty, is now designated as a late Ming copy.

Unlike Mr. Freer who became a patron of art through an innate love for it, the impetus of Senator William H. Clark was a pride of possession based on money values. When buying he was guided more by his own judgment than by the opinion of experts. He liked brilliant coloring, and for that reason one of his favorites was the French painter, Monticelli, to whom an entire room in his house was devoted. Once, in the absence of the Senator, I was shown around by his valet. Pointing to the Monticellis he asked me, "Can you see anything in these? To me they are just terrible daubs—certainly not at all like paintings an English gentleman would have in his house."

I went to Mr. Clark with a letter from Mrs. Fiske. She thought

z

he might like to have me make some color plates of his paintings. He was very cordial and told me I could come to see his pictures whenever I wished. "But," he added, "I won't permit color photographs to be taken of them, as it will diminish their value."

In the main gallery, high up on the wall, there was an interesting looking example of sixteenth-century German painting. I said to him, "Why did you hang that fine portrait way up there where it can hardly be seen?"

"It's by an unknown artist, and it is not signed," he replied.

While he had some first-rate canvases, he had a number of doubtful ones for which he had paid a large sum. In his opinion the price of a work of art determined its artistic value. There was a young Dutchman who had come over to New York to take a position in a bank. With him he had brought two canvases by Van Goyen which had been in his family ever since they were painted. As he wished to dispose of them, he had secured authentication from the director of the Rijks Museum in Amsterdam. Not knowing anything of the ways of the New York dealers, he went directly to Senator Clark, to whom he had a letter. Senator Clark glanced at them, asking almost immediately how much he wanted for them.

The young man quite innocently quoted the modest price of two thousand dollars each, which represented their value in Dutch money.

"They're not important enough for my collection," said the Senator, hardly glancing at the paintings.

After some months the young man, needing money, took the paintings to a leading art dealer who said that while two thousand dollars was reasonable, he was not particularly interested in Van Goyen, but would be willing to pay fifteen hundred dollars apiece for them.

When the sale was made, the dealer wrote to Senator Clark, who was an old client of his, that a fine Van Goyen had recently come into their possession, and he wanted him to be the first to see it. The Senator appeared the next day and the painting was sold to him for ten thousand dollars. Three months later he received another letter from the dealer. Through an extraordinary stroke of good luck, it said, he had acquired the companion piece to the Van Goyen. This time Senator Clark was told that since the picture really ought to belong to him, although it was an even finer example than the one he already had, he could have it for the same sum.

This reminds me of the tragedy of Ralph Blakelock. It was through the unscrupulous treatment of a dealer that his talent was disintegrated. In his beginning as a painter he had done some canvases inspired by the tribal ceremonies of the Indians among whom he had lived. As there was no organized market for them, he sold his pictures through a dealer who, knowing that he was pressed for money, always forced him to take less than he asked. One day he brought a large canvas on which he had spent a great deal of time—it was a group of trees by a river with the moonlight filtering through the branches.

"I consider this," said Blakelock, "my masterpiece. And I want seven hundred and fifty dollars for it." His top price thus far had been two hundred and fifty.

"That's absurd," said the dealer. "I'll give you five hundred. Take it or leave it."

"I can't let it go for that," replied Blakelock. "It's the best work I've ever done."

A week passed. There was illness in the family and funds and food were getting low. Blakelock went back to the dealer.

"Things are bad with me," he said. "I'm afraid I'll have to let it go for five hundred."

"I offered you that last week," said the dealer. "Now I will give you but four hundred."

Blakelock, hurt and indignant, refused the offer. A few days later, crushed by the pressure of his debts and the necessity for money, he returned saying he would take the four hundred.

"Oh, but that was three days ago," the dealer replied. "Now I'll give you three hundred and not one cent more."

Blakelock took it.

That afternoon passersby in the street were startled to see a man tearing twenty-dollar bills into bits and throwing them from his window to the pavement. It was Blakelock, completely broken in spirit and in mind. He was taken to an asylum where he was to remain for seventeen years. During this time his name as an artist was forgotten by the public. Then, one day in an auction sale at the American Art Galleries, the very painting for which Blakelock had received three hundred dollars came up for sale. The name of Blakelock did not mean much, but the poetic beauty of the painting stirred the audience. There was spirited bidding, and it was finally knocked down to Senator Clark for ten thousand dollars.

The press made much of this incident. Once more the forgotten name of Blakelock figured in the press and Blakelock paintings began to be in demand. It was only then that the long efforts of his wife and his faithful friends, Harry Watrous and Irving Wiles, were at last rewarded. He was removed to a home in the country where he could have pleasant surroundings and special care. The day he passed through New York, he was brought to my studio. Although he was somewhat emaciated he seemed all right mentally. He showed great interest in my art objects and I noticed that his eyes kept returning to an ancient Buddhist painting, mounted in screen form, that stood in a corner. "I have never seen anything like that before," he said. After a while he got up and knelt down in front of it to examine it closely. The painting represented the Buddhist Trinity: Amida, with his two companions, descending from heaven to enlighten the darkness of the world. He then spoke his first long sentence: "One doesn't have to know anything about Oriental art to understand the deep religious spirit that inspired this painting."

The doctor who was with him came over and whispered in my ear, "Not so bad for a crazy man."

For some time Blakelock talked quite simply and rationally. Then suddenly, without a change in the expression of his face or in the inflection and tone of his voice, he said, "You know if Morgan had only taken my advice about that Anaconda copper deal he could have made twenty million dollars with one stroke of his pen," and his voice trailed off into murmurings about large sums of money—millions and billions.

In the quiet life of the country, he showed signs of recovery. One day his wife brought me some drawings he had done. "See!" she exclaimed. "He is working again." The drawings, done in colored crayons, were such as any child of eight might do.

Henry E. Huntington I knew over a period of years, starting with my San Francisco days, when I had taken photographs of him and his family. He was, I think, not so much interested in art for its own sake as he was in giving a good account of his wealth. It was only after his marriage to the widow of Collis P. Huntington that he began his celebrated collection. He had the feeling that men of great fortune should do something of public benefit. He made no claim to being a connoisseur, and very wisely sought the advice of experts in whom he had confidence. The famous library, now in the Huntington Gallery in Pasadena, was started under the able direction of George D. Smith and Dr. A. S. W. Rosenbach.

It was Mr. Smith who suggested that Mr. Huntington should have some portraits made of himself in his library in his home on Fifty-seventh Street and Fifth Avenue in New York. After I made several photographs, Huntington said that he wanted to have one taken standing in front of his Caxtons. Mr. Smith, who was present, said he should also have a picture showing him holding one of his recent acquisitions.

Mr. Huntington called out to his secretary, "What book was that that I paid thirty thousand dollars for last week?"

It was the first edition of Shakespeare's sonnets.

Mrs. Huntington relied much more on her own taste than her husband did on his. If she liked a thing she wanted it, regardless of its authenticity. Among the objects she had bought was a Boule desk for which she had paid eight thousand dollars. One day a member of the firm through which she had acquired it came to have tea with her. Looking at the desk he said, "Really, Mrs. Huntington, you ought not to have that imitation Boule desk here with all of your fine things. Where did you get it?"

She told him it had come from his firm, and also what she had paid.

"Well," said he, "the old gentleman is not always accurate in his judgments these days. You know he's well along. Let me take it back and give you credit for that amount."

Mrs. Huntington did as he suggested. Some months afterwards a friend said to her, "I have just come from the Anderson Galleries and I saw a desk that looks exactly like your Boule."

"I know about it," said Mrs. Huntington. "It is too complicated to tell you the story now, but I want you to do me a favor. I like that desk and I don't care whether it is original or not. If I go to the auction they will bid it up, so I want you to go for me. I'll give you three hundred and fifty dollars and I hope you can bid it in for me." In a few days the desk was back with Mrs. Huntington.

A member of one of the best known galleries makes it always a point to approach his prospects by some subtle process of personal suggestion. There was a wealthy widow with a home on Long Island, who was just starting a collection. She had acquired a few good tapestries and bronzes, but had not yet got around to paintings. He succeeded in meeting her socially and was so attentive that she invited him to a house party which was to last several days. At luncheon he talked very little and every once in a while he would look in a melancholy manner at the vacant space above the mantel.

"Aren't you feeling well? You're so quiet," his hostess asked.

"I'm all right," he said, "but looking at the mantel there reminds me of a Renoir we have. It would be ideal for that space. I would love to see it there while I am staying at your house. It will add to my peace of mind, if you will permit me to send for it."

"All right," she laughed. "If you feel so badly about the bald spot on my wall, go ahead." The picture was sent for, and it is still hanging over the mantel today. At another time he contrived to dispose of a fine Corot in an equally clever manner. One of the clients of his firm was a banker who took a greater pride in his skill on the links than in the success of his financial transactions. The dealer managed to play several games with him and whenever the banker made a good drive he would exclaim, "That was a magnificent shot. But wait a minute! Just look what a beautiful view it is from here. It does remind me of a Corot we have. By the way, you ought to drop in some day to see it." He did that several times for the purpose of associating in the banker's mind the good shot with the painting. The Corot now hangs in the gallery of the enthusiastic golfer.

It sometimes happens that through false standards of evaluation the opportunity to secure a great work of art is lost to the collector. Several years ago a young German came to New York with a Rembrandt portrait he had inherited and which he wanted to sell. The canvas was in excellent condition and there was no doubt about its genuineness. It had been certified by Wilhelm Bode, considered the greatest authority on Rembrandt, and also by the Dutch expert, Hofstede De Groot. The young man, not knowing the ways of the New York art world, entrusted it to a dealer for whom he had a letter. Unfortunately, this dealer, who had handled only paintings of minor importance, did not know better than to exhibit the painting in his show window. When two weeks had passed and there had not even been an inquiry about it, somebody suggested to the owner that he should get my advice.

"To whom have you shown it?" was my first question.

When he informed me that it had been in the window of a dealer, who I knew was not the right man to handle it, I had to tell him that it would be practically impossible to interest an American collector in it. "You may think," I said, "that the painting, though nothing has been done to it, is the same now as it was when you arrived. It is not. With every day of public showing in

New York, before a buyer had been found for it, it decreased in value."

I sent him to Walter Ehrich of the Ehrich Galleries, an old friend of mine, who shook his head sadly but promised to do his best. He told me afterwards that he had two clients who would have bought it if he could have assured them they were the first to see it. The young man returned to Germany with the picture.

Often a good picture is ruined through overcleaning and repainting. I went once to look at a reputed Raphael with Rougeron, the well-known French restorer. The painting he had been asked to examine was a mere shadow of its original state. When I asked Rougeron his opinion, he replied, "Do you wish me to speak about it as if I were trying to sell it to a client, or do you want to know what I really think?" His remark, "It is like a beautiful bird without the feathers," could be fittingly applied to more than one painting that bears the name of a renowned artist.

A true patron of all the arts, one who became so from a deeply rooted knowledge and love of beauty and because of his desire to spread its gospel, was Otto H. Kahn.

A few weeks before his death I was a house guest at his country home in Glen Cove, Long Island. On Sunday morning, at breakfast, he noticed that I was looking at the pictures on the wall of the enormous room. They were large, purely decorative canvases by eighteenth-century French artists and of no particular distinction. Remarking the expression on my face he said, "Evidently, Genthe, you don't like those pictures."

"To be frank," I replied, "I don't."

"Neither do I," he laughed. "But sometimes, you know, one has to please the ladies of the family." He was silent for a moment, then said, "Do you want to know what I would really like to have in their place? A collection of modern American paintings. By that I don't mean so much the work of well-known ones who have arrived, but of the struggling unknown ones. Recognition is so often in the hands of the dealers that I know there must be many good painters who never have a fair chance, and if I could do my bit toward encouraging them, I would feel that I had done something really constructive. The only reason I haven't carried out my idea is that I haven't been well and if it became known that I was in the market, I would be besieged, and I just haven't got the strength for it at present."

After I went home I kept thinking about his words and I wrote to him, saying that his splendid idea should not be permitted to die and that I had a plan which might be worked out without taxing him too greatly. In reply I received a letter inviting me to luncheon at his office. He said nothing about the plan until we had finished. "Now, what's the great idea?"

I told him I realized that if it were known that he was going to specialize in modern American painting, an avalanche of indiscriminate canvases, good and bad, would descend upon him. To guard against this I suggested that he ask a few of his friends, men who had knowledge, taste, integrity, to submit thirty or forty pictures from which he could make a selection. "In that way," I said, "you would have a certain guarantee of quality and merit, and would not be deprived of the pleasure of making your own choice." I also suggested that he might make the experiment of hanging a few modern American paintings in his guest rooms, so that he could get the reactions of his friends without having to disturb the arrangement of other rooms.

"That is a very good idea," was Mr. Kahn's reply. We planned to have another discussion about it. It was not to be. He died the following week.

One of his last gestures was indicative of the man he was. A young girl who had graduated from a dramatic school in New York was anxious to get started in the theater. She had a letter of introduction to Mr. Kahn and he arranged for her to join a road company in the West, where she made steady progress. On her return she wished to thank Mr. Kahn personally for what he had done for her. She also wanted to surprise him by returning the loan which had been responsible for her successful start. In reply to her letter, the secretary wrote that Mr. Kahn was very busy, but if she would come to his office at half past four Thursday, she could ride uptown with him in his car and tell him all about it. In the subway, on the way to keep her appointment, she happened to glance at the evening paper which the man next to her was reading. Across the top ran the headline: "Otto Kahn drops dead in his office at noon today."

There are a number of wealthy art lovers in America who have succeeded in bringing together collections of great distinction and importance. I am mentioning here only a few with which I am familiar. Jules Bache's collection, though small, contains some superb examples of artists from the early Renaissance to the nineteenth century, from Petrus Christus to Goya. The pictures are

beautifully displayed in intimate settings and admirably lighted. When Mr. Bache is in New York, he keeps open house on Friday afternoon, when his friends may come and see his treasures. Their comments are sometimes a source of amusement to him. One day I had the pleasure of accompanying a lovely young Viennese Countess who had a letter to Mr. Bache. There happened to be many visitors there that afternoon and our host greeted us, saying, "I am so sorry that I can't show you around personally. But Genthe knows the pictures as well as I do, and you won't say what a beautiful girl said to me last week." I had to explain to her what Mr. Bache was referring to. It seems that while he was showing a young lady through his collection he would make remarks such as: "This is my best Gainsborough portrait," or "And my Fragonard here has become quite famous," whereupon the young lady exclaimed, "Oh, Mr. Bache! I had no idea that you were such a wonderful painter. I hope that some day you will do my portrait."

Of the men I know who enjoy their possessions, none finds such solace in them as Mr. Henry Goldman. For many years now he has been deprived of his sight but he knows every one of his paintings by heart. He loves to take his friends through his gallery as he points out to them the beauty he no longer sees but only remembers.

It was Mr. George Blumenthal who brought the first good examples of El Greco's art to America. He has since added many important canvases, chiefly of Renaissance artists.

Mrs. Chester Dale's understanding and appreciation have made the gallery in her home in New York an almost complete illustrated history of the modern French school. Beginning with its founders, the canvases carry down through the modernists and to the surrealists of today. Adolph Lewisohn has specialized in the modern French school and its founders, but on the walls of the rooms throughout his house are displayed works of representative living American artists. His son and daughter-in-law, Samuel and Margaret Lewisohn, collaborating with Stephan Bourgeois, who compiled the catalogue, have by elimination and addition achieved a collection which is unequaled in America.

Grenville Winthrop's tastes cover a wide territory—from ancient Chinese jades and Buddhist sculptures to William Blake, and to representative drawings and watercolors of great modern English, French and American artists. His interest in ancient Chinese art, especially in archaic jades, was fostered by A. W. Bahr, whose opinion in such matters is considered the last word both here and abroad. In bringing together the drawings, Winthrop had the advice of Martin Birnbaum, whose artistic perception has led him frequently to many exciting discoveries.

Joseph D. Widener, whose gallery (in Elkins Park, Philadelphia) is a legacy from his father, has gradually subtracted from it all objects which were dubious in quality. In adding to it he has shown admirable discrimination and taste.

Andrew W. Mellon, who has recently signified his intention of leaving all his art treasures to the nation, has, in the course of years, brought together a collection which includes some of the finest paintings in the world. As a matter of fact, it can be said that each work represents the artist at the peak of his career.

In none of these collections had there been a place for modern American paintings, with the exception of the Lewisohn collection. It was only when Mrs. Harry Payne Whitney (Gertrude Vanderbilt) founded her Museum of Modern American Art that the public for the first time was given a real opportunity to study contemporary American painting and sculpture. The museum not only contains a permanent collection of representative modern American art but arranges frequent exhibitions, thereby enlarging its importance and usefulness.

The Museum of Modern Art, which owes its existence chiefly to the initiative and enthusiasm of Mrs. John D. Rockefeller, Jr., follows a similar policy, but is international in its scope.

In the Phillips Memorial Gallery in Washington, Duncan Phillips has been successfully conducting an original and constructive experiment. By a novel and attractive manner of exhibition and a "policy of supporting many methods of seeing and painting," the best in art is made accessible to the public without concessions to traditional tastes. Here, in a quiet atmosphere that suggests more a charming home than the marble halls of a museum, the visitor is really made to understand the meaning and purpose of art. Duncan Phillips certainly deserves as much credit for what he is doing in the Phillips Memorial as do the great collectors such as Henry C. Frick, Mrs. O. E. Havemeyer, H. E. Huntington, Benjamin Altman, J. P. Morgan, and many others who have been animated by the same public spirit. They have all contributed to the spiritual content of our national life a gift of inestimable value, for which the nation should be eternally grateful.

THE BEAUTY OF WOMEN

SELDOM when I have been interviewed for the press have I escaped the question, "Who is the most beautiful woman you have ever photographed?" It is a question difficult, if not impossible, to answer. There are too many different definitions and conceptions of beauty. In what has been to me an endless search for the ideal, I have photographed hundreds of beautiful women. But I cannot designate any of them as "the most beautiful." However, I have to admit having used that expression. Once in answering a reporter who had asked the usual question, I replied that I considered Eleonora Duse "the most beautiful" woman who had ever sat for me. "You mean, of course, when she was young?" was the retort. "Not at all," I said. "I mean when she was sixty-four, and here is the picture she liked best." The bravery and wisdom with which she had fulfilled her destiny had molded her face into an unsurpassed sculptural beauty. And I recall another occasion, when I spoke of Rosamond Pinchot as being the ideal type of American girl, because I felt that she represented in a perfect manner the harmonious blending of fine physical and spiritual qualities.

The difficulty and futility of giving a satisfactory definition of beauty has been clearly shown by the beauty contests held in America. The purpose of the Atlantic City contests was to find the most beautiful American girl who then would be awarded a trophy and given the title "Miss America." Galveston, in later years, wanted to go Atlantic City one better by bestowing the title "Miss Universe" on the winner of their "international" contest, who thereby would become the most beautiful girl in the world.

The judges at these contests are artists of national reputation who have made the study and recording of feminine beauty their chief work. The first Atlantic City jury, of which I was a member, took their job pretty seriously. At a preliminary meeting we agreed on certain standards. Mere prettiness of the doll type would not be considered. Proportions and line were important, the manner of bearing and that indefinable essence known as personality would count more than mere regularity of features. The girls paraded down the boardwalk in bathing suits, with ribbons identifying them as "Miss Chicago," "Miss Boston," "Miss Wilkes-Barre," "Miss Newark," "Miss Kalamazoo," etc., until the gamut of the states and communities had been well-run.

Of the eighty participants about fifteen were selected as possible candidates. The next day this smaller group was judged separately. From the beginning we had been impressed with "Miss Columbus, O." She was not "a raving beauty," but perfectly proportioned, and there was a natural charm and radiance about her that made her stand out from all the others. When the vote was taken, two-thirds were in favor of "Miss Columbus" and it was thus that Miss Katherine Campbell became "Miss America." The choice was not very popular. When the verdict was announced to the vast audience assembled in the auditorium that evening, the applause was only moderate. Our verdict was vindicated, however, in the following year when Miss Campbell, again a contestant, was unanimously chosen as "Miss America" by an entirely different group of judges.

These beauty contests may be entertaining pageants, but as a means of selecting "the most beautiful" girl they have no real significance. There are many beautiful and lovely young women who shun the publicity and will not enter the field. And besides there are everywhere women whose beauty is not realized, not even by themselves, until the alert eye of one who knows "discovers" them. This is one of the happy privileges of a photographer who through his camera has the means of making visible to others the beauty which they failed to realize. I have had the good fortune to make several such discoveries.

One afternoon, walking on Broadway with a friend, I was startled by seeing in the crowd coming toward us a girl with per-

MRS. WOODROW WILSON

PROFILE OF AN AMERICAN GIR

fect classic features. "Did you see that Greek profile?" I asked my friend. "You mean the girl who just passed us?" my companion replied. "I know who she is. Do you think she's beautiful?" "Never mind," I said, "run after her and don't let her get away." I explained to the young lady that I wanted very much to make a photograph of her profile. "My profile!" she exclaimed. "I think it's awful."

I made some pictures of her, arranging the light in the studio so as to emphasize the Greek purity of her profile. When she returned to my studio after a few days to see the picture, she looked at it for a long time without saying a word. It was difficult for her to identify the profile's fine nobility with the features of the gum-chewing girl she saw in her mirror. Finally with a sob she said, "I suppose this is a picture of what I might have been." "No," I corrected her, "this is a picture of what you are going to be." And this remark proved prophetic. Since her profile bore such a striking resemblance to the Venus de Milo, I felt that there might be a story for the papers. I telephoned to my friend Karl Kitchen, who was then connected with the *Sunday World,* that I had a picture for him which would interest him. He came without delay, but when I showed him the picture he said, "That's a rather shabby trick to play on me. To have me come up all the way from the office and then show me a photograph that everybody knows." "What do you think it is?" I asked. "Well, of course it's the Venus de Milo in the Louvre in Paris," he replied. When I told him that it was Gertrude Eddington of Bozeman, Montana, a chorus girl in one of the musical comedies, he became quite excited. "That certainly will make a good story." Published as a full-page feature under the title, "Finding a Venus on Broadway," it created quite a sensation and in a fortnight the girl was on the Keith circuit at ten times the salary she had been getting. When she returned to New York, after a several months' tour through the country, she was given several minor rôles in musical comedies. Her great ambition was to become a "real singer." Through an introduction I was able to get her, she secured an audition with one of the best teachers. While studying with him, she met a wealthy rancher from the Southwest. She gave up her career as a singer and instead has made a success of marriage.

One day in the winter of 1912, I was in the studio of Robert Aitken, the sculptor, who had abandoned San Francisco some years before. He was deep in his work, so when the bell rang I went to the door. On the threshold stood a girl with black hair and finely chiseled features. She seemed troubled and discouraged and asked in a timid voice if there was any work for a model. Aitken, without looking up, said, "I never use models." "Let me have your address," I said. "I may be able to use you for some of my photographs." During the weeks following I made quite a number of pictures of her, among them several color plates. One of these, in which she had worn a thin drapery, revealing the graceful lines of her figure, happened to be on a table in my studio when Aitken came to see me. "You certainly are a lucky devil," he said, looking at the picture. "If I could get a model like this I certainly would use her. Who is she and where did you find her?" "Her name is Audrey Munson," I answered, "and I found her one rainy afternoon when she came to the door of the studio of Robert Aitken." From that time on she posed for several of Aitken's bronzes and marbles, and through him was brought in touch with many other New York sculptors. She soon became very popular: "The most copied girl in America." In the Panama-Pacific Exposition in San Francisco she was in many a court and over many a doorway. In fact, the beauty of Audrey Munson ran through the Exposition like a musical leitmotif.

In the winter of 1913 the *New York Times,* desiring to increase the circulation of their Sunday edition and to introduce the German rotogravure process in America, had arranged as a special feature a contest "The American Girl of Today," which was to be decided through photographs sent in by the readers. I neglected to send in any pictures, but as I was to find out later, quite a number of pictures I had made found their way to the

Times. The judges were James Montgomery Flagg, C. Allan Gilbert, Clarence F. Underwood, Philip Boileau, Penrhyn Stanlaws, W. S. Jacobs and Hamilton King. From the thousands of prints sent in, there had been no dissenting voice in selecting as the most distinctive and characteristic photograph, expressing "The American Girl of Today," a picture of Miss Helen McMahon of New York. It was a portrait I had made of a young girl whom a mutual friend had brought to my studio some weeks before. I had been impressed by the unusual loveliness of her face. In the photograph that I made, her large blue eyes, looking out from the half shadow cast by the broad-brimmed velour hat, had a mysterious fascination. It was a photograph of real pictorial interest, but its tone values were so subtle that it seemed hardly possible that it could be reproduced in a newspaper. The *Times*, however, with their new press, had succeeded in making a perfect reproduction, almost life size, covering the full 16″ x 20″ page. It created a widespread interest, really a sensation, and this hitherto unknown girl found herself suddenly a national celebrity. She received offers from theatrical managers, sculptors and painters, besides many proposals of marriage. Some years afterwards she became the wife of Mr. James Cox Brady, and after his death married Mr. Charles Suydam Cutting, the explorer, whom she has accompanied on some of his hazardous expeditions.

The photographs I made of Greta Garbo, when she first came to America in 1925, were destined to play an important part in her Hollywood career. It seems that Louis B. Mayer of M.G.M., while on a talent hunt in Europe, had seen in Sweden a motion picture, *The Atonement of Gösta Berling*, based on a story by Selma Lagerlöf and directed by Mauritz Stiller. The girl who played the lead impressed him, but he was more anxious to secure the services of the director. Stiller consented to come to America only if his protégée, Greta Garbo, went along. (Her name then was Gustafson.) Their arrival in New York did not cause much excitement. The "reception committee" consisted of an M.G.M. publicity man, an interpreter and a photographer.

My friend Martha Hedman, the beautiful Swedish actress who was for several years a Belasco star and of whom I had made many studies, brought Greta Garbo and Mauritz Stiller to my studio. Stiller had known Miss Hedman in Sweden where they had worked together under August Strindberg. The newcomers were very much interested in the photographs they saw in my studio. That kind of photography was something entirely new to them. "I would love to have you make some pictures of me sometime," Miss Garbo said. (We spoke in German, as she knew hardly a word of English at that time.) "Why sometime?" I inquired. "Why not now? You're here and I'm here and I must make some photographs of you to have a visible proof that you are real." She smiled, but protested earnestly, "No, not now. Look at my dress, and I don't like my hair." "Never mind that," I said. "I am more interested in your eyes and in what is behind that extraordinary forehead." And without any further preparations, Greta Garbo let me make a number of pictures of her. Her face had an unusual mobility of expression and in the course of an hour my camera had captured a number of distinctive poses and expressions, all so different that it was hard to believe they were of the same girl. Both she and Stiller were delighted with the result. Later on I took the pictures to Frank Crowninshield, the editor of *Vanity Fair*. I wanted to give him, I said, the opportunity to discover a great cinema star. "The pictures are very interesting, but who is the girl?" he asked. "Greta Garbo," I answered. "Never heard of her," he said, "but perhaps I might use one of the pictures." "You can have it only," I insisted, "if you give it a full page." Reluctantly he agreed. By the time the issue with the picture was on the stands, rumors of a discovery of a phenomenal new star in Hollywood had reached New York.

It had not been an easy matter for Greta Garbo to secure a contract. While in New York, she had had weeks of tests (cinema and stills) and interviews with directors and officials, but with no results. "We cannot use her" was the verdict. "She's a type. Maybe for one or two films, but that's all." They were very

GRETA GARBO (1925)

ELEONORA DUSE

anxious, however, to sign up Stiller, who was considered the greatest motion picture director in Europe. He absolutely refused to go without her. In these weeks in New York I saw a good deal of the two. That Stiller was deeply devoted to his young protégée was evident, and she certainly admired the great man and fine artist that he was. She was the one great love in his life. It is touching to learn that he died clutching in his hands one of the pictures I made of her.

One night I went to the Commodore Hotel, where they were staying, to take them to a dinner which my friend Albert Rothbart was giving for them at the Five-Fifty Club. Stiller met me in the lobby, looking upset. "Greta has a terrible headache," he informed me. "What a pity," I replied, "as the dinner is being given for her, not for you or me. May I speak to her on the phone?" She answered in a very cheerful voice and was delighted that he was worried and really believed that she was not coming. She had merely wanted to tease him. The guests that evening were charming, intelligent people who knew the art of appreciating an excellent dinner and adding to its enjoyment by brilliant conversation. Greta was in the best of spirits, charming and witty, so different from the mysteriously silent, diffident and lonely person which Hollywood has made of her.

One morning she appeared at my studio looking rather sad. "I've come to say good-by," she said with a resigned smile. "They don't seem to want me. They say I'm a type. I'm going back to Berlin." When I asked her if she had shown the pictures I had made of her to the M.G.M. people, she replied, "No, I wanted to keep those for myself. They have so many of me already." I said, "You go right back to your hotel and send those pictures over to the M.G.M. offices without delay." I had seen in the papers that some of the important officials had arrived from the Coast that morning. Miss Garbo did as I told her, and from a report heard later from someone who was present, I learned that the pictures arrived during a directors' meeting. Great surprise and consternation! "Is that the blond Swede who has been hanging around here these last weeks? Great heavens! If she can look like that we better sign her up. Don't let her get away. Give her what she wants." And she signed a contract for $350 a week and went to California with Mauritz Stiller. It took Hollywood some time to discover her fine dramatic qualities. The phenomenal success of her first picture, *The Torrent,* is cinema history. To her great disappointment it was not directed by Stiller. He did not get along with the officials and could not adapt himself to Hollywood methods. After a year he returned to Sweden, disillusioned and broken in health. Without Stiller, Greta Garbo would never have been the great artist she is today. Losing him, she lost not only her best friend but the best influence in her life.

Another portrait made just on the spur of the moment, without having been planned, was that of the second Mrs. Woodrow Wilson. Gertrude Gordon, who is now the wife of Dr. Cary T. Grayson, was a pupil at the Finch School in New York, and an appointment was arranged to have her portrait made. She came accompanied by her friend, then Mrs. Edith Bolling Galt. After I had finished with her pictures, she urged Mrs. Galt to have hers done. "I'd like to, but it will have to be at some other time. I don't like this dress. It's too fussy." I suggested that she put on one of my simple dark Japanese kimonos which give a good neck line. "All right," she said, "we can try it anyway." It was in this unexpected way that, without the slightest inkling of what its fate was to be, I took the photograph that was reproduced oftener than any other I have made.

Some weeks later I received a morning telephone call and was informed by the long distance operator that the White House was on the line, Mr. Tumulty calling. "After five o'clock today," he said, "the representatives of the newspapers will come to you for copies of your picture of Mrs. Galt—you know the one she likes best—and you are authorized to let them have it. I ask you, however, to keep this message confidential until they arrive. You probably know what it is all about."

The next morning the papers announced the engagement of

President Wilson and Mrs. Edith Bolling Galt and my picture of her was the only one that was used. In fact, it was the only portrait of her that the President ever authorized for publication, here as well as abroad.

Dr. Grayson, one of the closest friends of President Wilson, told me that this photograph of Mrs. Galt had rendered the President a very valuable service. "There had been," he said, "some criticism in certain circles of his wanting to marry again. The morning of the announcement, I happened to be at the house of Mrs. George Dewey, the widow of the Admiral, whose opinion, as you know, counts a great deal in Washington society. When she read the announcement she exclaimed, 'So he's going to marry again. Mrs. Edith Bolling Galt. I don't know who she is. I've never heard of her, but I can tell from this photograph that she must be a woman of extraordinary charm.' And this," Dr. Grayson concluded, "was the impression the picture produced throughout the country."

From President Wilson I received a letter saying, "It was very fortunate, indeed, that we had such a splendid photograph of Mrs. Galt to give to the press."

Sometimes more than the artistic merit of a photograph is needed to make an impression. A well-worded title may have to be found before the picture will attract attention. To give just two examples:

A young singer who had a minor part in a musical comedy was bemoaning the fact that she had not been able to get any publicity whatsoever. All attempts to get her picture in the paper had failed. Someone had told her that perhaps I might be able to help. When she came to see me, I was struck by the strange similarity, especially of the mouth, between her profile and that in Rossetti's painting, "Beata Beatrix." There was the same softly rounded and full upper lip as in Rossetti's famous model. In the photograph I made of the girl, this likeness was even more evident than in reality. I telephoned to one of my newspaper friends and told him about "The Girl with the Rossetti Mouth."

"That sounds interesting," he said. "I'll send one of my men to see you right away." The reporter who came announced that he was not the fellow who wrote "this art stuff." He was a baseball reporter. He asked that I dictate the story to him. "Great stuff," he exclaimed, "but say, who was that guy Rossetti anyway?" . . . The story about "The Girl with the Rossetti Mouth" was copied in many newspapers to the great advantage of the ambitious young singer.

In a similar way I was of some assistance to Hilda Biyar, the dancer, who inspired many of Mario Korbel's most successful sculptures of the dance. Korbel, Walter Goldbeck, the painter, and I had planned to arrange a benefit for the Polish Relief Fund, chiefly as an expression of our admiration and affection for Paderewski, who was giving all his energy and means to help stricken Poland. This was in 1916. The featured artist on our program was Hilda Biyar. Goldbeck had painted a striking full-length portrait of her in a costume of red and gold brocade. We had tried in vain to have the papers publish, as propaganda for our planned benefit, a photograph of this painting. It was not of sufficient news interest. The picture was exhibited on the ground floor of the Reinhardt Galleries on Fifth Avenue. I had observed that passersby would stop in front of the window, as if someone had pulled them by the sleeve. Men in taxis ordered their drivers to stop, though they were in the middle of the block, so that they could get out and look at it. This gave me an idea for a title: "The Picture That Stopped Traffic on Fifth Avenue." This title did the trick. The photograph was published in several newspapers and the *World* reproduced it in color for their Sunday magazine. That was the beginning of the publicity we needed. The benefit was a success and we received the following letter of thanks from the great artist and patriot:

MY DEAR DR. GENTHE:

Such a beautiful tribute as you and your fellow artists Mr. Korbel and Mr. Goldbeck, have given to me for my suffering countrymen reaches the chords of my heart and draws me, if possible, closer to you.

I can only say that, sorely as the money is needed, I appreciate even more deeply than that itself, the sentiment which prompted you to organize the benefit and give the proceeds to me. I know that from its distribution many thankful hearts in Poland will take courage and go plodding on with renewed energy.

Again I thank you for all you have done.

Believe me, now and always

Faithfully yours,
I. J. PADEREWSKI.
HELENA PADEREWSKA.

In discussing the degrees of beauty, I have denied the verity of the term "most beautiful." I will have to modify my assertion. There are cases where the expression "most beautiful" is justified. I do not hesitate to say that of all the women of the various nationalities I have seen and photographed, none can compare with those of America. It is true, I have found a high degree of beauty and loveliness among other nationalities. But nowhere else are there as many beautiful women of all types and classes, who approach the ideal of perfection, as here in America. Each generation seems an improvement on the preceding. Fashions change in beauty. The change in our day has been chiefly a closer approach toward the Greek ideal, away from the rounded lines of the indolent harem type once so popular. The modern American girl moves with a free stride that marks her wherever she goes. A souvenir of Spain comes to my mind. It was in Cadiz. I had seen marvelous sights in my travels through the country, but the famed beauty of the Spanish women had been somewhat of a disappointment to me. Lustrous dark eyes, smiling lips revealing the most perfect teeth—yes, but instead of fine strength and freedom there was a suggestion of plumpness and laziness. Late one afternoon I saw coming toward me the slender figure of a girl. She was not accompanied by a duenna, which marked her at once as a foreigner. Yet even if she had been thus chaperoned, one would have recognized her as an American by her gracefully proportioned body and the free rhythmic swing of her gait. When she was quite close and I could admire the radiant beauty of her features that bespoke intelligence and charm, I took off my hat and bowed, saying, "I had to salute the most beautiful woman I have seen in Spain. I hope you are not offended." "No, I rather like it," was the reply, and thanking me with an enchanting smile, she pursued her way and I continued in the opposite direction.

The chief factors that have contributed to this supremacy of the American woman are her activities in all forms of sports, her interest in the classic dance which she prefers to the meaningless shuffle of some of the ballroom "dances," the joy of outdoor life—all this is responsible for the fresher, the finer, the more truly beautiful woman of our day. She is frankly proud of the grace and strength of her body. She realizes her responsibility in preserving and improving it through sensible exercise—and sensible eating. She is taller than the former average. Her legs are longer, and a shorter waist increases the impression of height: a definite trend toward the Greek ideal. Some time ago I was able to give an interesting illustration of the truth of this theory. I had photographed a young girl of quite unusual beauty. Her mother, at the end of the sitting, asked if it would be possible to make a photograph that would give an idea of the beauty of her daughter's body without showing the head. I explained how it could be done. "You know," the mother said, "at my daughter's age, I knew that my figure was beautiful, and I have always regretted that no picture of it exists." The photograph I made of the girl had a sculptural quality which gave the effect of a classic Greek torso. When I showed it to a famous archeologist in Athens, he exclaimed, "But where is that sculpture? I don't know it." And he was relieved when he learned that I had made it with my camera.

The mixing of races, which in other countries would hardly have the chance to amalgamate, is another element in favor of producing a new and distinctive type of beauty: Norwegian father and American mother, Cherokee mother and New England father, Italian mother and Danish father, Chinese father and Spanish mother, etc.—the endless variety of unions made possible in this "melting pot of races." And another element that must not be overlooked is that America offers its young people a freedom unknown in the old world, a freedom in thought and action, facilities for spiritual and physical growth and other advantages they could not find anywhere else. Whoever has the chance of observing groups of young men and women at athletic contests in our schools and colleges, seeing the grace and strength of their bodies, the spirit and intelligence that give their faces something more than mere surface handsomeness, will agree with me that a country that can produce such men and women need not worry about the future.

American Freedom

173

PAVLOWA, ISADORA, TERRY, DUSE

PAVLOWA, Isadora Duncan, Ellen Terry, Eleonora Duse! They were an immortal coterie who held a special niche in my mind because of the common bond that drew them to me. The bond was Isadora.

I met Pavlowa in San Francisco when she was there with Mordkin. It was some time after the fire when what we called the "Barbary Coast" had been rebuilt and was getting back into swing. She wanted to see the new dances she had heard so much about—the Turkey Trot, the Texas Tommy and the Grizzly Bear. I arranged a party for her and Mordkin, inviting some of my newspaper friends.

As a preliminary I consulted the Chief of Police, since a risk was involved in taking Pavlowa to the Barbary Coast. There was the danger that the crowd might get out of hand. Or there might be a raid, which happened now and then. The Chief assured me that there would be no raid, but he sent a detective along in case of emergency.

Into the harbor of San Francisco came freighters and sailing ships from the South Seas and the Orient. Their crews were a dangerous lot composed of the dregs of many countries whose rendezvous, when in port, were the dance halls of the notorious Barbary Coast. The most famous, as well as the most infamous, of these was the Olympia, a vast "palace" of gilt and tinsel with a great circular space in the center and around it a raised platform with booths for the spectators. We took our place in one of these. Below us on the floor, to the barbarous sound of tomtom, cymbal, horn and banjo, a medley of degenerate humanity whirled around in weird dance steps. Pickpockets, dope fiends, sailors, longshoremen, Negroes, Mexicans, attired in bright sweaters, checkered suits and waistcoats, danced with streetwalkers who had come in their tawdry finery from the crib-houses of Commercial Street.

The exotic music and the strange wild steps of the dancers fascinated Pavlowa. After discussing it with Mordkin for a while, she asked us if it would be all right for them to go out on the floor and dance. We thought it safe enough, and she and Mordkin stepped down to the floor. It was difficult to explain to Mordkin that he had to pay the customary ten-cent fee to the floor manager for the privilege of dancing with his chosen partner.

Pavlowa had on a simple black frock and toque and Mordkin a dark street suit. Nobody knew who they were, and nobody noticed them as they began to feel out the barbaric rhythm with hesitant feet. Gradually they were carried away by it and, oblivious to their sordid surroundings, they evolved, then and there, a dance of alluring beauty.

Gradually, one couple after another stepped aside to watch, forming an astonished circle at the edge of the floor. When Pavlowa and Mordkin had finished, there was a moment of silence, followed by wild bursts of applause. The men stamped and threw their caps into the air and the women clapped, calling out, "More! More!" They made no attempt to crowd in around Pavlowa or to speak to her, and when she passed through the circle to get to the booth, a respectful lane was made for her.

This incident has always seemed to me a thrilling example of the power of great art. Pavlowa was touched to tears by it, and she said, years afterwards, that the tribute of the sorry rabble that night had meant more to her than decorations she had received from the crowned heads of Europe.

My acquaintance with her then was brief and there were no opportunities for photographs. The next time I saw her was during one of her visits to New York, when she came to my studio. Pavlowa seldom went to a photographer's studio, preferring to have him come to the theater during rehearsals. She knew the pictures I had made of Isadora, whom she greatly admired. "I love the pictures you made of her," she said, "and I want you

SCARF DANCE (MARGARET SEVERN)

ANNA PAVLOWA

to make some of me that Isadora will like. Perhaps some in my Orfeo costumes would please her. You will have no difficulty, I am sure, as I can hold any dance pose for several seconds."

"You can, I know," was my response, "but your draperies can't." "Never mind about that, but before you take the pictures let me limber up a bit," she said. "I know I don't have to worry about the camera as you cannot take pictures in this light when I'm moving so quickly." According to all rules photographic, it should have been impossible to obtain a picture in that studio light, but since she was paying no attention to me, and danced in absolute freedom without a thought of photographs, I took a chance with the small camera which I always kept at hand.

I made a number of exposures. Only one was successful. It is one of the best photographs of the dance I have ever made and the only one in existence showing Pavlowa in the free movement of the dance. Upon seeing the proof a few days later, she threw her arms around me and actually cried. "This is not a photograph," she exclaimed, "it is a miracle."

I had made some motion pictures of Isadora's older pupils, chiefly of Anna, Irma and Lisa. Taken without benefit of any of the apparatus available to motion picture operators today, they were purely an experiment. At that time all efforts to record the dance on the screen had failed. The smooth coherence of dance rhythm was always lacking. I knew that if the pictures were taken two or three times faster than the normal speed and projected at the standard tempo, this fault could be rectified. My experiment proved this theory to be correct. Occasionally in my studio I had run off the reels for my friends.

Pavlowa asked me if I would show them for her. "Isadora told me," she said, "that they are the only dance pictures she has seen on the screen which are smooth, fluent and harmonious."

An appointment was made for her to come and see my films, but she was unable to keep it, as she was always rehearsing. This happened several times and finally she called me up. "It is just impossible for me to keep an appointment," she said. "My work always interferes. I wonder if you could show them here at my hotel after the performance?"

One midnight I appeared at the McAlpin Hotel. When I asked at the desk for Madame Pavlowa's rooms, a man whom I recognized as the house detective eyed with evident suspicion the mysterious looking box I was carrying. He followed me, believing no doubt that one never knows when a Russian may be blown up. Pavlowa greeted me at the door in a negligee. It was not one of those sumptuous creations one sees in the shop-windows on Fifth Avenue, but a none too elegant flannel wrapper. The champagne supper which the public envisions as the midnight repast of great stars was a glass of milk and some crackers which she was eating out of a box. She and her husband, Monsieur Dandré, were enthusiastic about the way I had maintained the harmony of the dance movements in my films. Dandré was particularly eager to have me explain how it had been done. After I told him, he said, "Very simple. Now that I know how, I will take all of Madame's pictures myself."

No good dance motion picture was ever taken of Pavlowa. One might say that the only thing approaching it is the splendid frieze that Malvina Hoffman did of her with Mordkin in the *Bacchanal* in about thirty different poses. It now rests in Miss Hoffman's studio in New York, but it should be reproduced and given a place in colleges as a memorial to the immortal artist and as a study for all who are interested in the art of the dance. It is sad to realize that no motion pictures of Isadora Duncan's dances exist, nor are there any of Nijinsky. The art of the dancer is a fugitive thing and the only way it can be preserved as an inspiration and guide for future generations is through the cinema. That there are no such memorials to these three incomparable artists is a sin of omission to be charged up against the motion picture industry of their day.

Of Isadora Duncan I write from a friendship which endured through many years. Like all those who knew her, I had a deep

ODERN TORSO

DUNCAN DANCERS

ANNA DUNCANLISA DUNC

affection and admiration for her. But when I think of her, it is with a measure of sorrow for her tragic impulses.

As a creative genius she was both artist and liberator, releasing by her courage and heavenly grace, not the dance alone, but womankind, from the fetters of puritanism.

Where her work was concerned she had integrity and patience, knowing no compromise with what she felt to be the truth about beauty. In her personal life she had charm and a naïve wit. Of tact or self-control she had very little, nor did she wish to have. She was the complete and willing tool of her impulses.

I met her first at the home of Mary Fanton Roberts, now editor of *Arts and Decoration,* who had known her for years and was her most devoted and understanding friend. It was during one of those periods, frequently occurring in Isadora's career, when she found herself short of funds. She had just started her school in New York, and Mrs. Roberts had invited a few friends —Percy Mackaye, Marguerite Namara, Max Eastman, and Mr. and Mrs. Louis Anspacher—to talk over ways and means for creating an interest in it. Isadora had taken a barn-like place on Fourth Avenue and Twenty-third Street. By covering the floor with a carpet, veiling the lights with Liberty scarves and hanging blue curtains as a back-drop against the wall, she had turned it into a semblance of a studio. Some low couches and cushions for seats were the only furniture. It was there that an afternoon reception was given to which a number of influential people were invited. Walter Lippmann and Mabel Dodge had arranged to have John Purroy Mitchel, the mayor of New York, meet Isadora so that she might explain to him the problem of her school. When he was presented, Isadora looked up at him with her child-like eyes and said, "You, the mayor of New York? You certainly don't look like a mayor of this big city. You look like a very intelligent and handsome young man."

Leading him to a couch she sat down beside him talking animatedly, but not about the purpose of the meeting. She had talked with him for some time when there was one of those sudden silences in a room that are sometimes fatal. Plainly her voice could be heard: "Who are these people? What do they know about art or what can they understand of my work? Who are these women? Wives with feathers!" There was a confused buzz and some hasty and embarrassed leave-taking. Nothing came of the meeting.

Things were getting serious, and Mrs. Roberts and some others thought it would be a good idea for Mr. Otto Kahn, who was doing so much for the theater and the opera, to meet Isadora. An evening program in the studio was planned. The girls were to dance and Isadora was to talk about the school and its aims. Mr. Kahn accepted the invitation. This time Isadora's friends had given some urgent advice, and she was in a more receptive state of mind.

As nine o'clock approached, she appeared in her draperies and assumed a graceful and fetching pose on one of the low couches. "Now," she said to the girls, "I hope you understand the importance of the occasion. We must do everything we can to make a hit with Mr. Kahn."

Mr. Kahn came attired in full evening dress. Isadora, in the most innocent manner, asked him to be seated. He looked around for a chair. There was none. Isadora, with a graceful gesture, invited him to sit beside her. For a moment the only sound to be heard was the creaking of his stiff shirt as he negotiated the distance between them. Isadora turned the full spell of her radiance upon him. Before the evening was over he had placed the Century Theater, of which he was a patron and subsidizer, at her disposal. She was to give a performance there and he further arranged that her girls could live in some of its upper rooms, and she could also have her school there.

When the great night arrived, I was standing at the back of the theater as Mr. Kahn came in. I shall never forget the horror on his face when he saw that Isadora had covered the elaborate gold of the founder's loge with unbleached muslin, and had had the first ten rows of seats taken out so that the orchestra would not be too close to the stage. Under the soothing influence of Isadora's art—she put on a beautiful program—he appeared to relent, but not for very long. Her unfortunate tendencies created so many complications that after a few weeks she had to move her girls and herself into a boarding house.

Practically the same thing happened in Athens. The Venizelos Government, anxious to show its appreciation of what she had done in reviving the art of the Grecian dance, sent a cabinet minister to ask her what was the most helpful thing it could do for her. She said she would like to have a place for her school. So a small, unoccupied palace was made ready for her and she moved in. The minister who had been instrumental in paying her this tribute asked her if he might bring some of his political colleagues to attend the opening with him. Isadora said she would be delighted.

They arrived, dressed in frock coats and high hats. When Isadora saw them she froze up. "Who are those people?" she asked. "I don't know them. I did not invite them. And I'm not going to have my girls dance for them." That ended the school in Greece.

When Isadora first came to Athens in 1904, she and her two brothers started to build a house for her school on Kopanos Hill, just outside of Athens. A small fortune was spent to drill an artesian well, but the well proved a failure—after they had started building it was discovered that there was not a drop of water on the whole mountain, and building was abandoned. On her last visit to Athens (in 1920) Isadora found the house in ruins, inhabited by shepherds and goats, but she decided to have the grounds cleared and to start rebuilding. Doors, windows and a roof were put in, the floor of the high living room was covered with a carpet, a piano was moved in, and she started to work with her six pupils whom she had brought from New York, the same girls she later legally adopted. But the school was not to last. When in the revolution following the King's sudden death Venizelos and his party were forced to leave the country, Isadora's stay in Athens came to an end. Kopanos and the idea of a school in Greece were abandoned.

When I visited Athens, three years after Isadora's death, the walls of the Kopanos house were still standing. The old caretaker and his wife had remained, faithfully trying to prevent refugees and others from carrying away the stones for building material. The old couple, who had not received any wages in all these years, refused to believe that Isadora was dead. I learned that several artists had formed a plan to rebuild the house and make it into something like a monument to Isadora, by letting Vassos and Tanagra Kanellos, the foremost dancers of Greece, who worked toward the same goal that had been Isadora's aim, use it for their school. (I have spoken of the Kanelloses and their work in another chapter.) The City Government was willing to name the road leading up to Kopanos after Isadora. I was asked to communicate with Augustin Duncan, Isadora's brother and chief heir. Time was pressing. The property was in danger of being sold for unpaid taxes. I explained the situation in a lengthy cable to Augustin, only to learn that he had turned over all his rights to his brother Raymond in Paris. Raymond was not interested. The appeals of many friends brought no results. Isadora had called the house on Kopanos "a beautiful ruin and a hope for the future." Her last words to Vassos Kanellos were: "When will we be able to have the school in Athens?" Perhaps there is still a chance to have at least a part of Isadora's dream salvaged. Who knows?

Among the friends who stood by her through her many vicissitudes, none was so long-suffering, so devoted and so valuable as Paris Singer. It is no secret that he is the "Lohengrin" of her memoirs. There were intervals during their association when Isadora's tempestuous moods drove them apart. But he had always kept in touch with her, and their quarrels had been patched up.

During the war, after one of their reconciliations, he took the Metropolitan Opera House and financed a matinée performance for her. This was the first time that she danced in public after the death of her two children. In honor of the occasion Mr. Singer had asked about twenty of their close friends to a dinner at Sherry's. About a hundred guests were to come in afterwards to dance.

Isadora's appearance at the Metropolitan was a triumph and she arrived at the dinner radiantly happy. When I arrived Mr. Singer called me to one side. "I have placed you next to her," he said. "You know she never eats before a performance—she's had nothing all day but a cup of coffee at breakfast. I want you to see that she doesn't drink anything until she has had some solid food."

Isadora had scarcely sat down when she said, "I'm dying of thirst. I just have to have a sip of champagne."

I have never seen her in better form than she was during the dinner. As a rule she paid very little attention to clothes. And she cared nothing at all for jewelry. But that evening, to please Singer, she wore an exquisite white chiffon frock and a diamond necklace which he had just given her. All went well until the dancing began. I was talking to Isadora when all of a sudden her face lit up. "Do you see," she said, "that dark, handsome young man over there?"

"A typical lounge lizard," said I.

"What do you mean?" she exclaimed. "He's the most famous tango dancer in the Argentine. I want you to go over and bring him here."

I did as she asked and they proceeded to dance a tango that astonished the guests by something more than mere grace and rhythm.

Paris Singer stood watching them, a giant of fury—he was six feet six—until they were half through. Then he strode into the middle of the floor, took the Argentine by the scruff of the neck and slithered him out of the room.

Isadora turned pale, and with the air of a prima donna, she called out, "If you treat my friends like that I won't wear your jewelry." She tore the necklace from her throat and the diamonds scattered on the floor. As she swept from the room, I was standing in the doorway. Without looking at me she whispered, "Pick them up."

There was a coolness for days, and as usual Singer forgave her.

Galen Stone, who was an old friend of mine, had never seen Isadora dance, nor was he interested until I persuaded him to go with me to one of her matinées. She danced César Franck's "Redemption." Stone was so moved that tears were in his eyes. "You are right," he said. "It is something that I shall never forget. I would like," he added, "to do something as a token of my admiration for this great artist."

Knowing that she would like nothing better, I suggested that he give a party for her.

"All right," he said. "You fix it up. Ask anyone you think ought to be there, but don't forget me."

As I wanted something in the way of a novelty, I got Michio Ito, who had just come to New York, to give an hour of Japanese dances, with two Japanese girls in costume playing the koto and the samisen, and two Japanese boys with the drums. For a background we used one of my large Chinese banners to cover the ornate decorations of Sherry's salon. Isadora loved to make speeches. "I may not be a good dancer, but I do know how to speak," she said, and she gave a splendid talk on the dance. The evening was a great success and Isadora was especially delighted with Ito's Japanese dances, which were something new to her.

It was my embarrassment to be present when the final break came between Isadora and Paris Singer. Isadora's version of it, as recorded in her book, is incomplete. For some time Paris Singer had had a big plan in his mind. He wanted to do something for Isadora that would carry on her memory and her work for all time. George Gray Barnard, the sculptor, had suggested the endowment of an American Art Center where sculptors,

JEANNE EAGLES

ELLEN TERRY

MAXINE ELLIOTT PARIS SINGER

ISADORA DUNCAN

RUTH ST. DENIS

painters and dancers could develop their talents in an atmosphere conducive to work and without financial worry. It was to be a testimonial to Isadora and she was to direct the School of the Dance. Singer took to the idea at once. As he wanted it to be a surprise, he said nothing about it to Isadora. He was going to Florida to visit the home for convalescent soldiers which he was supporting, and before leaving he had taken an option for a large sum of money on the old Madison Square Garden. On his return he gave a dinner at the Plaza for the purpose of telling Isadora about his plan. Among those there were Augustin and Margherita Duncan, Isadora's sister Elizabeth, Mary Desti, George Gray Barnard and myself.

Unfortunately, Singer started to talk of what he was doing for the wounded soldiers.

"Is that what you brought me here for?" said Isadora. "I'm sick and tired of hearing about the war and the sick soldiers. Can't you think of anything else?"

We all began to talk, in the hope of clearing the air, and after a few minutes everything was peaceful again. Then he told her about Madison Square Garden and the plan, mentioning that he had already negotiated for the purchase of Madison Square Garden.

"Do you mean to tell me," asked Isadora, "that you expect me to direct a school in Madison Square Garden? I suppose you want me to advertise prizefights with my dancing."

Singer turned absolutely livid. His lips were quivering and his hands were shaking. He got up from the table without saying a word and left the room.

"Do you realize what you have done?" we asked in a chorus of dismay. "You could have had the school that was your life's dream, and now you have ruined everything."

"He'll come back," she said serenely. "He always does."

He never did. She sent her brother, her sister-in-law, Mary Desti, and finally the pupils to plead with him. He was adamant. Her letters to him went unanswered. All funds were stopped.

She did not hear from him for years, not until a few weeks before her death when Mary Desti called upon him at his villa on the Riviera, telling him that Isadora was penniless. He finally consented to come to her rescue, but it was too late.

All my memories of Isadora are not overwrought with shadows. By some odd twist of Fate it was only where her own best interests were at stake that her destructive instincts came to the fore. At other times she had an endearing charm and spontaneous wit that were irresistible. I feel that if it had not been for the shock of her children's death, the pattern of her later years would have been different. Her children and her art were the only things that really mattered to her. After the children's death her life seemed finished. She would never have danced again if it had not been for the continued insistence of her friends. Her one desire was to escape from the horror of reality. And parties, continuous parties, were her outlet. They were not, however, the orgies so often attributed to her. I have many happy recollections of little gatherings in delightful company in which the real Isadora was the leading spirit.

There was the day we went out to George Gray Barnard's studio and he took us through "The Cloisters," that fine treasure house of Gothic sculpture which John D. Rockefeller, Jr., has since given to the Metropolitan Museum of Art. In the collection was a Madonna so much like Isadora that she might easily have sat for it. Barnard said to her, "I have always wanted to do a marble of you, but you have never given me the opportunity. I have had to be satisfied with looking at this Madonna."

It was a perfect summer's day and we had luncheon at a restaurant overlooking the Hudson. Isadora was in one of her best moods, and there was not a discordant note in the two hours we were together. She talked at length about Greek sculpture, and about the work of Michelangelo and what it had meant to her. Isadora suggested in her movements and posture and in the modeling of her head and body some of Michelangelo's work. Barnard, who more than any other of our sculptors admired and understood her, could have done a sculpture that would have revealed the beauty of her spirit.

One summer Isadora with her pupils had taken a house at Long Beach. Many interesting guests came and went, among them Eugène Ysaye, who sometimes would bring his violin. One evening when he had been playing for us for a long time, he put his violin down, saying to Isadora, "Now it is your turn to entertain."

"Very well," she said. "You men sit here. We'll close these folding doors, and I'll prepare a spectacle that will be better than the Ziegfeld Follies."

When the doors were opened, Isadora and the girls in diaphanous draperies gave an amusing burlesque of the Ziegfeld Follies that would have done credit to Mr. Minsky.

At her request I had taken Isadora one evening to Henri's famous restaurant at Lynbrook, a short motor ride from Long Beach. Henri Charpentier, one of the most distinguished French chefs in America, insisted that we leave the menu entirely in his hands and he composed for our benefit a dinner that was a veritable Lucullan symphony. Isadora was delighted and told Henri that she had not thought it possible to get in America a meal of a perfection that no Paris restaurant could surpass. My enjoyment of the excellent food and wine was curtailed by the thought of the accumulating check. When after reverently sipping a real Napoleon brandy, which Henri poured from the only bottle left in his cellar, I asked for the check, I was more than relieved and delighted when Henri, with an inimitable French gesture, said, *"Monsieur, tout est payé. C'était un grand honneur de servir Madame."* Needless to say, the gesture was not repeated on my subsequent visits.

One Sunday when Ysaye came for luncheon, Isadora showed him in the gravure section of the paper a photograph of young women in chaste draperies, with their heads thrown back. It was titled "Modern Maids in an Ancient Greek Dance."

"This," said Isadora, "is the kind of thing that the general public blames me for."

The great virtuoso then told us the following story:

"Once when I was walking with my accompanist through the streets of Brussels, we passed a blind man playing on a squeaky violin a tune that one could scarcely recognize. My accompanist said, 'Even you, Master, could not play on that instrument.'

"I asked the blind man to let me have his fiddle and I proceeded to play the same tune, probably a little bit better than he had. As we turned to go, my friend said to the blind man, 'Do you know that it is the great Ysaye who has just played on your violin?'

"A week later I passed that way again. The blind man was there playing the same tune no better than he had before. But around his neck was a large sign—'Pupil of Eugène Ysaye.'"

Turning to Isadora, Ysaye said, "I am sure we both have many pupils we will never know."

Isadora had a certain kind of humility with those whom she considered truly great. A touching illustration of this was a morning in Long Beach when we were out for a stroll on the Boardwalk. Sarah Bernhardt, recuperating from an operation, had been taken to Long Beach, and Isadora had often said how much she would like to meet her. But when I suggested taking her to call, she always held back. "How do I know she wants to meet me?" she would say. "What have I to give to one of her divine genius?"

This day Sarah was being wheeled toward us in her chair. "Now," said I, "you'll have to speak to her. Her doctor has recognized us and Sarah will be hurt if we don't go up to her."

When the introduction was made, Sarah, pointing to the place beside her in the chair, said: "Sit down here beside me." "Ah," replied Isadora, with a moving sweetness, "that would be too great an honor. I ought to be at your feet." In the excitement of the meeting, she had forgotten that Sarah had had one of her legs amputated.

I had known Isadora for quite a long time before she would let me take photographs of her. "No," she would say, "I am not good for the camera. Perhaps before I go back to Paris I'll let you take some, but not now."

One day she came to my studio without having made an appointment. "I've come to keep my promise," she announced. "I will let you take my passport picture."

When she saw that having her picture taken was a rapid and painless process, she said, "Let's try some more." She got into her dancing costume, which she had brought with her, and the photographs I took were the first of my studies which were published after her death in book form by Mitchell Kennerley, in 1929, with a preface by Max Eastman.

Through the long period of our friendship, she seldom spoke to me of her children. That day while I was photographing her, she felt like talking about them. One of the portraits I liked particularly and I was disappointed when a few days later she took it away without making a comment. When I called for her at her hotel some days later, I noticed that she had placed the photograph on the mantelpiece. "There's something peculiar about that picture," she said. "When I am alone and look at it, after a while my face fades out and the faces of my children take its place." This is the portrait of which she says in her book: "It is not a representation of my physical being. It is my very soul indeed."

Isadora's life was as Greek in its pattern as her art. No Greek dramatist could have devised a more fitting end. It was an automobile that brought her children to their death. So it was with her. She had just received an advance payment on her book and had bought a car, the first she had owned. About to start out on a demonstration trip, she looked at the driver and turning to her faithful friend, Mary Desti, who was standing on the sidewalk, she said, "He is not a chauffeur—he is a Greek god." Waving gaily to Mary, she called out: *"Adieu, mes amis. Je vais à la gloire."* The automobile started and the red scarf, the symbol of her art, became entangled in the wheels. With one turn her lovely neck was broken.

Although I met Isadora long after she had left Gordon Craig, she and his mother, Ellen Terry, were still devoted friends, and it was through Isadora that the great English actress, on her last visit to New York, came to me to have her picture taken. I made a portrait of her alone and several with Anna Duncan, one of Isadora's pupils, of whom she was especially fond.

Ellen Terry was very much interested in Chinese and Japanese art and liked to look at my collection. I showed her a Japanese seventeenth-century book about marionettes. She went through it with little bursts of delight. "This is charming," she said. "But it really ought to belong to Ted [Ted was her name for Gordon Craig]. He just has to have it."

My response was not one of generosity. I explained to her that the book was rare, and in fact I knew of only one other copy

of it. "I'm afraid I'll have to be stingy. I don't want to part with it."

I might just as well have given it to her, for later when I moved into my second New York studio, a suitcase with some of my most cherished books and curios was stolen, the marionette book among them.

Ellen Terry was old when I knew her, but there was something luminous about her. Her voice had lost none of its timbre and she had the same vitality that distinguished Bernhardt. She hated to be alone and she loved to be entertained. Several times when she had appointments, she called up and said she did not feel like going out, and asked if I would come to see her. When I arrived she would say: "I want to be amused. Bring up a chair and sit down here and tell me some of your entertaining stories." She spoke often to me of Eleonora Duse, and said that she had seen her the night before Duse sailed for America in 1924. "I knew her and loved her for many years," she said, "not only for the great artist of the theater that she was, but because of her glorious soul. And that night—it was the last time I was ever to see her—she looked even nobler and more beautiful than in her youth."

When Duse was finally persuaded to come to America under the management of Morris Gest, she was living in poverty in a small villa in the Italian countryside. She had thought her career in the theater was over, and it was only the—to her—fantastic salary which Gest had offered her that induced her to come to America. Her performances in New York were given at the Metropolitan Opera House. She was sixty-four then and she used no make-up. On the opening night I had to sit very far back, as it was almost impossible to get seats, and when she came on the stage, this frail, elderly little woman looked like a being from some other world, so startling was the contrast between her pallor and the heightened color which artifice had given her company. But when she began to speak, she stood out like a bright star in the night sky, so compelling was the magic of her acting. I could not hear what any of the other actors and actresses were saying, but, because of the way in which she knew how to project her voice, not one word of hers was lost to me.

Naturally I wanted to photograph her. But I knew that she would be besieged by requests from all the other photographers, and so I made no attempt to reach her. To my great joy, one day her secretary, Lady Onslow, came to see me. "It's very strange," she said. "The Signora has refused to let anybody take her picture. But today she said that she wanted you to do so. You know she loved Isadora Duncan, and she has some of the pictures you did of her. But you will have to come to the hotel as the Signora's throat is weak and she does not want to risk going out, if it can be avoided."

In due time I went forth with my camera to the old Majestic Hotel on Seventy-second Street and Central Park West. The first thing I noticed when I got there were two oxygen tanks in the narrow hallway leading to her suite. The door was opened by the faithful maid who had been with Duse ever since her early days in the theater. The maid said that the Signora would come into the drawing room as soon as the camera was ready.

While I was waiting I noticed with horror that no attempt had been made by the management to create any kind of beauty in the surroundings which were to be the home of this great woman for some weeks. The furniture and hangings were of the typical old-fashioned hotel style. On the walls were the engravings that the average hotel deemed indispensable—"Three Horses in a Thunderstorm," "The Return of the Prodigal Son," "Alone at Last." I was thinking that it would not have hurt the manager to have gone to some of our big department stores and asked them to lend a few good etchings and some tapestries, etc., to add a touch of beauty to the room. When Eleonora Duse came in, even before she had greeted me, she said, "Oh, don't look at these horrible things. I try not to. They hurt my eyes."

As she shook my hand in greeting she pointed to her hollow cheeks. "I don't think it is possible to make a good picture of me," she said, "but I know if anybody can, you can."

She was both pleased and astonished when she saw that I was not going to pose her, but was taking her pictures as an incident in the conversation. Among the subjects she brought up was the Moscow Art Theatre and she spoke in glowing terms of the Russian actors, particularly of Stanislavsky. "Just compare their attitude toward their work, and what they accomplish with such simplicity and frugality, with the lavish expense and the mediocre achievement of Hollywood."

As I did not want to tire her, I made the pictures as rapidly as I could. When I started to leave, she insisted on my staying for another quarter of an hour. "This has been a most refreshing experience. I'm not tired at all. And if you find that the results are not what you want, you shall try again. Sometimes we all have to try again."

She was as naïvely happy over the photographs as a child at Christmas. "They are the only pictures which I have had in twenty-five years that I really like," she remarked.

From San Francisco I had a telegram from her. It said, "Am sending you greetings from your San Francisco. I ask you again to put me on the list of your regular clients. I need some more of my photographs, the profile which I like best. Please have them ready for me when I return to New York after Easter. And this time don't insist on sending them without a bill, but do as I ask. I am very grateful to you and I want to see you again."

Such a privilege was never to be mine. Eleonora Duse died in Pittsburgh on her trip back across the continent. From Lady Onslow I have the story of her death. On a cold, sleety day she was driven to the theater. The chauffeur stopped at what he thought was the stage door, and drove off. The door was locked, and she stood there in the wind and rain for several minutes, until someone in the theater heard her knocking. The cold she caught that day proved fatal. The name of the play was *La Porta Chiusa*— The Closed Door.

*The
Closed
Door*

THE DANCE

SURVEYING the changes which have taken place in American life during my years in this country, I cannot fail to be deeply impressed by the magic growth in its artistic perception and achievement. When I arrived there was little in dancing, painting and sculpture that could be called truly American. This was but natural in a young nation that had covered so much ground in so short a time. Men who must be concerned with building cities, planting the soil and exploiting its resources, and must conquer the obstacles that stand in the way of such pioneering, have neither the mind nor the energy for the amenities. But what puzzled me then, as it did for some years, was the utter indifference of its artists to the rich material this country had to offer and their lack of originality in conception and treatment. Art, if it is to be an authentic part of national culture, must find its inspiration in its own soil and environment, and the life that springs from them. In 1895 there was little, if any, of that kind of self-expression. In 1936 America is becoming recognized, the art world over, for what it has done, not only in creating its own pattern of beauty, but in wielding a new and vitalizing influence on the older civilization of Europe. America is no longer an imitator. It is a forerunner. This is true of all the arts. I shall speak only of the dance, because it has had a special significance for me photographically.

My interest in it came through my desire to capture its rhythm and to suggest it adequately through the camera. Most of the photographs of dancers I had seen were of the kind in which the subject was taken in an arranged pose, simulating movement. Such pictures can never give any suggestion of life or movement.

I fully realized what a difficult problem the dance presented

to the camera. Though modern photographic devices permit one
to arrest any movement in the smallest fraction of a second, it is
quite a difficult matter to seize with certainty that one moment
in the dance in which the pose of the body and the lines of the
drapery form an harmonious and graceful design; and unless a
pose—here the photographer has a task similar to the sculptor's—
indicates the preceding as well as the following movement, be it
rapid or slow, a suggestion of motion—fluent, dynamic, natural—
cannot be conveyed. I had made innumerable attempts to capture
with my camera the dance in motion. Twenty years ago one hundred of my dance pictures were published in a volume, *The Book
of the Dance* (Kennerley). It was the first attempt to record in a
pictorially interesting manner, and in a diversity of patterns, impressions of the charm of dance movement, of the fleeting magic
designs made by the human body, of the nobility of gesture called
forth by the dance. Though the book—now long out of print—
was very well received, I realize today that in only a few of the
pictures had I succeeded in solving the problem of suggesting
movement in a convincing manner. I have faithfully continued to
study the dance and the many phases of its evolution, and I want
to comment briefly on its high development here in America.
Here, during the last twenty years, it has blossomed forth into a
variety of plastic symbols, creating new schools, bringing release
from the stilted technique of the ballet and transmuting itself
into a living art. This is true even of "jazz," which came to us
through the Southern Negro by way of the Barbary Coast in San
Francisco, and which now may be considered the great American
folk dance.

The liberator and prophet was Isadora Duncan. Hers was
not a mere talent finding an outlet through accepted technique,
but the flame of genius driving its way through the narrow conventions of the classical ballet. Her idea was not to be a Greek
dancer, but to use the Greek dancing legend handed down in
statue, frieze and painted vase as an inspiration for a play of
rhythmic motion and gesture that would have grace and beauty

and freedom, synchronizing the body and spirit of the modern woman and making it the implement of a great plastic art.

Whoever has seen Nijinsky in *Le Spectre de la Rose,* or Pavlowa as she floated along the stage in a conquest of the laws of gravity, must be eternally grateful to the ballet. But at its best, as Diaghileff brought it to us, it was no more than a gorgeous pageantry hiding monotony of movement and a repetition of formula and posture. It was not in any way an expression of the Russian spirit, but an adaptation from the Italian and French schools designed for the delectation of the Czar and his court. And the dances were often lacking in unity, disturbing the mind through sudden pauses in the middle of chorus movements to give the two principals the chance to demonstrate poses that had no relation to the dramatic action of the piece. Because of the corset, which restricted the bodies, and the ballet-slipper, necessary to obtain extraordinary elevations, there could be no reality in this kind of dancing.

Isadora had no formula of technique. She saw no beauty in conventional postures and overdeveloped muscles. Nor did she need elaborate costume or background. Barefooted, clad only in simple draperies and with a dark curtain for a back-drop, through her divine fluency she could create a tone-poem out of her thoughts, feelings and moods. Her only outside aid was the music of the great composers. She did not limit herself to music that had been created for the dance, but went beyond it to the symphonies of Beethoven and César Franck. Her teachers were the Greek sculptors and vase painters, and Walt Whitman and Nietzsche. Whitman, for her, more than any other poet, best knew and expressed the spirit of America, and Nietzsche was Dionysos, the god of wine and drama and dance, come to life. The dance was a great liberating force.

America was her free land, as free as Greece was in the Golden Age. And she felt that the bodies of the American youth, approaching, as they do, the Greek ideal, should be used for beauty and with the same lightness and grace as those of the young in that fabulous era when the creative arts came to their finest blooming.

A curious thing about Isadora was that her body was not exactly beautiful from a classical point of view. But when she danced, the nobility of her gestures could make it into something of superb perfection and divine loveliness. This was true even during her last years and after disaster had come upon her.

During her last sojourn in New York, I went to see her one day when she was in one of her dark moods. As she was going on I said, "It is a blessing that there is such a difference between the woman that you are and the artist that you are."

"How stupid of you," she replied. "The woman I am is the artist I am. There is no difference."

"I, for one, am grateful that there is," said I.

She looked at me in dismay. Then a charming smile spread over her face. "Wait," she said. "Sit over there and I will dance for you." And in those few minutes, without an audience, without music or any outward inspiration, she danced a poem of ineffable beauty.

Of her many dances, one of the most compelling, because of its tremendous drama, was the *Marseillaise*. No one who has seen her can ever forget her in that red drapery, on the stage of the Metropolitan Opera House during the war, as she danced the indomitable spirit of France under attack, fighting with a mighty fury to preserve herself from destruction. With superhuman power that day Isadora did something that no painter could do with his colors and no sculptor in bronze or marble.

That I was accorded the opportunity to make some photographs of Isadora Duncan in the dance, is something I must be particularly grateful for. She had always refused to have photographs made in dance poses. But when she discovered that it was possible to take pictures while she was in motion, she was eager to collaborate. These photographs are the only dance pictures made of her during her visits to America. If my pictures suggest some of the nobility of gesture that was so much a part of her, it will be at least a small contribution to the record that should have been made of her.

Fortunately, a number of painters who understood Isadora's great art have given us a series of drawings made of her in dance movements. There is the portfolio of seventy marvelously vital sketches by the Spanish artist, José Clará; we have the powerful drawings by the greatest of French sculptors, Rodin and Bourdelle; the chalk drawings of Van Dearing Perrine, so closely related in treatment to the charming pastels by Grandjouan; the sensitive pen drawings of Dunoyer de Ségonzac. No other artist has devoted himself more faithfully to the making of a complete record of Isadora's dances than A. Walkowitz. Within a period of almost twenty years he has made actually thousands of drawings, while watching Isadora dance. It is the most complete record ever made of the work of any dancer.

Of course, the only perfect way to preserve for posterity the fugitive art of the dance would be with the aid of the motion picture camera. That Isadora could never be induced to let the cinema camera record any of her dances is a calamity. But in the absence of such a record, the work of A. Walkowitz assumes a special significance and it is something for which we and future generations should be grateful.

Although the genius of Isadora lives on in the spirit of the modern dance, of which she was the vital spark, the great pity is that the school, which was her life-dream, was not realized in the way it should have been. She had hoped to have studios in all the capitals of Europe and America, from which her disciples would have gone forth spreading her precepts of grace to the world and carrying it down through the generations. She made several good starts and some progress was made. But each time they failed because of her inability to carry on. Her first school was in Berlin, where her sister Elizabeth, who had a great gift for teaching, took charge when she was on tour. Then for some years, through a subsidy from Paris Singer, she had the magnificent studio near Paris. During the war she brought twenty-four pupils to New York, where she had a series of studios, one following upon the other, and all of which failed to endure.

Back in Paris in 1921, she accepted an invitation from Soviet Russia to open a school for a thousand children in Moscow. She was to stay there ten years. She set out with high hopes that at last she would have the kind of school she always wanted. Alas, her temperament and emotions got her into difficulties, and after her marriage with the Russian poet, Yessenin, she departed for France, leaving her faithful pupil Irma to go on as best she could. In the meantime her sister had bravely continued to teach her ideas in the Elizabeth Duncan School here in America, and to some purpose, as not a few good dancers were developed there.

Since Isadora's death, several professional dancers have falsely claimed to have been her pupils. The truth is that of the twenty-four children with whom she started her school in Berlin, only six had genuine talent and were her real pupils. They were the six girls who traveled about Europe and came to America with her and whom she finally adopted legally, giving them her name. Anna, whose dancing in company with her pupils drew large and enthusiastic audiences at the Lewisohn Stadium in New York, is at present living in Berlin. Therese, now married to Stephan Bourgeois, the art dealer and connoisseur, has appeared with success, under the name of Maria Theresa, in a number of recitals. She has created some interesting new forms and has in New York recently started to work in group dances with some native Greek girls, "The Heliconiades." Lisa, whose lyric beauty and grace always brought overwhelming applause from her audience, has established a school in Paris and her dancing is being acclaimed by the press and the public of France and Belgium. Irma, who remained in charge of the school in Russia for several years, is now teaching in New York. Margot, known as Gretel to her friends, died of pneumonia nine years ago in Paris. And Erica, the youngest of them all, lives in New York, where she has given up the dance for painting and designing, in which field she is meeting with gratifying success. Besides these, several pupils of Elizabeth

Duncan, among them Anita Zahn, Erna Schultz and Katherine Hawley, are conducting classes and giving performances in New York. And there are Margherita Duncan, Augustin's wife, who in her teaching is a devoted follower of Isadora; and Diana Huebert, now active in Chicago, who studied with Raymond Duncan the archeological traditions of ancient Greece.

In many studios, and in the colleges and fashionable finishing schools, a kind of dancing called "classical" or Greek, but without the faintest kinship to either, is being taught. It has little or no meaning, and no artistry. On the other hand, there are a number of serious and inspired teachers with ideas of their own who, without connecting themselves with Isadora, owe a great deal to her in the way of method and inspiration. They are training young women to dance in a manner that is of real physical and spiritual benefit.

Ruth St. Denis is another revolutionary artist who, like Isadora, felt the need for breaking through the limitations of the ballet. She saw the salvation of the dance not so much in the rhythms of classic Greece as in those of the Orient—Japan and India. Knowing that the Western mind could not assimilate the content of these dances of the East, with their gestures and movements that had come down through long generations as symbols of faith or legend, she made no attempt to reproduce them. Her aim was to give a free and beautiful translation that would make clear the enduring and universal truths of which they were the parables.

With absolute integrity, as artist and woman, Ruth St. Denis has never tried to deceive by resorting to the cheap or the spurious for the sake of effect. From her dancing we have gleaned much more than the enjoyment of exotic charm and color. We have been brought nearer to an understanding of those spiritual concepts which had their roots in the Orient. In her school, Denishawn, in southern California, and now in her studio in New York, she has instilled these precepts into the minds and hearts of her pupils, teaching them how to apply them to life as it goes on around us.

The ritual pageants given at the church of St. Mark's-in-the-Bouwerie in New York City, under the direction of its rector, Dr. William Norman Guthrie, are another tribute to Isadora. Without her they might never have been. And too much praise cannot be given Dr. Guthrie, who has had the courage to use the dance (which probably preceded the hymn, the prayer and the sermon in the history of worship) as a leaven to raise the spirit of religious reverence through its appeal both to the imagination and the senses. In spite of the drastic opposition of higher authorities, the congregation as well as the press have realized the healing and uplifting power of the dance as presented at St. Mark's. One must hope that there will be others with the understanding and the bravery of Dr. Guthrie to take pattern from him.

Two of the most gifted of our younger artists of the dance are Doris Humphrey and Martha Graham, who studied with Ruth St. Denis and are deeply indebted to her for turning their talents into rich channels.

Doris Humphrey, through her deep spiritual insight, her sensitive touch, and her instinct for thinking in choreographic terms, has given us some of the most stirring dance compositions of the day. She draws her inspiration and material from the stuff of the times. She is capable of a satire presented with such depth and vitality that it never loses its point in the ridiculous or the grotesque.

Martha Graham and Ruth Page, working honestly and seriously with the same intention, have gone a long way toward their goal, the discovery of entirely new forms of the dance and the enlargement of its limited vocabulary of motion. Like Doris Humphrey, they are trying to express in a new language themes that were formerly the exclusive province of the theater or the written word. It is an original kind of pantomime which will become in time so much a part of the American consciousness that the audience will need no program notes to interpret them.

Entirely outside of this coterie is Angna Enters, not so much a dancer as she is a pantomimist. She has an amazing facility in

MARION MORGAN DANCERS

LA ARGENTINA

FE ALF (WIGMAN SCHOOL)

THE DANCE: ANDANTE
ALLEGRO
ALLEGRETTO

creating original effects which delight her enormous audiences.

Mary Wigman's visit to America has made a definite impression, and various groups, without clearly understanding Wigman's theories and methods, are trying to imitate her. An authentic pupil of Mary Wigman is Fe Alf, who has established a successful school in New York, and guided by Wigman principles has developed a method of her own.

The schools founded in many of our cities by Florence Fleming Noyes have gone on quite successfully since her death and are a vitalizing, important influence in the life of the dance in America.

The desire to create new forms, to increase the limited vocabulary of dance gestures, has in some instances resulted in compositions that go beyond the confines of intelligible dance expression. So long as one may feel that this search for a new form of expression is sincere and not merely the result of wishing to mystify and astonish, one ought to view these attempts, however nebulous their significance may be, with a sympathetic eye. I sometimes doubt, however, that a genuine earnestness of purpose is back of these strange modern spectacles—just as often the work of some of the super-modern painters and sculptors cannot convince me that they are seriously seeking a new form of expression. I have the faint suspicion that to fool the public is their main object.

When I see such exhibitions, my memory goes back to the first showing of the work of the modernists in New York. It was the exhibition held in an armory in 1913. Its most discussed canvas was Marcel Duchamps' clever stunt, "Nude Descending the Stairs," which one critic described as an explosion in a shingle factory. One day when I was looking at it, a nice old couple were standing near me. They stared at it for some time and suddenly the wife, still deeply engaged in studying it, exclaimed, "Oh, I'm just beginning to see her." "All right, Ma," said he, "then it's time for us to go home."

A few days later an old Gloucester sea captain whom I knew came to New York for a visit. We were having a Sunday together and I thought it would be amusing to get his reactions on the exhibition. While he was taking it in, he was strangely silent. At the end of half an hour he was ready to go. Walking along the street I said, "Well, Captain, what do you think of it?" He stopped chewing.

"Well," he drawled, "it may be art, but I tell you, my Aunt Melinda can knit better pictures than them."

To those who have grave doubts about the sincerity of a modernistic work of art, I recommend Andersen's wise fairy story, *The Emperor's New Clothes,* in which a child exclaims at the end: "But the Emperor has not anything on."

But to get back to the dance. Whatever may be devised and invented in new forms and gestures and pantomime, in an attempt to express the spirit of our modern machine age, I do not believe that there can ever be a nobler aim for the dance than to develop, as Isadora Duncan expressed it, "the highest intelligence in the freest body."

SCENES IN AMERICA AND SPAIN

T HE desire to travel and see something of the world—a true Genthe characteristic—had to remain unfulfilled while I was a student in Germany. My early travels, because of lack of funds and leisure, were confined to long walking trips in Germany. These wanderings were for me a school in the art of intelligent sightseeing, which was a good preparation for my later travel experiences.

In my San Francisco years I used much of my leisure time to explore the marvels and beauties of the California scene. A horseback trip to the Yosemite Valley, a bear hunt in the wilds of Siskiyou County where for weeks we did not encounter a living soul, a trip in a fishing schooner to the Farallon Islands, where I was marooned for ten days on account of storms, a complete tour of the Spanish Missions of California, and similar excursions gave me a taste of the wonders of this new world. It was Charles Lummis' *Strange Corners of Our Country* that turned me toward the desert of Arizona and New Mexico. In the summer of 1899 I set out on a camping trip with Frederick Munson, the lecturer, who knew the Southwest thoroughly.

My first night in the desert will always be an unforgettable memory. We got off the train at Adamana. At that time there was no station, no house, just a water tank. We set up our cots and tried to sleep. The stillness of the desert was like a singing silence, broken only by the occasional distant howl of a coyote. The sky, a velvety black, was strewn with stars of incredible brightness. They were so big they seemed like young moons. At dawn I was awakened by a terrified whisper from Munson. "Don't move," he cautioned, "but look at the foot of your bed." There on the top of the blanket was a rattlesnake quietly investigating the intruder. I lay perfectly still, and after a few minutes the snake, probably bored, wriggled quietly to the ground and no harm was done.

After leaving the Petrified Forest, we went to the Reservation of the Hopi Indians to witness the Snake Dance at Walpi. This ritual, handed down to the Hopis through many centuries, is a prayer to the gods for rain. Its exact date is announced nine days in advance, and the priests must be pretty good weather prophets, since the dance is always followed by an answer from the clouds.

The dance is a weird and most dramatic spectacle. Each priest holds in his teeth one or two snakes by the middle, while a companion strokes the snakes with an eagle feather to keep them from coiling and biting. But often the snake manages to strike. I saw one of the dancers—I was only two yards away—being bitten on the forehead by a rattler. The dance went on without interruption. The priest was taken to the underground ceremonial chamber (*Kiwa*) where he was given an antidote, the secret of which has never been revealed to any white man. The last part of the dance is a purification ceremony, after which the snakes are carried by runners to the plain below, where they are released and sent on their mission to convey the prayer to the gods. Though this ritual has now become almost a tourist's spectacle, it retains for the Hopis its ancient religious significance.

Acoma, the "Sky City," situated on top of a precipitous rock near the Enchanted Mesa in central New Mexico, has preserved more than any other pueblo of the Southwest its old architecture and customs. The inhabitants, as a rule, are not particularly friendly to the white man. They have not forgotten the terrible slaughter of the population by Juan de Oñate (in 1599), the story of which has been handed from father to son. But if the visitor shows in his attitude a consideration and respect for native traditions and customs, he will have no difficulties.

Our journey carried us into the land of the Navajos, the nomads of the desert, where we visited the Canyon de Chelly (the name is a corruption of the Navajo word *Tseyee,* meaning "within the rocks"). The rock formations here are incredibly fantastic in shape and color, and I often regret that the color camera had not then been perfected.

It was in this vicinity that I had my initiation into the perils of quicksand. My Indian pony, a docile little animal, had stopped to let me take some pictures. While I was holding the camera above my head, he had what might be called a real sinking spell. I saw that he was about to disappear into the ground. To save my camera I rolled off. Not at all perturbed, he quietly worked himself out, and without any ill effects, except that he acquired a coat of yellowish mire which dried into something like a plaster cast.

On our way back to Gallup we went off the beaten track to one of the most interesting historical monuments in all America— the "Inscription Rock" near Zuñi, known as El Morro. Because of its proximity to a water hole, ever since the day of Cortez the military expeditions sent out by the Spanish stopped there and upon leaving carved their names on the surfaces of the rock with their swords. The oldest decipherable date is 1602. When I first visited the rock, there was neither guard nor railing to protect it, and alongside the autographs of the illustrious conquistadores were carved names like "John G. Jones." Since then it has been made a National Monument and now there is a guard.

Munson and I spent the night there. In the morning as we were about to leave, a troop of villainous-looking men came galloping toward us. The leader called out roughly, "What are you doing here?"

"Taking pictures of the inscriptions," was my reply.

They scowled at us for several moments. "I guess they're all right," said the leader. "Just bug-hunters." And giving the rock a vicious kick, they rode off. A week later at Gallup, we saw them again. Horse thieves and murderers, they were being marched through the streets handcuffed. Their distrust of us had come from the suspicion that we were a sheriff's posse.

Subsequently I took several trips to the Navajo country accompanied only by a guide who drove the supply wagon and acted as my cook when necessary. The Navajos do not live in villages or pueblos, but wander over the desert, building shelters of cottonwood branches in summer. In winter they make their homes in adobe huts known as "hogans." As a people they have a rugged beauty, a kind of haughty nobility both in manner and feature. They are not talkative with the stranger, and yet they are hospitable. My Navajo guide knew about thirty words of Spanish. I knew about twenty words of Navajo. But we got along famously. And when at the end of my trip we said good-by to each other, he slapped me on the shoulder, giving me what I still consider a great compliment: *"Tu buen Navajo* [You are good Navajo]."

Spanish
Courtesy

208

In all my travels I have seldom been given a more gracious welcome than that accorded me by a fine old Spaniard at his rancho in New Mexico. I had revisited the pueblo of Zuñi and was on my way to see again the Inscription Rock. There were no signposts to go by and I soon saw that my driver did not know the direction. Toward evening we were hopelessly lost. The driver refused to go any farther but I insisted that we go on for another hour, telling him that he must drive straight ahead. It was not long before we saw a light in the distance and never was the sound of barking dogs more welcome. Following the light we came to a ranch house. Through the window I looked upon a touching scene.

At a table surrounded by his family sat a white-haired patriarch reading the Bible. It was Sunday and he was conducting the service. When he had finished, he came out, asking me in Spanish what he could do for me.

I told him that we had lost our way and asked if he could put us up for the night.

"It will make me very happy to do so," he said with a warm smile, as he invited me to come in.

Two young girls, his daughters, were in the large living room and he told them to bring some dinner. They went out into the kitchen, returning shortly with a dish of steaming *olla podrida.* "Please pardon the humble meal," they said.

Afterwards my fine old host came in with a candle, lighting the way for me down the hallway to the guest room, having assured me that my horses and the boy had been looked after.

In the morning, after a hearty breakfast, I thanked the girls, and drawing the old gentleman aside, I asked him what I owed him.

He smiled and raising a deprecating hand, he replied, *"Nada* [nothing]. It is always my great joy to welcome a stranger."

He hesitated for a moment, adding, "But I have a favor to ask. You are a doctor." (He had heard my driver call me "Doc.") "One of my daughters is suffering with the toothache. Can you do something about it?"

I had no chance to explain that I was not that kind of a doctor, but it happened that I had a medicine chest with me containing some toothache drops. I took it into the living room where the patient was in a chair waiting for me with all the family and the ranch hands assembled to watch the operation. Saturating some cotton with the drops, I applied it to the aching tooth and the pain stopped immediately. My audience thought I had performed a miracle. I told them that if the pain came back they were to use the medicine which I was leaving with them.

It was now my host's turn to take me aside and ask, "How much do I owe you?" My reply, made with the same gesture as his, was, *"Nada."*

Taking my hand, he said, "Please remember that whenever you are in this neighborhood my home is yours."

Another host whose geniality gave flavor to my journeys through the Southwest was Lorenzo Hubbell, the Indian trader at Ganado, New Mexico, who was also sheriff of the territory. He had a great affection and understanding for the Navajos, and a respect for their traditions. It was he who induced them to use the old native patterns and vegetable dyes in the making of their blankets. Everyone who went through that part of the country knew him and loved him. Among those who counted him a friend were Frederick Remington, the artist, Henry Ford, and Theodore

Roosevelt. He conducted an enormous trade with the Indians but kept no books, yet no transactions escaped him. He told me that he had never suffered through this method which would scarcely be appreciated by the modern efficiency expert. One year when a drought destroyed the corn, killing off the flocks, Hubbell came to the relief of the Navajos, who were threatened with famine, by letting them have whatever they needed without exacting payment. Altogether he dispensed eighteen thousand dollars' worth of goods and promptly forgot about it. "I have made money enough through you in times past," he told them. "Now that times are hard with you, I am glad to be able to help."

The last time I went to New Mexico was in 1926. Many changes had taken place in the twenty-five years that had elapsed since my first visit to the pueblos. Their essential character had not changed, but much of their primitive charm was gone. The young men and women were wearing store clothes. One little boy was playing with a model of an airplane made by his father. The houses had been modernized. Doors had been cut in the walls of the ground floor which formerly could be reached only by a ladder through an opening in the ceiling.

The venerable stone towers of the old fortress church at Acoma had been repaired with a covering of cement, giving them quite a commonplace look. This thoughtless manner of restoring and repairing has ruined many a building of historical interest. Some of the California Missions have suffered from it. The Spanish Missions in Texas, near San Antonio, fortunately have escaped this fate. The Concepcion Mission as well as the San José Mission are impressive and picturesque: partly ruined, but without disturbing repairs. The door of the Espada Church might have graced the entrance of an old Chinese monastery.

Of the Grand Canyon I have already spoken. It is something beyond the power of poet or painter to tell of. To have seen it will always be a great spiritual experience. To depict it seems almost an impossibility. Thomas Moran, who devoted so many years of enthusiastic and reverent work to transferring its elusive and unbelievable colors to canvas, has come nearer to achieving the impossible than any other artist.

When Walter Gropius, the renowned German exponent of modern architecture, was in America, at the end of his stay he asked me what I considered the one important architectural monument that he should not miss.

My reply was, "The Grand Canyon. It will take you three days to get there but I guarantee that you will not regret it." I showed him my color photographs of it, the rainbow and the view from Hopi Point at sunset. He decided to go.

As he was pressed for time he expected to spend but a day or two at the canyon. After his arrival there he sent me a telegram: "Most marvelous thing I have ever seen. Have changed our plans. Staying ten days."

The plan to make a series of photographs of New Orleans, first suggested by some of Cable's romances, and particularly by certain vividly descriptive passages in letters and articles by Lafcadio Hearn (most of them written while he was on the staff of the *New Orleans Item* during the years preceding his stay in Japan), assumed more definite form when I first became familiar with Grace King's fascinating biography of the old town, *New Orleans, The Place and the People*. My enthusiasm, aroused by this delightful volume, was somewhat dampened by discouraging observations of people well acquainted with New Orleans. They claimed that the city of today bore only faint resemblance to the New Orleans of twenty years ago: many historical buildings and old residences had been destroyed, and the inroads of modern business life had abolished so much of what was beautiful and picturesque that it might be too late for my camera, which after all had to depend on visible realities. It was a passage in an article by E. L. Tinker on the charm of old New Orleans that finally decided me. It ran somewhat like this: "New Orleans, like the rest of the world, is beginning to destroy her old glories in her ambition to become an up-to-date American city. But the damage has not yet been done, only commenced. There is still time, not much, for an artist with sympathy in his touch and reverence in his heart, to preserve for future generations the full flavor and charm of old New Orleans, and in the doing, give himself a claim to the gratitude of the American People."

My idea, when I set out, was to get the material for an illustrated article on Lafcadio Hearn's impressions of things as they were when he lived in New Orleans.

I admit that my first reaction on arrival was one of disappointment. Wherever my eye turned it met the evidences of indifference and decay. Many of the historic buildings I had looked forward to seeing had been demolished. Not a trace was left of the St. Louis Hotel which had been the hub of the city's social life in colonial days.

Fire had completely destroyed (in 1919) a most celebrated landmark, the French Opera House, which was so intimately associated with the musical and social history of the city. And the levees, in former days one of the most famous and interesting sights, lining a river that was crowded with innumerable ships, had lost much of their picturesque character. Prosaic sheds and immense warehouses now look out upon the lazy Mississippi, from which the railways have taken most of its old trade; nevertheless, New Orleans has become the second largest port in the United States.

The old French quarter was bustling with the noise and hurry of a modern thriving American city. Gaudy signs and large advertisements disfigured fine old dwellings; nets of telephone wires marred charming vistas, and in the narrow thoroughfares electric cars were a distressing element of modernity. That there was no real feeling of civic responsibility toward the preservation of the old architecture was shown by an astonishing example of wholesale destruction on Royal Street. An entire block—and it contained some of the finest examples of old Creole residences—had been razed in 1918 to make room for the new Court House. This splendid and costly building of shining white marble forms a strange contrast with the noble simplicity of the old Bank buildings opposite; indeed it looks hopelessly out of place—an arrogant parvenu in the midst of proud though impoverished aristocrats.

Of the original French buildings, very few survived the conflagrations which devastated the greater part of the city toward the end of the eighteenth century, but fortunately the most ancient and noteworthy of them is still extant. This is the venerable Ursuline Convent, built in 1727 and occupied by the Ursuline nuns for over a hundred years; later on it served for a time as the official residence of the Archbishops of New Orleans. During recent years it has fallen into an alarming state of neglect. The beautiful garden with its tropical plants and tiled paths has vanished altogether, and the massive walls and planked floors of the old building are showing signs of decay. But the vast stairway, composed of solid cypress blocks and guarded by a wrought-iron balustrade, is still one of the most beautiful things to be found in the Vieux Carré. I learned that the priest in charge of the building was planning to have the worn-down stairway replaced by a modern cement one. Fortunately I knew some influential Catholics, who prevented the threatened sacrilege.

One can say without exaggeration that no American city contains as many fascinating picture-motifs in such a small area as can be found in the Vieux Carré of New Orleans, even today. It is true that much sympathetic search and patient experimenting are required before one can hope to secure photographs which will actually suggest something of the vanished beauty and charm of the old days. For much of the real picture-material lies hidden under the ugliness superimposed upon it by modern utilitarian life, and charming designs and impressive silhouettes, unnoticed in the glare and noise of a work-a-day world, will be revealed to the eye only under the spell of a moonlight night, when merciful shadows hide disturbing unsightliness; and in the mellow light of the early morning or the late evening the camera can be made to convey something of such impressions.

The months I was in New Orleans covered two visits, when my little hand-camera and I became as familiar to the passersby as we had been in San Francisco's Chinatown. Often I had to wait for hours until the sun created the desired effect in light and shadow, or until the figures I needed for my composition came along. I waited a whole afternoon in front of the gateway of the Armory until two Sisters of Charity passed its portals, which gave to the picture the added authentic touch that I wanted.

The more I roamed the streets with my camera, the more I came to see the romance and beauty that could be found if one had the patience to look for it. Gradually I was led to abandon my original purpose for the larger one of making a picture book that would be a faithful collection of all that remained of the early Spanish, French and American colonial flowering.

The French heritage is ever present in diverse ways: the Absinthe House which is said to have been the stronghold of Jean Lafitte, the buccaneer; the eighteenth- and early nineteenth-century French dwelling places—the home of Sieur George and the old planter's house on Dumaine Street known as "Madame John's Legacy"; the ancient Cathedral of St. Louis; the French Market, busy and colorful, surviving the vicissitudes of changing centuries. And it requires no effort to imagine one's self in Spain, when contemplating the simple dignity of the Cabildo (the Old Spanish Town Hall), the arched ruins of the old barracks, or the courtyard of the Commandcia (now Antione's) celebrated restaurant.

A most distinctive and universally admired feature of the streets in the Vieux Carré is the decorative iron work which embellishes the façades of many buildings. Much of the notable wrought-iron ornament adorned houses that have since been torn down, and are now to be found in the shops of antique dealers. Yet many fine examples of the ironworker's art are encountered in all parts of the old quarter. Particularly remarkable are the window railings of the Cabildo, and a number of private dwellings have

A
NEW ORLEANS
MAMMY

THE OLD ARMORY IN NEW ORLEANS

balconies of great elegance of design to which here and there are added the interwoven lines of a family monogram. The infinite variety of patterns in the cast-iron ornamentation of the galleries and verandas furnishes other fascinating themes for the camera: here the lace-like iron arabesques of a balcony make a charming frame for an unexpected vista; there they paint a delicate pattern on the sun-lit stucco wall; and hardly less picturesque is the effect of the slender posts which, resting on the outer edge of the sidewalk, support the iron fretwork of wide galleries above which furnish shade and shelter to the pedestrian—a unique feature of the architecture of the Vieux Carré.

The Negroes, young and old, as picturesque in speech as in type and costume, were always a camera delight. One of the noblest heads I have ever seen was that of an old colored woman who had been a faithful servant in the same family for over fifty years. In her face was the strength and gentleness of one who had known life and surmounted suffering without bitterness. She had in her face something of that rare quality which I had found in the profile of Eleonora Duse.

My book, *Impressions of Old New Orleans,* was published in 1926 by George Doran. Though out of print now, it had its reward. I had pointed out what a calamity it would be if the old French quarter were to be lost to future generations. "Private individuals," I said, "have acquired some of the old residences and are restoring them with taste and understanding. Recently a commission of influential men has been created to act in an advisory capacity with the city council to see that no inappropriate buildings or repairs crowd into the historic section. This is at least a start in the right direction. But it is not enough. Repairing an old building can easily destroy its character and charm, if it is put into the hands of a mere mechanic who has neither architectural knowledge nor artistic conscience. Unless a body of competent local architects is given official authority to direct and supervise all restorations and repairs, the future of the representative architecture of Old New Orleans cannot be considered safe."

It was this comment that moved the Chamber of Commerce to appoint a committee of architects, who now see to it that if an old building can be saved, it is saved by restorations and repairs that do not destroy its original design. If it must be torn down, it is photographed and a careful record made of its measurements, so that the America of the future, with its constantly developing artistic appreciation, may know something of its vanished glory.

Mexico

216

Both my journeys to Mexico were undertaken in the summer, which is supposed to be a bad time on account of the rains. It is true that it rains almost every day, but only for an hour or so, and as a rule in the afternoon, so one can easily arrange one's day accordingly. The absence of dust and the cloud effects add to the enjoyment of one's wanderings. It was during the rule of Porfirio Diaz, when traveling facilities were not as numerous and well organized as they are today, that I visited Mexico.

The government and American expeditions had not yet conducted excavations which in recent years have thrown light on the early civilization of this amazing country. The temples and palaces of Yucatan were still hidden in the jungle and Monte Alban had not yet yielded up its treasures. In the south, the ruins of Mitla had been partly unearthed and restored. In Oaxaca, Dr. Sologurren had assembled a marvelous collection of Aztec, Mayan and Toltec antiquities. The Duke of Aosta had offered him a large sum for them but he refused. "No," he said, "they shall remain where they belong, in my country." He took me to several places where excavations were conducted under his direction. Once we were present when a small golden figure was dug up that looked strangely like an ancient Chinese Buddha. The possible connection between Chinese sculpture and the pre-Columbian art of Mexico and Central America is a subject that puzzles and intrigues our archeologists more from year to year. In the ruins of Xochicalco, not far from Cuernavaca, I recall seeing some sculptured ornaments which resemble the designs on Chinese Chou bronzes. Each year

LOOKING FROM ACOMA TOWARD THE ENCHANTED MESA

IN THE CANYON DE CHELLY (TSE-YEE)

END OF THE HOPI SNAKE DANCE AT WALPI

new finds are being made which will bring the question of a possible link between the two civilizations nearer to its solution.

Mexico, with its temperate and tropical climates; its architectural monuments, ranging from the early Aztec to Spanish and later periods; the ever-varying charms of its scenery, far more colorful than Spain's; its picturesque and hospitable people, make a visit to Mexico one of the most thrilling chapters in a traveler's journal. What a variety of entertaining experiences one can enjoy in a brief space of time! I bought in Querétaro for little money a fire opal from a man in the street only to have it stolen from my pocket before reaching the hotel. I hunted alligators in the jungle, just a few hours from Mazatlán. I nearly became engaged to a charming Señorita without realizing or knowing anything about it, simply by taking a moonlight stroll with her in her garden. I had my camera stolen in Mexico City and was enabled to buy it back in the "Thieves Market" the following day for a small fraction of its value. I was offered an Aztec jade mask by a rancher who was unaware of its value and importance. I traveled in a dugout canoe paddled by Indians over a lake of magic beauty to an Indian village with the fascinating name of Tzintzuntzan, "Place of the Humming Birds," to study in its little church a jealously guarded painting by Titian of the Entombment of Christ.

I have often wondered why Americans do not avail themselves more frequently of the opportunity they have as neighbors, to visit a country to which bonds of closest friendship should attach us, and where the traveler can find more fascinating attractions than many European countries offer him.

When I was in the south of Mexico, it was difficult to resist the temptation to visit Guatemala, the largest and most interesting of the Central American states. But it was many years before I had my first glimpse of this picturesque republic. Starting from the Atlantic port of Puerto Barrios, I interrupted the journey to Guatemala City by spending some days at Quiriguá for a visit to the Mayan ruins there. They are among the best preserved monuments of that mysterious and highly civilized race. Instead of staying at the comfortable quarters provided by the American Fruit Company—their famous hospital is located here—I preferred to go to the little jungle village of Los Amates, nearby, where from a hammock in a clean Indian hut I had a glimpse of the river and listened to the symphony concert of the monkeys and parrots in the treetops. The train steadily ascends, first through miles of banana plantation, until it reaches the capital. Guatemala City, five thousand feet above sea level, has quite a cosmopolitan air. Though it was almost entirely destroyed by the earthquake of 1917, when I visited it ten years later it had been rebuilt completely and gave the impression of an up-to-date and prosperous city. For me its chief attractions were the magnificent view from the high plateau of the Cerro del Carmen, and the Market Place. Here Indians of various tribes living many miles away congregate, bringing their wares, chiefly pottery, blankets and other textiles. Each village has a distinct pattern for its embroideries and weaves.

I was particularly eager to explore Antigua (its full name was San Diego de los Caballeros de Guatemala la Antigua), the former capital. It was destroyed in the terrible earthquake of 1773 and completely abandoned by its inhabitants who then founded the present capital.

Antigua is a ghostly city of half-ruined churches, monasteries, palaces and private dwellings dating from the time of Pedro de Alvarado (circa 1524), one of the chief lieutenants of Cortez. The architecture of the sixteenth-century buildings of Antigua is puzzling. It does not seem to belong to any known style or period, unless one concedes an earthquake style, one of the characteristics of which are the enormously thick short pillars supporting low arches, as in the Convento de los Capuchinas and in the Palace of the Captains-General; such buildings could withstand the frequently occurring earthquake shocks.

It is a curious fact that some of the most beautiful places all over the world are situated in earthquake zones. Fortunately man is basically a fatalist. Here, in an incredibly beautiful valley dominated by the two volcanos, "Agua" and "Fuego"—a constant warning—people go on living blissfully in an ideal climate, unmindful of the fact that disaster may overtake them any day. And it is not only the native Indian who has that attitude. There are quite a number of Americans and Englishmen who have bought some of the old houses and restored them to new life.

To the traveler who can spend only a short time exploring the ruins and the picturesque surroundings, the little inn "El Manchen" offers all the comfort he can desire. When the owner, who is a Swiss, found that I spoke German, he said, "I will have a nice surprise for you at dinner." It was indeed a delightful surprise to have in this out-of-the-way place a bottle of Rhine wine of a precious vintage, placed beside my plate and served by a barefoot Indian. The coffee of Guatemala is of a particular excellence. The plantations cover a vast area of the valley and reach up to the high slopes of the volcanos.

Even when pressed for time, the traveler today can see a good deal of Guatemala within the short space of a week, since good roads make travel by automobile possible also in the highlands. For instance, the trip to Chichicastenango (Father Rossbach there has the finest collection of jade in Guatemala), situated north of Lake Atitlán, with the bluest water to be found anywhere, used to require over ten days on horseback, and now takes less than ten hours by motor.

The stimulating and exotic experiences which the visitor will have enjoyed in this colorful country will make him wish to retrace his steps no matter what distance he has traveled.

After the death of my brother Siegfried in 1904, who, as I related previously, had been murdered in Fez, I went to Morocco to straighten out his affairs. I had had several unsatisfactory conferences with the Berlin Foreign Office concerning the case, and owing to certain political complications my dealings with the authorities in Morocco—in Tangier and Fez—were equally unsatisfactory. It was only after Wilhelm II visited Morocco that the government was forced to make amends and erect a memorial in honor of a man who, during the years that he had been connected with the *Cologne Gazette,* had rendered his country most valuable services.

At that time I was not in a frame of mind to appreciate the rich possibilities this North African country offered to my camera. I wanted to leave Morocco behind me and depart for Spain.

I spent a month in Spain, making my headquarters in Madrid. The Museum of the Prado is one of the great treasure houses of the world. To see and study the chief works of Velasquez, which are so admirably displayed there, is one of the most memorable experiences in the life of anyone to whom art has a meaning. To follow in the footsteps of El Greco in Toledo, to seek out what exists of his work in public and private collections, enables one to form a just estimate of this strange genius. Of Goya the same holds true—one cannot form a complete picture of his greatness unless acquainted with the wide range of Goya's activities. To wander through the cathedral towns like Burgos, Cordova, Avila, Segovia, so inexhaustibly rich in architecture and ornament, is an equally unforgettable experience.

I am not ashamed to confess that the bull-ring of Spain had a great fascination for me. In Mexico I did not see a bullfight, as they are held in winter and I was there only in the summer, but in Spain I went whenever I had the chance to see one. Its dramatic splendor held me spellbound. The most brilliant of the many I attended was held at San Sebastian. Fuentes, one of the greatest of matadors, was the hero of the day. Both the King and Queen were present. The Queen wore dark glasses so as not to see what was going on in the arena. There is no more colorful spectacle to be witnessed in these days of our civilization than the scenes of a bullfight. The gorgeous costumes of the participants, the feverish excitement of the crowd, the dramatic intensity of the rapidly shifting events in the arena, the almost supernatural skill and grace of

A COURTYARD IN SEVILLA

SPAIN: ON THE ROAD TO SEGOVIA

MARKET DAY IN BURGOS

the matador, seem to cast an hypnotic spell that changes one's normal reactions in an incredible manner.

In Jerez, I saw a good deal of Bombita Chico, one of the best known of the younger matadors. One night I arranged a dinner for him and his whole troupe. He presented me with one of his swords (*espada*) and also with the permission to enter with my camera the narrow runway directly adjoining the bull-ring. This runway offers an escape, when any of the participants are too hard-pressed, through narrow openings big enough for a man to squeeze through but too small for the bull. Sometimes, however, the bull decides to jump over the wall into this narrow runway, necessitating a sudden exit into the ring for all concerned. I had this exciting experience more than once.

There was a breathless minute when Bombita, in executing one of the passes with the *muleta*—a maneuver in which the matador, by just the slightest movement of his body, avoids the horns of the bull—miscalculated the distance and before the bull could be diverted, Bombita was tossed high in the air. There was a terrified silence while Bombita lay motionless. Then he slowly arose and finding no bones broken, got the bull into the position he wanted and with a masterful thrust of his *espada* brought the bull in collapse at his feet. Indescribable enthusiasm and wildest applause rewarded the victor. Unless one has seen a bullfight, and knows something of the Spanish tradition, one cannot understand the hold it has on the public, nor can one appreciate the honor and veneration shown a famous matador. He is admired as a great artist and beloved for his generous gifts to charity.

Ignacio Zuloaga, the painter, has a private ring of his own in his villa at Zumaya near San Sebastian where he sometimes arranges bullfights to entertain his guests. One of his closest friends is Juan Belmonte, the most celebrated matador of modern Spain. On his last visit to America, after his return from a triumphal tour of South America, Belmonte happened to be in New York at a time when Zuloaga was also visiting there. Mrs. Rita Lydig was giving a dinner in honor of the painter who had done many portraits of her, and Belmonte was invited. The dinner took place in a private dining room of the Colony Club. Zuloaga was seated on the right of the hostess and Belmonte on her left. Next to him she placed Mrs. Charles Lanier, who has done so much for music in America. When the men had joined the ladies after dinner, Mrs. Lanier wanted to know who that interesting man was who had sat at her right.

"He is the most famous bullfighter in Spain," I explained. "He is just back from a triumphal tour of South America."

"A bullfighter?" she gasped. "That's even worse than a prize-fighter. The idea of his being here!" Turning to Mrs. Lydig, she said, "I'm not feeling very well, Rita; I think I must be going."

GUATEMALA: STREET IN ANTIGUA

PLAZA AND VOLCANO
OF ANTIGUA

MISSION "CONCEPCION" NEAR SAN ANTONIO, TEXAS

CLOISTERS OF SAN JOSE MISSION NEAR SAN ANTONIO

JAPAN

THE promise I had made to myself in 1906, when all my possessions were burned up in the San Francisco fire, that my next investment would be something that neither earthquake nor fire could destroy, was fulfilled in 1908 in a six months' journey through Japan. I had prepared myself quite carefully for it by learning enough of the colloquial language for ordinary needs. It is not such an arduous task as one might think. The pronunciation does not offer the same difficulties as Chinese, where every word has four "tones," each with a different meaning of its own. But the construction of sentences is entirely unlike that of any European language. To cite just one example: the Japanese expression for "I am glad to meet you" literally translated means "For the first time I hang on your august eyes." I even made an attempt, with the aid of an old Japanese teacher, to learn something of the writing, including Chinese ideographs. I mastered about three hundred, which does not help one very much when one ought to know at least three thousand, and though I papered the walls of one room with large copies of these graphic symbols so as to have them constantly before me, I found after a week's absence that I had forgotten most of them. Our memory evidently is not built for remembering Japanese and Chinese writing.

I wanted to learn as much as possible of Japanese customs, the Japanese point of view and Japanese mode of travel. My meeting at Shuzenji, a popular Hot Springs on the peninsula of Idzu, with an elderly gentleman and his family, was to give me an ideal chance to realize my wish. He had belonged to the feudal warrior class, the Samurai, and when the new régime came in, leaving him without a position, he had, like others of his class, gone into business, selling his family possessions. He had become a curio dealer and was spending a few vacation weeks with his son and the latter's young wife. I suggested that they travel with me as my guests and that we visit together some of the noted places I wanted to see and which were not yet known to them. They spoke no English, but with the aid of pocket dictionaries we managed quite well. Though our conversation could not be considered brilliant, we soon became more than speaking acquaintances and in the weeks we traveled together, I saw and learned a great deal about the real Japan that without my new friends would have remained unknown to me.

The first thing I learned was to bathe in the Japanese manner. Being the only foreigner at the baths, I had hesitated to be an active participant in the "community bathing" at the inn where men, women and children bathed together in the nude in a large tank which accommodated about thirty, or in one of the small tanks large enough for four. Before one enters the bath a thorough scrubbing with soap, rinsed off with water from a bucket, is the prescribed preliminary. Then one steps cautiously into the tank and proceeds to boil, the bath water in Japan being much hotter than we use. While I was stewing in my tank, the only one that happened to be unoccupied, two young girls, veritable Botticelli-like figures, appeared. Seeing that my tank was the only one that had room for them, they approached demurely and murmuring the conventional formula, "I beg your honorable pardon," slid into the tank. And there we sat, facing each other, squatting on our heels in respectable and respectful silence.

It is amazing and consoling how easily one can translate one's accustomed attitude into another language. Once in a small mountain village the little servant-maid (*nesan*) who had been assigned to look after me happened to be a very diminutive person, and when in preparation for the bath she started to scrub me and found that she had to stand on a stool to reach my shoulders, she called in the landlord to come and look at the "stranger whose head almost touched the ceiling." He thought it would be a good réclame for his inn, and sent word through the village to come and look at this strange phenomenon. In a short time a crowd had assembled, staring at me with amiable curiosity. At times my Samurai friend's daughter-in-law, at his suggestion, would act as my bath attendant, and she did so in quite an impersonal and entirely business-like manner.

Staying at a Japanese inn has other surprises for a newcomer. Upon arriving, the guest hands the tip he intends to give—it is called *chadai* (tea money)—to the proprietor, telling him how long he expects to stay. The quality of the food is regulated according to the amount of the *chadai*. To show that he considers the money not a tip but a present, the proprietor returns after a few minutes with a gift for the guest, something characteristic of the place, a lacquer or pottery bowl, some towels decorated with the large crest of the inn, etc.

The inns have no public dining rooms. The meals are brought to one's room on low lacquer table trays. The food as a rule is very palatable: bean soup, mushrooms, pickles, sliced raw fish (*sashimi,* a great delicacy), broiled and boiled fish, an omelette, and at the end of the meal always a bowl of rice, a meal in itself. The food is served in lacquer or porcelain bowls, and of course eaten with chopsticks. The accompanying drink is tea and *sake,* a kind of rice-wine tasting faintly like sherry. It is always served hot.

In a fair-sized town we sometimes would have Geishas to entertain us or we would go to the theater or marionette show, or we would remain at the inn and enjoy a different kind of performance. My friend would have sent word to the curio dealers of the place that a distinguished collector from America was with them and wanted to see some of their wares. Along they would come in the evening with large bundles, and before an audience which included the entire household, the servants in the background at a respectful distance, they spread out a fascinating array of embroideries, hangings, kimonos, *netsukes, kakemonos,* prints, illustrated books, ancient swords, etc. There were long sessions with much bargaining and tea drinking in the best Japanese manner, and some of the finest objects of my Japanese collection were secured during such evenings.

In some of the famous temples we visited we were shown, thanks to the prestige of my friend, some of the treasures that were seldom brought out: marvelous screens, paintings and sculptures by early masters.

No matter what the future may hold in store for Japan, no matter what far-reaching changes may be brought about in the political and social life of the country, the great arts of old Japan will forever remain a noble inspiration to us.

Most of our traveling was done by jinrikisha, one for each person, the honorable stranger heading the procession, then the old Samurai and his son, and the lady following last before the two jinrikishas for the baggage. The strength and endurance of a rikisha man are remarkable. He never seems tired, and takes it as an insult if the passenger expresses a desire to walk a stretch.

The only place where in these rapidly changing times the life of old Japan can still be studied is the theater. The plays either depict the life and manners of the everyday people (love stories, etc.) or they are historical plays about the deeds of famous warriors and heroes. They are performed with a high degree of realism, with much shouting and fighting and killing, but one thing is never shown—a kissing scene. When American motion pictures invaded Japan, all kissing scenes had to be cut out. It is related that the censor entertained his friends by projecting films composed entirely of cuttings representing a long variation of the soulful caresses of our motion picture stars.

The *No* plays are the drama of the nobility and the learned. One might say that they bear a certain resemblance to the ancient Greek drama with its chorus, or to the Elizabethan masque. The costumes are most elaborate, often being ancient ceremonial court robes, and the masks worn by the actors are often the work of great sculptors.

Hamada, my Japanese boy in San Francisco, had written to his father telling him of my visit to Japan and I was invited to be

IN THE
INLAND SEA
OF JAPAN

MT. FUJI FROM LAKE HAKONE

A STREET IN OLD JAPAN

a guest at his home in Dogo, in the southern island of Shikoku. Upon my arrival I was met by his father, a distinguished looking old gentleman, and a reception committee of prominent citizens. Staying at his house for a week, I had the chance to fully appreciate the beautiful simplicity of a Japanese home, the absence of furniture and the charm of natural wood, polished but left without paint or varnish. In the *tokonoma,* the niche where the only ornament to "decorate" the room is placed, hung a *kakemono,* a seventeenth-century painting of horses. This had been selected in my honor from the family storehouse, where the treasures are kept. Hamada had written of my fondness for horses.

One evening I was taken to the fashionable inn where at the "Bathers Club" (which probably was the bankers club of Dogo) an elaborate dinner with Geishas had been arranged. The Geishas are there to entertain the guests with singing, dancing, the reciting of poetry and above all with charming and gay conversation. They are prepared for this task by a several years' course of education at the Geisha schools where they learn the complicated art of flower arrangement, the intricacies of the tea ceremony, the art of dancing, singing and of playing several musical instruments, etc. They often make very good marriages.

Returning to Kyoto I spent several weeks exploring the temples and gardens of this ancient capital and its surroundings. A visit to the temple of Horiyuji, the oldest Buddhist building in Japan, and to the monastery of Koyasan were the most interesting incidents of my travels in the heart of Japan. In such a monastery, among other things, one learns to be a happy vegetarian. I did not know that there existed so many edible plants, and the monk who had been assigned to look after me reported, "The stranger ate everything."

The Japanese love for nature finds a beautiful expression in the making of their gardens. Often a small space, not more than fifty feet square, will be laid out so as to give the impression of a celebrated scene. Waterfalls a few feet high surrounded by dwarf pines, a rock (frequently large sums are paid for a rock because it resembles a mountain famed in legend), a lake several yards square—all this, because of its perfect proportion and carefully calculated scale, will suggest the full sweep of a hallowed landscape.

One of the ancient ceremonies that is still universally practiced is the tea ceremony, *cha-no-yu,* which goes back to the fifteenth century. It is difficult for us to fully appreciate the significance of this solemn social rite. It is an exercise in repose, intended to detach the mind from the outside world. Every implement used in it, every gesture, has an esoteric meaning which to us is quite obscure. The guests sit around the floor while the host, with movements that are fixed by an elaborate code of rules, prepares the tea. The tea used is in a form not of leaves but of powder, so that the resulting beverage resembles pea-soup in color and consistency. The bowl, like a loving cup, is passed around to each guest, who takes three sips according to a ritual which must be scrupulously observed. The tea itself has a delicate and elusive flavor. One Kyoto hotel keeper used it for ice-cream, which became very popular.

Everywhere I went in Japan, even in remote villages, I found that the great desire of the young men was to learn English. Frequently an ambitious student would attach himself to me to act as my guide and at the same time have a free lesson in English. I am sure that I was a better English teacher than the old schoolmaster whom I encountered in a village, where for once I felt sure of not being bothered. I was walking along the deserted street, when I heard rapid footsteps approaching. Turning around, I looked into the smiling face of a gray-haired old man who greeted me with these words: "Sir, or Madam, as the case may be, do you speak English?" I replied that I was surprised to find anyone in this village who could speak English so well. "Yes-s-s," he said. "American nation very great nation. American ladies very beautiful." I discovered that he could not understand a word I said, but to give the villagers, who by this time had assembled, the impression that we were carrying on a real conversation, I continued, while he recited the textbook phrases he had memorized. He was a teacher of English in a neighboring town.

My visit to Japan would have been incomplete without ascending the sacred Mountain Fuji. It is about a twelve-hour climb, and does not require any mountaineering skill, just endurance. One has to take provisions and blankets along to spend the night in the rest house on top of the mountain. The view from the rim of the crater is marvelous when the weather is good. Though it was in the middle of August, I was marooned there for two days and nights by a snowstorm that made everything invisible. The first night, just when I had rolled myself in my blankets, two English navy officers appeared on the scene. They thought it would be a jolly thing to go to the top of Mount Fuji, and taking a guide they had started off without any provisions or blankets. I had to share mine with them. They were thoroughly disgusted when they found, the next morning, that to get back was a physical impossibility. There was no radio at that time, and there was no means of communication with their boat which was leaving that evening. The glorious sunrise, which rewarded my long wait on the third morning, meant nothing to them.

Traveling with the camera in Japan has its exciting moments. There are many taboos: No photographs may be taken within a radius of thirty miles of any fortification, and since the country is a network of military defenses, visible and invisible, some of the most picturesque scenes are situated in the forbidden zone. No pictures may be taken of any place visited by the Emperor; and even the visit of merely an Imperial commission to a temple to catalogue its treasures renders it immune from camera attacks.

I had obtained an official permit from the Japanese Minister of War, but with it came a long list of restrictions. Before taking any pictures I had to notify the chief of police who would detail an officer to go around with me. I found my police companions very courteous, but always inflexible. They would not permit the slightest deviation from the official rules, but at least I was spared unpleasant experiences.

The month I spent among the Ainu in the island of Yezo (Hokkaido)—it is the northernmost of the large islands of the Japanese archipelago, not far from Saghalien—was a voyage far back in time to the beginning of an almost vanished civilization. The Ainu are not Japanese. They are the remnants of an Aryan tribe that once inhabited the whole of Japan. Gradually driven north, they are to be found now only in Yezo and the lower part of Saghalien. They carry on their communal life isolated by custom and language from the Empire whose subjects they are. Their position can best be compared with that of the American Indian in the United States.

After crossing the stormy straits of Tsugaru to Hakodate, I had to proceed by wagon. The springless horse-drawn vehicle (*bassha*) is a miniature of the prairie schooner, and taxes the endurance of the traveler to the utmost. After a three-day trip over roads that were either stretches of running streams or muddy ruts, through a country that at first was indescribably bleak but gradually became green and fertile, we approached the wooded hills of Piratori, the Ainu capital—if one may use that term for a one-street village. The street, with substantial thatched huts, each with its little storehouse on the opposite side of the street, raised on poles from the ground, winds through the valley between the wooded cliffs.

My guide and cook was a Japanese who had come to me in Yokohama with excellent references—I discovered only later that all his references bore a date of ten years back. He acted as interpreter, knowing several hundred words of Ainu language. Upon our arrival at Piratori, I was greeted by a venerable looking man in a long kimono-like robe. His high cheek bones and long white beard and hair gave him the appearance of a distinguished Russian. He supported himself on a long stick. To my great astonishment he shook hands with me in American fashion, and with an amiable smile said, "Sank you." He was one of the Ainu group that Professor Frederick Starr had exhibited at the World's Fair at St. Louis where, he informed my interpreter, he had learned

A KYOTO TEMPLE WALL

A JAPANESE FAMILY (A. G.'s TRAVEL COMPANIONS IN JAPAN)

AINU CHIEFS AT PIRATORI

CRANE DANCE OF AINU WOMEN

English. His entire vocabulary consisted of the two words which he used with great pride, whenever there was a chance. He conducted me to the hut of the chief, the son of old Penri who had been a friend of Mrs. I. B. Bishop and the Rev. John Batchelor, the missionary and great Ainu authority. Penri II was a splendid looking old man, not very tall, but with a fine physique, broad shouldered and thick set. The ceremonial totem crown (more like a wooden fillet), which he wore on his head, added to his impressive appearance. There was a certain air of nobility about him. In the center of the room was the large sunken hearth; over it hung the black pot hooks from rafters which the smoke had polished to an exquisite bronze. There was no chimney; the only outlet for smoke was a small opening in the roof. During the winter, when for six months the country is buried under snow and ice, the people have to remain indoors most of the time. Spending weeks and weeks in the smoke-filled rooms affects their eyes, and many cases of blindness result. In a corner near the sacred east window—a paneless opening, which must be neither approached nor peered through for fear of offending the gods—stand rows of precious old Japanese lacquer boxes and bowls. On a rack were several Japanese swords, gifts of some Japanese prince of centuries ago. These are jealously guarded treasures.

Clothes are made of the fiber of the inner bark of the elm and are decorated with symmetrical designs similar to the one of the mat that covered the floor near the hearth. The pattern of the design was curiously reminiscent of the prayer rugs of the Klikitat Indians of North America.

Some of the younger Ainu women are quite handsome, but whatever beauty they may have is spoiled by a bluish black mustache of quite Imperial shape that is tattooed around their lips. It is not done to add to their beauty. It has a fetish-like significance to ward off evil spirits, and is started in childhood and completed upon marriage. The Ainu women are very fond of their children, though they often leave a few months' old baby alone for hours at a time in its cradle, which is suspended from the rafters near the fireplace. To let a child lie in its cradle and cry is not only thought to be good for its lungs, but is a part of its education. "Babies are like talkative men and women," the Ainu believe. "They must have their say, so let them cry as much as they will."

In the evening there was a drinking feast. Drinking with the Ainu is a religious rite. To drink for the gods is part of the ritual. The elders of the village and the chief squatted around the fireplace with me between them. A drinking bowl was placed before each. The feast began with the ceremony of beard stroking. They solemnly stroked their long white beards with both hands. It was the customary greeting accorded guests and politeness required that I imitate the gesture, beard or no beard. My "St. Louis" friend arose and coming over to me grasped my hand and said, "Sank you." He wanted everyone to know that he was acquainted with the foreigner's ways and language. Chief Penri dipped a carved stick (which I was to discover was the ceremonial mustache lifter) into the *sake* bowl and sprinkled a few drops on the hearth and then toward the sacred east window. No matter how intoxicated an Ainu may be, this ritual is never omitted. Then the drinking started in earnest. The women, who were sitting back of the men, could drink only when their masters deigned to hand them a cup. They wasted no time on ceremonial gesture, but eagerly gulped down the contents of the cup.

Ainu religion is a strange mixture of animism and superstition, and their numerous legends are poetical and picturesque. Though there is no written tradition—writing being unknown to them—the legends and stories are handed down from father to son in a definite fixed form. Some of the expressions have quite a poetical touch. For instance, to die is "to sleep the other sleep," and they speak of "the iron gate of heaven."

The bear plays a most important part in the Ainu religion. The bear festival is a curious ceremony. When a bear cub has been captured, it is reared with great care, and lives with the family and children until it gets too big and strong, when it is placed in a cage. Often the very young cubs, too young and helpless to take food, are nursed like babies by the women. When he is two or three years old, the time has come for the bear to be sacrificed. It is a great occasion to which the people of the village and guests from other villages are invited. There is much dancing, singing and drinking. Before the bear is killed (as a rule by strangling) a formal apology and prayer is addressed to the victim. It runs somewhat like this: "O thou precious little divinity, we have brought thee up with much trouble, because we loved thee so. Now that thou hast grown big, we are about to send thee to thy father and mother. Pray, be not angry. Speak well of us and return to us, so that we may sacrifice thee again." The bear's meat is boiled and is distributed among the people so that everyone present may partake of some, and thus obtain communion with "his dear little divinity."

One morning the women performed for me the crane dance. Efforts to suppress it on account of its erotic character seem to have been successful. It was now just a faint echo of the dance that had, in the past, shocked the missionaries: a circular parade with the women flapping their arms and gyrating their bodies in an innocuous imitation of the wooing of the bird.

I had no difficulty about taking photographs. I knew that the Ainu, like the Chinese, looked upon the camera with suspicion. They believed that reproducing the human face upon paper destroyed the soul of the subject. This superstition has disappeared to some extent, and since I went about it quite diplomatically, arousing their curiosity and interest concerning the working of the camera, there was no trouble. The old wife of Penri insisted on being photographed with me. I arranged the camera on a tripod and showed Penri how to press the bulb. The villagers stood around, silently watching the scene with amazement, but were disappointed when nothing exciting happened. The picture, however, was a success.

Returning from an excursion on the river, the Ainu who was paddling the canoe had, while I was taking pictures, refreshed himself too freely with *sake,* with the result that the boat was overturned. I managed with some difficulty to reach the shore with my camera, which was in a waterproof case. When I mailed a print of the picture, which Chief Penri had taken of me and his wife, to one of my newspaper friends in San Francisco, to whom I had casually mentioned the accident, he put the two together with true reportorial imagination. On my way home the boat stopped at Honolulu and I bought a San Francisco paper. There on the front page was my picture with the Ainu lady. The title read: "Arnold Genthe Rescued from Drowning—Refuses to Wed Ainu Princess."

During my stay in Hokkaido, I had found the Ainu to be a gentle, childlike people; and even when the men were quite intoxicated, which was frequently the case, they were never boisterous or aggressive. It is due to the work of the English missionary, the Rev. John Batchelor, who has devoted his whole life to the welfare of the Ainu, that nowadays the visitor can travel with safety through the Ainu country. Formerly there was an element of danger, since the legends carried from generation to generation had created a feeling of terror and contempt of all strangers. To Mr. Batchelor I am indebted for much valuable information.

One day while I was waiting for him in his office in Sapporro, an Ainu came in. On a wall was a picture of Michelangelo's "Moses." Pointing at it, he turned to me with broad grin and said, "Him Ainu." There may be a grain of truth in it. Who knows?

Where the Ainu came from, to what lost Aryan branch their language is related, has not yet been definitely established. The number of the Ainu is rapidly diminishing and it is to be hoped that before it is too late, the puzzling problem of their origin will be solved.

GREECE AND RHODES

TO one whose imagination has been fed by the Homeric legends as mine had been ever since I was a boy of twelve, the desire to visit Hellas, to follow the trail of the Odyssey and to see what remains today of the Glory that was Greece was an ever-present dream. A tourist's glimpse of Greece, or to seek only the ruins of the classic era, would not have satisfied me. I was eager also to study the castles and monasteries of Byzantine times and of Frankish and Venetian occupation. I wanted to know the real people—the peasants and shepherds who in the solitude of mountains and the protection of islands have preserved much of the ancient tradition—and I also wished to record something of the Greek landscape, the bold rhythm of mountains and valleys. To do all this would require many months of well-planned traveling. And it was only after I had passed my sixtieth year that I was able, in the summer of 1929 and again in the autumn of 1930, to arrange my affairs so that I could devote altogether seven months of leisurely travel through the whole of Hellas and the islands.

No matter if one lands at Patras or at Piraeus, the harbor of Athens, the first impression is bound to be disappointing. The usual activities of a busy seaport town—warehouses, sheds and factories, and noisy crowds dressed in ordinary store clothes and caps—nothing of this suggests the Greece one has dreamt of. And there are other disappointments awaiting the traveler. So many of the places celebrated in classic history and literature today offer nothing to the eye but a vast field of ruins. At Eleusis, for instance, it is difficult to imagine when one is standing in the midst of the scattered debris that this is the place where the sacred festival of the Eleusinian Mysteries was celebrated in the temple of Demeter. In Sparta very little has been brought to light by the excavations of the ancient town. In Delphi, besides the ruins of the theater and the stadium, only the foundations of the famous Apollo temple remain; and at Olympia two columns of the Hera temple are all that is left standing. The columns of the temple of Zeus that housed Phidias' greatest masterpiece are lying on the ground, their drums still in line just as the earthquake had left them. If one looks at these ruins with only the outward eye they may be just "painfully archeological," as a famous English traveler expressed it. And one can almost sympathize with the wife of a professor of archeology who, after having traveled all over Greece without being able to share her husband's enthusiasm, was finally taken up to the Acropolis. Her husband explained, "Now you are about to see the Parthenon, the finest example of classic architecture in the world." When around the bend of the road the golden columns of the temple of Pallas Athena came into view, she merely said, "What? Ruins again? I say, 'Let bygones be bygones!'"

I could appreciate then a story Ethel Watts Mumford once told me. On a Mediterranean cruise, she had heard enough on the voyage between New York and Athens to make her decide to visit the Acropolis alone. With this in mind she had waited patiently for the cruise taxis to depart before setting out by herself. It was a hot day and she had taken the climb slowly. When she caught her first full view of the Parthenon she was so overcome by its incredible beauty that she slumped onto a rock by the roadside and actually cried. Just then around the bend came the returning cruise party headed by Ethel's pet aversion, a school teacher from the Middle West, who called out, "I know just how you feel, dearie, my feet hurt, too."

But to one who has eyes to see, the Parthenon—shining in the morning light against the deep silvery blue of the Attic sky, or when the last rays of the setting sun add a golden touch to its ivoried columns, or in the moonlit night when the noise of the city is but a vague murmur and every voice is hushed in an ecstasy of meditation and worship—makes one feel that the ancient gods are not dead and that the temple of Pallas Athena is not a shattered ruin but the noblest living monument ever built by man.

In Athens I had selected a modest Greek hotel on Stadium Street for my headquarters. Aside from the Acropolis and the museums, there is not much to hold the traveler in the city, but excursions to many points of note can be made from Athens by automobile. The treasures in the National Museum and the smaller Acropolis Museum could hold the attention of the student for many months. Most of the sculptures of the Parthenon frieze were taken to London by Lord Elgin; a small part of it is in the Acropolis Museum and only a portion of it remains on the west front in its original site. Photographs of it had always been taken from a scaffolding at a level from which it was never intended to be seen, thereby giving a wrong perspective. By the use of a tele-photo lens I succeeded in making a picture of it from the ground, showing it without distortion in its original architectural frame.

Among the hundreds of photographs that I took of the Parthe-non under varying conditions, in the early morning or toward sunset, with bright sunlight or threatening clouds, there were sev-eral which really showed the effect I wanted to picture. When a Greek friend of mine showed them to Mr. Venizelos, he asked if the man who made them also took portraits. Upon being told that this was my profession, it was arranged for me to photograph him at the hotel where he was staying in Kephissiá, a summer resort. I was there punctually at the appointed time. After waiting for an hour, I was about to start back to Athens when Mr. Venizelos appeared, followed by a deputation of some thirty politicians. Holding out his hand, he said to me in French, "I am sorry you waited so long. After all, it will not be possible to have the picture taken today. I have another important conference in a few min-utes. We'll make it for some other day." I was not going to be put off. "Your Excellency," I said. "I was here at the time appointed by you. I have waited a whole hour. Surely you can give me three minutes of your time." "All right," he said smilingly, "if you promise not to make it any longer." Since everything was in readi-ness, I made a number of pictures in less than three minutes. This was the shortest sitting I ever had, but the result was gratifying. Mr. Venizelos looked in every way the clever diplomat that he was; tall and dignified of bearing, with penetrating yet kindly eyes, his manner and expression made one surmise something of his ability to handle all sorts of political difficulties. A friend of his told me that whenever a controversy arose demanding a solution that might not be acceptable to his followers, he would take a trip on a man-of-war to one of the islands and remain until minor complications had cleared up, and he could come to a decision that would please both sides.

One afternoon when I was making photographs of some of the sculptures in the Museum, the only other visitor in the room where I was working was a dark, heavy set, studious man who was making numerous entries in his notebook. It was Edouard Herriot. His learned and charming book on Greece, *Sous l'Olivier,* is the work of a scholar and poet and should be made accessible to the English reading public.

Now that many good roads have been built, trips of interest can very conveniently be made by automobile that heretofore required many days. For instance, a visit to Cape Sunion—with its temple of Poseidon set high on the promontory, its white columns, seen against an azure sky and silvery clouds—can easily be accomplished in one day by automobile. It was a favorite shrine of Byron's whose name is one of many cut into the face of a marble slab. It is always pointed out to visitors as the chief sight of this noble temple which for so many centuries was a guide to mariners seeking safe harbor. One afternoon, when I happened to be there, an Englishman and his daughter came up the hill, accompanied by a guide carrying a tea basket. They did not even look up at the temple, but wandered around in search of the "Byron stone." When he had found it, the father turned to his daughter and said, "Well, here it is. Now let's have tea." And there they sat in the shadow of the magic columns, sipping tea and chatting about the people back home.

But traveling by automobile is not the ideal way to see

Greece. The Greek chauffeur, competent and skilful driver that he is, is also utterly reckless. He will refuse to diminish his speed when taking the sharp curves on the mountain road, and barely making the turn, he will grinningly remark, "That was a hard one." It was difficult to induce him to slow up or stop so that I might enjoy a view and make use of the camera. Though many good roads tempt one to travel by automobile and save time, one must forget about hurrying in the desire to adhere to a definite itinerary.

To travel by horse or mule is the ideal mode of transportation, one animal to carry the baggage and another for the rider. Before setting out, an agreement, called *symphonia,* is made with the guide who furnishes the animals for a stipulated sum and accompanies you for not longer than two or three days—his knowledge of the country not going beyond that limit. Then a *symphonia* with another muleteer has to be made, time never being "the essence of such an agreement." The Greek saddle is something like a wooden pack saddle covered with blankets, the stirrups are loops of rope and the bridle is just a rope halter. Riding astride with such a saddle for an hour or so is enough to make one abandon all equestrian pride and reluctantly adopt the custom of the country, sitting sideways with one foot in the stirrup. Going up and down steep mountain trails in this manner, a new mode of balance has to be acquired. I made many trips in this way through various parts of Greece, often being "on the go" for fourteen or fifteen hours, sometimes walking long stretches, without feeling any fatigue. There is a strange, sustaining quality in the Greek air that keeps up one's energy in a most astonishing manner.

It is a truly Arcadian experience to travel for hours up hill and down without meeting a soul, hearing no sound except the tinkle of the horse's bell and the resonant voice of the guide as he entertains one with song and legend, or to meet in an olive grove a flock of sheep tended by a young boy playing a folksong on a pipe of reeds as he sits by the roadside. The only disagreeable note on such trips is provided by the shepherd dogs, enormous mongrels, who will set upon the traveler in a ferocious manner. I did not have the courage to do what the returning Ulysses did—get down on all fours making strange noises. Instead I followed the advice of my guide and threw stones and swung a stout stick above my head. The dogs are trained to guard the flock against thieves and the shepherd will not call them off until the very last moment.

My first mountain trip was to the village of Astros. We started on mule from Kastri early in the morning, fortified by the traditional Greek breakfast of a small cup of Turkish coffee, a glass of water and a spoonful of jam. It was two hours after dark by the time we reached Astros. The only available room in the inn had four beds in it, for all of which, according to the custom, I had to pay. When the negotiations were completed the landlord, who was also the village barber, appeared with a Flit gun which he used, not as if he were ashamed of its necessity but with an air of pride as if he wanted to show that he knew the proper thing. He then led me down the street to a tavern which would have delighted the soul of Max Reinhardt, with its enormous six-foot barrels, the dim flickering light from wicker oil lamps, and the swarthy, bearded men with their bright headdresses looking like a gypsy band. The tavern keeper asked me what I would like to eat. Astros being on the sea, I answered, "Fish." "The day has been hot," was the reply. "You will have eggs and roast lamb." The latter, I was to find, is an inevitable feature of a Greek meal. The wine that went with it was the famous *retsina* which so few travelers get accustomed to, but which plays such a great part in all native hospitality. Made from grapes, it is mixed with the resin from pine trees, which is supposed to act as a preservative and also a preventive for malarial fever. It is not difficult to get used to its slightly turpentine flavor. My ability to drink it and enjoy it enabled me to get closer to the people and I was never bothered with an attack of malaria. The *retsina* in this tavern, drawn fresh from the huge barrels, had a most agreeable flavor and without reluctance I responded to the friendly glasses that were raised in honor of the stranger.

When I finally said good-night I asked them if they remembered a young man by the name of Giorgios A. who had come from their town and now lived in New York (for many months he had read modern Greek with me before I started on my trip). They excitedly answered that his parents still lived in Astros. Next I asked if there was a phonograph. The barber said he had one. "Very well," I told them, "have it here in the morning. See that the young man's parents are present, and I shall have a great surprise for you." Before sailing from New York I had suggested to my young friend that instead of giving me a letter to his parents he prepare a phonograph record (which could be done very easily and inexpensively with what is known as the "speakophone") and surprise them by letting them actually hear his voice. I had brought the aluminum disk with me and I had not forgotten the fiber needles that have to be used with it.

The next morning an official holiday was called. Not only the parents but all the inhabitants assembled outside of the tavern where the phonograph had been placed on a table. I am sure that no radio broadcast was more appreciated than was this squeaky disk in the little seaside village, so remote from the great world. When the mother and father heard the first words of their son, "This is Giorgios A. speaking," tears of joy ran down their fine old faces.

Astros, obscure today, was famous in history a hundred years ago as the place where the first assembly met after the Turks had been driven out. I knew by heart some of the patriotic poems written about the War of Independence and my recital of them was greeted with great enthusiasm, followed by a series of many toasts. When it was time for me to leave, one of the men who had been mysteriously absent for an hour, handed me a farewell document signed by all my newly acquired friends. It was written in English and read: "Dear Sir and Stranger: You have surprised us in many ways. We were delighted to hear you recite our poems. We wish to surprise you by showing you that we know something of your language. We hope you will return to us soon. Farewell!"

Sometimes instead of traveling on horseback, I secured a place in one of the freight-carrying "busses" on which passengers and goods were packed together in hopeless confusion. At each stop the driver and the passengers refreshed themselves with *retsina* until the road was made merry with their singing as we bumped and jolted and creaked along. There was much hilarity but never any drunkenness. My entrance into these busses seldom varied. Sometimes when I inquired from the driver what the fare was, he would quote an amount two or three times in excess. I would respond with what I had learned was the correct amount. Then the passengers would laugh, saying to one another, "He knows," and I would at once be welcomed as one of them.

An unforgettable experience was my visit to Megalopolis in the summer of 1930 at the time of the Pan-Arcadian Festival held there in honor of the hundredth anniversary of Greek Independence. In the forenoon there was the ceremony of the dedication of a monument to the heroic dead who had fallen in the War of Independence. The monument had only been planned, funds for its execution not being available. Not even a symbolic cornerstone marked the site where it was to stand in the town square, but the speeches delivered by the Mayor and leading citizens and by the Commander of the Garrison were full of fire and patriotic fervor. The prayers and the chanting of the Clergy attired in their ancient and gorgeous ceremonial robes made one almost forget the invisibility of the monument. Folk dances, in which the city officials and the military officers joined the peasant dancers who were clad in the native fustanella, concluded that part of the program. But the main event of the day was the performance in the ancient theater late that afternoon. The theater of Megalopolis was one of the largest in ancient Greece, seating twenty thousand. All that remains intact today are the three lower rows of seats; the stones of all the others, built in a semicircle into the slope of the hillside, have gradually been carried away by the inhabitants to serve as

ISADORA DUNCAN

HERA TEMPLE AT OLYMPIA

COLUMNS OF THE PARTHENON

AT THE THEATRE OF EPIDAUROS

building material for the houses and the bridge that spans the river. The orchestra space had been completely cleared for the performance, which had for its theme the myths of Pan and the Nymphs, familiar to all Arcadians. This was rendered in panto-mime and dance and music by Vassos and Tanagra Kanellos and their dance group from Athens, supplemented by local talent. It was a memorable spectacle to which the picturesque audience contributed a most effective note. Hundreds of men in native costume, peasants and shepherds, had come from all over Arcadia to do honor to the ancient god, Pan, who is still a living force with them. Besides myself there was only one other non-Greek spectator present: the painter and author, Mrs. May Mott-Smith, a friend since the old San Francisco days. She was touring Greece to add some Hellenic notes to the vast number of sketches she has painted in many strange corners of the world.

The Kanellos couple are not unknown in America, having given performances of Greek plays and dances in New York, Chicago and California some ten years ago. In Greece for a number of years they have been the foremost exponents of ancient Greek music and drama. Under the auspices of the Greek government they have arranged a series of choro-dramatic festivals in the ancient theaters of Delphi, Argos, Epidauros and Athens, with the enthusiastic cooperation of the leading archeologists, musicians and poets of Greece. It is to be hoped that we may soon be given an opportunity to witness in one of our open air theaters, some of the recent Kanellos productions which, as far as dances, costumes, music and pantomime are concerned, represent an authentic reconstruction of the classic choro-drama.

Even if the remaining architectural ruins of places bearing such illustrious names as Megalopolis, Olympia, Sparta, Corinth, Delphi may at first glance be disillusioning to the traveler, he will always find ample reward in the treasures housed in the museums there and in the picturesque and colorful scenery. If one could see nothing else of Greek art but the pediment figures of the temple of Zeus and other sculptures preserved in the Museum of

Olympia, the traveler's journey would not have been in vain. Damaged as they are, there is a magnificent strength and simple nobility in these figures which makes the popular Hermes of Praxiteles, found in the Hera temple, look rather weak and pretty. Here as well as in other local museums, such as in Sparta, Corinth and Delphi, fine examples of the great periods of Greek Art are to be found. Many of these sculptures exist in several duplicates and I have often wished that an arrangement could be made with the Greek government which would enable our American museums to acquire them, to say nothing of the sculptures hidden away in seldom visited "museums" (sometimes they are nothing more than a shed) of small towns and villages which the traveler can see only if he can find the schoolmaster who keeps the key.

Among the oldest and most renowned of the many Byzantine monasteries and churches which are to be found all over the country is the monastery of Hosios Loukas. Its mosaics are considered the best preserved of any belonging to an early period. I had been told that the abbot was not particularly amiable toward visitors, since he had been offended by the bad manners of several tourists. When I arrived he happened to be standing at the entrance of the court talking to some monks. Dismounting, I approached respectfully, addressing him in the orthodox manner as "Holy Leader," and as is the custom, kissed his hand. He was visibly pleased to have this mark of deference shown him by a stranger in the presence of his monks and he invited me to remain as his guest. I had brought him a small gift, which I knew would be a novelty: a small automatic electric light which requires no battery but is worked by a little motor from within; a repeated pressure of a spring turns on the light. Incidentally, I found that these pocket lights, and a boy scout knife with many blades, were always welcome gifts in the monasteries, similar in effect to the presents with which the explorer, Charles Suydam Cutting, told me he had ingratiated himself with the Dalai Lama of Tibet: a Swiss cuckoo clock and a self-winding wrist watch.

That night after supper, the old abbot and I sat late, drink-

Ancient Monasteries

244

ing the excellent monastery wine, munching dried almonds and discussing some rare books on the history of the monastery. "It is a long time since I have had as my guest a stranger with whom I could talk and drink like this," he told me. The next day services in the church were suspended for two hours so that I might have ample time to make some portraits of the abbot in his ceremonial robes.

The Metéora ("In the Air") Monasteries, situated in the north of the wild mountain regions of Thessaly, may not have much to offer in the way of Byzantine treasures and manuscripts, but the scenery is of an incredible and fantastic beauty. Against the russet mountains, with their blue depths and purple haze, the giant rocks seem to have been carved by an angry Nature into an army of monstrous phallic symbols. Perched high, hundreds of feet in the air, are these extraordinary strongholds of the medieval monks, who fled to these heights to be away from the world and to be safe from attacks of pirates. Until recently, the only way of access was by ladder or in a basket pulled up by windlass; now trails have been cut into the rock and the four monasteries that are inhabited—formerly there were over twenty of them—can be reached on foot. The number of monks is diminishing from year to year, since the admission of novices is prohibited by the Greek government. The rich lands will eventually revert to the State. When I asked how it had been possible for the first monks to build on these inaccessible heights, the answer invariably was—"Angels helped them." When I asked if there ever was an accident in hauling people up and down in the basket, the naïve reply was, "Only when the rope breaks." Finding that the rope at the St. Stephanos Monastery was a good American steel cable, I took the chance and had myself lowered from the dizzy height to where my muleteer was waiting.

Comparatively few travelers who visit Greece and see most of the places famous in classic times manage to include in their itinerary a visit to Mount Athos, that unique monastic republic where life has gone on unchanged in the monasteries for almost a thousand years. The conservatism of Mount Athos is such that a description published by a French traveler, P. Belon, in the middle of the sixteenth century still fits present-day conditions.

To be admitted as a guest, a number of official credentials are required. In addition to a letter from the Minister of Education and Religion in Athens and letters from the Governor-General of Macedonia and the Chief of Police in Saloniki, I had an impressive looking document from the Archbishop of Corinth, explaining to the Holy Synod of Athos that I was coming to the Holy Mountain "not as a curious and casual tourist but as a serious student and reverent pilgrim." It is only a twelve-hour journey by steamer from Saloniki to Daphne, the official port of Mount Athos on the eastern arm of the peninsula of Chalkidike. Two monks and the head of the military guard, a white-bearded, imposing looking man in native costume, are a reception committee whose duty it is to prevent the landing of any female passenger, no matter how good her disguise may be. The law, dating from the foundation of the first monastery in the tenth century, "No woman must set foot on the Holy Mountain," is strictly enforced to this day. Even female animals are barred, though in some monasteries exception is made of hens and cats. The story that a French woman writer and a young Greek girl (who had gained some publicity as "Miss Europe" in 1930) had succeeded in smuggling themselves into one of the monasteries is journalistic fiction. Even Queen Marie of Rumania, one of whose ancestors had richly endowed one of the oldest monasteries, was forcibly prevented from landing when she tried to visit the Holy Mountain some years ago.

There are no roads on Mount Athos, no wheeled vehicles; everywhere one has to go on foot or by mule. It is a three-hour ride through magnificent forests from Daphne to "the capital," Karyes, the seat of the monastic government, where I had to present my credentials to the Holy Synod, composed of a representative from each one of the twenty monasteries. After a brief consultation I was given an open letter (bearing the ancient seal) to the abbots of all the monasteries, commending me to their hos-

LANDING PLACE IN ISLAND OF THERA

IN ARCADIA

ABBOT OF THE MONASTERY OF HOSIOS LOUKAS

ABBOT AND DEACONS OF THE MT. ATHOS MONASTERY OF ZOGRAPHOU

pitality. I was now free to go from monastery to monastery, knowing that food and shelter and transportation by mule would be provided for me free of cost.

Before starting out I lingered a few days in Karyes, exploring its picturesque surroundings and devoting many hours to studying the frescoes of its church, the Protaton, the oldest building on Athos. The town consists chiefly of a "Main Street" with several narrow lanes branching off on either side. It is paved with rough irregular cobblestones. The houses, mostly two-story buildings, are painted gray or black. No one may ride through this street; the traveler must dismount. And to smoke a cigarette in passing the church is a punishable offense. The whole place seems phantom-like—no gay voices of women or children, no animals, no sound of conversation—only the ghost-like figures of monks, in long black gowns and curious brimless high hats, treading their silent way. In a number of shops monks were busy. The carpenter, the grocer, the blacksmith, the tailor (working a sewing machine) —all monks; only the keeper of the small inn and the pharmacist were laymen. The latter was a curious wizened old man, who must have had a strange life. He had been at Karyes for over twenty-five years. He showed me with pride diplomas from various learned societies of Europe of which he was a member. His laboratory was a room of truly Faustian character, filled with weird instruments, retorts, phials, strange stuffed animals, etc.; a wall cabinet marked "Poisons" was invitingly open.

Twenty of the medieval monasteries are inhabited today, but many of the monks live in single secluded houses or in organized groups called *Skites* which are built around a central church almost like a village. A number of hermits live in most primitive fashion in caves on the slopes of the mountain, out of touch with monastery activities. I visited fourteen of the monasteries during my month's stay on Athos. The ceremony of arrival is always the same. Upon approaching, one dismounts some distance from the gate and hands in the letter of introduction at the porter's lodge, from where it is taken to the abbot, who in turn will have the guest-master conduct the visitor to his room. These guest rooms vary in quality and comfort according to the resources of the monastery. Some are very simply furnished, with divans, instead of beds, ranged along the wall in Turkish fashion. One has to be pretty tired to sleep on these cement mattresses. Sometimes the rooms are quite luxuriously furnished, with brass beds and good blankets and mattresses. As a rule the rooms are well kept and free from the little animals that so often disturb the traveler's sleep. Yet sometimes the use of the Flit gun is commendable. Once a guest-master came into the room when I was busy "Flitting." Realizing what I was doing, he reprimanded me, saying, "They, too, want to live." I convinced him that I was only putting "them" to sleep for a few hours. Washing facilities vary; sometimes there is running water or a basin and pitcher in the rooms. Sometimes the fountains in the courtyard must serve for both. On one of them was an inscription: "Wash not only your face and hands but also your sins."

My first stopping place, after leaving Karyes, was the monastery of Zographou, two hours and a half away by mule. It is chiefly inhabited by Bulgarians. Only the guest-master, Father Daniel, and the abbot spoke Greek. The room to which I was shown was spacious and comfortably furnished; and the evening meal which the guest-master himself brought on a tray was most palatable. I had hardly finished when I was startled by a weird sound in the courtyard. Beginning with slow notes, the sound gradually increased in tone and tempo ending in an almost barbarous rhythm like the beating of savage dance drums. When I looked out I saw a monk beating with a hammer a large wooden board, the *simandron,* calling the monks to the first evening service. There are four services during the night and four during the day and it is the polite duty of the guest to attend at least one of them. The next morning when I was about to start out with my camera—the light being perfect for a picture of two enormous cypresses in the court (with those in the monastery of Lavra, they are said to be the oldest in the world)—Father Daniel announced that it was now time to go to church. So I followed him, taking my camera with me. The walls with their ancient frescoes, the jeweled icons hung with votive offerings (among them a *croix de guerre*), the brocaded robes of the officiating priest and somber black of the monks made an unforgettable picture in which I, in my khaki riding things, must have presented a discordant note. When the service was over and the monks were filing out, the abbot and three deacons happened to be standing in front of a wall covered with Byzantine frescoes of the saints. I asked the abbot if I might take a picture of this group. "Not today" was the reply given with a quiet finality which I felt meant "Never." I asked if he minded if I looked into my camera to see how I might take the photograph the next day. There was no objection, and I rapidly made the necessary adjustments for taking a picture then and there. Though the light was scarcely strong enough for an exposure without a tripod, I made a picture of that group, raising my voice so that the noise of the released shutter should not be heard. Perhaps as a reward for my pious devotion the picture turned out well. When on the third day the arranged hour of my departure was approaching, the guest-master informed me that no mules would be available until the next day; they all had to be used to carry the olive crop to the harbor. When I remarked that this would upset my itinerary and make me lose a whole day, he replied, "My son, what is a day when you think of eternity?"

I had been particularly anxious to go to the seldom visited monastery of Esphigmenou. Aside from its impressive situation—it lies directly on the sea, the waves dashing against its walls—it held a special attraction for me. I had read that its library possessed a fifth-century palimpsest of the Gospels which had never been deciphered. Father Parthenios, the guest-master, who was quite a scholar, was pleased to learn of my interest. Leading me into the church, he opened a small door and with lighted candle preceded me up the dark and narrow spiral stairway, which led to the top of the tower where monastery treasures are kept to preserve them against fire or piracy. In a room not larger than twelve by twenty feet sat a grizzled librarian engaged in cataloguing the few hundred volumes of the library. He brought out the ancient volume with great eagerness. Underneath the dark and distinct writing of a fourteenth-century text the letters of a very early period were faintly visible. By the use of modern photographic methods (infra-red plates, etc.) it would be possible to render the fourteenth-century writing practically invisible and to bring out clearly the ancient lettering which might reveal some important text.

The two finest libraries on the peninsula are in the monasteries of Lavra and Vatopaedi. Here in spacious rooms, the manuscripts and books are carefully kept in glass cases and looked after by competent librarians who have compiled a scholarly catalogue. I found that the name J. Pierpont Morgan is venerated almost like that of a saint. It was through Mr. Morgan that the publication of several early Athos manuscripts of the Gospels had been made possible (most of the work being done by Professor Kirsopp Lake of Harvard University), thereby adding to the fame of the monasteries. A great many of the treasures of the library are manuscripts of authors of classic Greek literature and of the later Hellenistic period. Many of them are elaborately illuminated and illustrated.

The last shrine of my monastic pilgrimage was the monastery of Simonópetra. On a steep cliff rising a thousand feet above the sea, it presents a fantastic picture, suggesting rather the palace of the ruler of Tibet than a Greek monastery. The lower floors, used for storerooms, have neither doors nor windows. The six upper stories, where the monks have their cells, are encircled by wooden galleries where most of their time is spent. To walk along these galleries when they are creaking and swaying in the wind is an experience not meant for nervous people. Many of the footboards are missing and when stepping carefully over the space left by them and looking down at the rocks hundreds of feet below, it is difficult to overcome a feeling of dizziness. But

I quickly got used to these new surroundings and enjoyed sitting in a corner of one of the gently swaying galleries, chatting in the cool of the evening with my monastic friends, less about religious problems than of world affairs.

Though the guest of a monastery is not obliged to pay anything, even if he stays several days, it is customary and proper for him to make a donation to the church. I found that an amount about equal to what I would have had to pay in my Athens hotel, plus a small gift of cigarettes and a pocket-knife, was always welcome. It seems little to give in return for the gracious welcome and kindly hospitality I received in the monasteries. To have breathed the atmosphere of the splendid forests, the only ones that in all Greece remain unspoiled, to have had a glimpse of an existence so utterly remote from our hurried machine age, to have realized in the religious peace of the monastic life new spiritual values which will continue to be an influence in my life—all this is an experience which cannot be measured by material standards. My visit to the Holy Mountain will always be one of my most treasured memories.

One could spend many months tracing the charm of the Greek islands and every day come upon some new adventure in an old beauty. But the mode of travel as a rule, on the small steamers which ply between Piraeus and the various islands of the Aegean, is not without its hardships. The cabins are small, the deck space reserved for first class is often completely occupied by the steerage passengers or by an overflow of freight which the captain has taken on the last minute. The food as a rule is quite decent.

No more thrilling sight will greet the voyager in the Aegean Sea than the first view of the island of Thera (Santorini) just north of Crete. A sheer wall of volcanic tufa, of russet, black and yellow strata, rises from the narrow landing place, where there is room for only a few warehouses with vaulted roofs. This awe-inspiring cliff is the side of an extinct volcano, which goes down into a bay so deep that no ship can anchor there. A solidly built zigzag road winds its way to the summit—it is a thousand feet to the row of white houses of the town perched on the top of the cliff. Broad steps enable the mules (the Fords of Thera) to carry the traveler safely to his destination. The houses are built in terraces, the flat roof of one being the front yard of the house above. The view from any of these terraces looking out over the sea is one of enchanting beauty. The semi-circular bay (three miles wide) is dotted with small islands marking the rim of the ancient submerged crater. Somewhere in the center, stretching out like a dark hand, is the volcanic island where in 1925 occurred the terrible eruption that threatened to destroy the whole town.

One can truthfully say of the people of Thera that they are living on the rim of a volcano. Any time another eruption may bring about destruction to the whole island group. However, the inhabitants are fatalists. When the government, believing the island doomed, sent a man-of-war to take the populace to a place of safety, they refused to leave. "When the fumes of the volcano are sweet," they said, "there is no danger." And their faith was justified.

The volcanic soil of the main island yields a wine of peculiar excellence, Mavrodaphne, which is a blessing in more than one way, as there is no water whatsoever on the island, rain water carefully collected in barrels being the only water supply.

Thera would be a painter's paradise. Will an artist, endowed with vision and imagination, record for us some of the unique charm of this unbelievable isle before it is too late?

Though it is only a short distance from Thera to Crete, one has to go back to Piraeus and make a fresh start to reach Crete. At Candia (Heraklion), the main harbor of Crete, the sculptured lions set in the old fortress walls denote the Venetian occupancy that has left a more lasting mark than have the subsequent three hundred years of Turkish rule. The chief sight in Candia is the museum where all the finds excavated at Knossos, Phaestos and Hagia Triada are assembled and properly catalogued. The English archeologist, Sir Arthur Evans, is responsible for the work at Knossos. The uncovering and restoring of the palace of the legendary King Minos at Knossos is due to his unceasing efforts, and though at times he may have let his imagination carry him too far in the restorations, he deserves the greatest credit for having brought to light a civilization which as long as four thousand years ago must have been equal to our own in certain phases. Incidentally there are authentic reproductions of most of the important Cretan antiquities in our museums.

Unless one is really interested in things archeological, the best part of a visit to Delos, which with all its past glory is today but a vast area of ruins on a barren island, will be Mykonos, where one charters a sailboat for the trip to Delos. Mykonos is without a doubt one of the loveliest and most picturesque islands in the Aegean. Its white, flat-roofed and balconied houses, its windmills and its innumerable small churches and chapels (there seems to be one for every inhabitant, each chapel being a votive offering put up by fishermen in gratitude for rescue from storms) present a fascinating picture. The friendliness of the inhabitants and the inviting inn close to the shore tempt one to linger, but the wind is favorable for the sail to Delos and the captain urges immediate departure. It took only an hour and a half to reach the stony shore of Delos, while the return trip, in a choppy sea and against the wind, required over five hours. There are no accommodations for visitors but I was permitted to stay at the little house of the School of American Archeology. A significant piece of furniture was a large jar marked "Quinine." It seems that the sacred lake on whose shore Apollo was born, was drying up and had become a breeding ground for malaria mosquitoes. Of the great temple of Apollo, the most interesting remains are in the Avenue of Lions which led to its entrance. They are primitive sculptures looking more Egyptian than Greek, belonging to an early period. Through the French and American archeologists who are constantly at work on the island, much has been brought to light of the ruined palaces and private dwellings, the markets and temples and the innumerable monuments that were the glory of Delos. Taken all in all, Delos offers more to the student and scholar than to the seeker of the picturesque.

The island of Corfu is in the Ionian Sea off the western shores of Greece. My itinerary brought me to Corfu during the holiday of St. Spiridon, the Christian Martyr whose miracle-working mummy reposes in the church. The festival in his honor was a spectacle worth seeing. With all the pomp and circumstance of the Greek ritual, he was carried through the streets to the firing of guns and the playing of sacred music by a military band. The procession was headed by the impressive and venerable figure of Athenagoras, then Archbishop of the Ionian Islands, now Archbishop of the Greek Orthodox Church of North and South America. He and all the priests were clad in the resplendent robes of their office. On the sidewalks, along which the procession passed, were laid the bedridden sick and invalids so that the sight of the martyred saint might help to cure them.

The buildings and the costumes of the women are more Italian than Greek in character, but in the ancient olive groves, which are the island's greatest attraction, one might imagine oneself in the very heart of Arcadia. Corfu, in spite of its Italian costumes and its British fortress, is after all Greek, just as it was in the days of Homer.

The island of Rhodes, famed in classic literature for her beauty of scenery and mildness of climate, seems to be known to some people today chiefly through the Colossus of Rhodes. Recently, a young lady who knew I had been to Rhodes said that she hoped I would let her see the pictures I had made of the Colossus, since she had never seen a good photograph of it. Well, I hadn't either. This celebrated bronze figure of Helios, the sun god, over a hundred feet high, bearing in his hand a torch to light the mariner's way, was erected some time in the

"HERE'S HOW" (GREEK STYLE)

ABANDONED METEORA MONASTERY (THESSALY)

ATHOS MONASTERY OF SIMONOPETRA

GUESTMASTER

LIBRARIAN

STREET OF THE KNIGHTS IN RHODES

HARBOR OF LINDOS (RHODES)

third century B.C. at the entrance of the harbor. It stood there for only fifty years, when an earthquake overturned it. Undisturbed, it lay at the bottom of the harbor for almost a thousand years. There was a superstition that calamity would overtake anyone who dared to touch it. The Saracens, invading the island in the seventh century A.D., had no such fear. Breaking up the bronze, they shipped the pieces to Asia Minor, where all trace of it was lost.

Rhodes has in the course of centuries known many different rulers—the Greeks, the Romans, the Crusader Knights of St. John, and the Turks. The latter finally defeated the Knights in 1522 and were in possession of Rhodes for four hundred years. During the Turkish domination the whole of the island gradually fell into decay, but since 1922, when it became an Italian colony with several other islands of the Dodecanese (through the treaty of Lausanne), a new life has sprung up. First an effort was made to restore the old buildings to their original state. It was no small task to remove the Turkish disfigurements.

The splendid fourteenth-century palaces in the Street of the Knights, which had housed the various "Tongues" of the French, English, Italian, and German crusaders, were "decorated" with wooden balconies (built for the Turkish women so that they could sit outside without being seen); windows with marble crosses of the Knights had been walled up; fine old residences had been completely transformed into commonplace Moslem dwellings; the Hospital of the Knights, which had been used by the Turks as military barracks, had very little of its original architectural beauty visible. All the Turkish defacements have been removed by expert Italian architects and now the noble simplicity of Gothic structure has come to light. The Hospital of the Knights houses the archeological museum where the finds of the recent excavations are admirably displayed: painted vases; early Minoan jars, much like the enormous vessels found in Crete; a great number of inscriptions; sculptures of various Greek and Roman periods, among them a small crouching Venus and a torso of extraordinary beauty. Much excitement was caused recently in the art world by the finding of a funeral stele, a life-size marble relief of a farewell between mother and daughter. It is of such exquisite workmanship that some authorities believe it to be an original work of Praxiteles.

One form of Turkish vandalism is beyond repair. As it was against the Mussulman creed to make graven images, the fanatic invaders had mutilated with vicious strokes of the axe every sculpture, Greek or Roman or Gothic; even the relief of the angels holding the Grand Master's crest has been hacked to pieces.

All the modern buildings erected since the beginning of the Italian era, the Palace of the Government, the hospitals, the schools, the military barracks and likewise the new private residences, follow the plan of the old architecture, so that there is not one inharmonious note—even the comfortable and quite up-to-date hotel, the Albergo delle Rose, fits into the scheme. The walls, ramparts, gates and towers of the fortifications that encircle the old town in a line six miles long—they had enabled the Knights to withstand the siege of the Turks for so many years—have been restored to their original state. A market to which the fruit, vegetables and fish have to be brought by the peasants is a model of modern sanitary methods. Excellent roads traverse the whole island so that the country produce can readily be transported, and incidentally the visitor is now enabled to see without much loss of time some of the magnificent scenery of other parts of the island, such as the harbor and Acropolis of Lindos, to mention only one notable place. Not enough credit can be given to Governor Mario Lago, a man of fine courage, vision and culture, for the splendid work of restoration and colonization which his régime inaugurated.

After returning from my first visit I spoke with such enthusiasm about what I had seen in Rhodes that one of my New York friends, John Hemming Fry, the painter and writer, who is a great admirer of modern Italy as well as of classic art, was moved to contribute a generous sum of money for the archeological explorations. Governor Lago directed that the money be used for one project, the excavations that had been begun in the neighboring island of Cos, the home of Hippocrates. Among several sculptures of no great importance there was discovered, under the foundations of a small theater, a full-length statue thought by the authorities to be a portrait of Hippocrates. The old scholar, called the Father of Medicine, seems to have been far ahead of his time (fourth century B.C.). He was well acquainted with what we consider modern discoveries: the healing powers of sunlight and water, the curative use of hypnotism and even the principles of chiropractics. The ideals of his profession, expressed in what is known as the Hippocratic Oath, to this day administered in our universities to graduates in medicine, have never been formulated in more concise and adequate terms.

It happened that when I arrived in Cos, due to a delay of the steamer, the museum, which is housed in the fine old castle of the Knights of St. John, was closed. Darkness had set in but I was eager to get into the museum. There being no electric lights, the curator arranged to have a soldier accompany me with a torch. It was then that I fully appreciated Rodin's remark: the best way to see a Greek statue is by the light of a candle moved about at will, so that none of the subtle and sensitive nuances of the modeling will be missed. It was an amazing and revealing experience.

The series of photographs which I had made of Rhodes during my two visits were shown at the International Colonial Exposition in Rome, where they were awarded a diploma. I had hoped to add some airplane views, but during my flight (in an Italian plane) from Piraeus over the Aegean Sea to Rhodes, my cameras were officially sealed for the benefit of the Greek and Italian governments and my enjoyment of the beautiful scene was sadly diminished by my inability to take a single picture. Mr. Fry acquired the collection and donated it to the Library of the Archeological Institute at Rhodes. Several of my friends, after seeing my Rhodes photographs here in New York—among them Chester Aldrich, the architect, and William Howard Gardiner, the eminent camera pictorialist—were induced to spend some weeks on that enchanting island. They returned full of enthusiasm and ready to urge others to share their experience. I almost felt that I was encroaching on the work of Franco Benetti, Governor Lago's right-hand man, whose office it is to prove to the world that there are other things worthy of attention in Rhodes besides the Colossus.

PROGRESS OF PHOTOGRAPHY

I N my earlier years as a photographer, I was often haunted by the ghost of my old desire to be a painter. As time went on and I became more and more aware of the power that lay within the camera, this sense of frustration vanished. Today I have only gratitude, untouched by regret, for my part as one of the pioneers in the development of an art which has done so much to spread the gospel of beauty.

It is not generally known that the first photographic portrait was not done in France by Daguerre, the inventor of photography, but was made in America. It is a story of particular interest to New Yorkers. Daguerre had to expose a plate even in bright sunlight for about twenty minutes. Portraits were out of the question. Human beings could not remain immobile as statues for that length of time. Samuel F. B. Morse, the distinguished American painter and inventor of the telegraph, visited Daguerre in Paris and obtained from him the working formulas of his discovery. Returning to New York, he evolved in collaboration with Professor John W. Draper of New York University, a method of concentrating light (by the use of concave mirrors) with such intensity that a picture could be made with an exposure of about two minutes. Before the end of the year 1839, through this device the first photograph of a human being was successfully taken. The subject was Draper's sister Dorothy.

The top of the old university building on Washington Square was turned into a photographic studio and here Morse and Draper carried on for over a year their photographic work, taking pictures of their friends in quite a professional manner. Philip Hone, then mayor of New York, relates in his memoirs how city notables flocked to the studio to have their portraits done with this new process.

Few of these earliest American daguerreotypes have come to light. Some of them, probably forgotten heirlooms, may still exist. A search ought to be made for them. Any daguerreotype taken between 1839 and 1840 in New York must be the work of Draper and Morse. There was nobody else who could have done it. This early chapter of American portrait photography has never received the attention it deserves.

A year or so later, after Daguerre's process had been published, a number of professional studios sprung up in many cities, and it must be admitted that some of these early daguerreotypes, in spite of stiff poses due to the long exposures, possess a quaint charm. The sitters had not yet learned how to "pose."

The Frenchman's metal plates did not permit the making of duplicates. In 1841 W. H. Fox Talbot of England had succeeded in substituting a sensitized paper for the metal plate, and now any number of prints could be made from these paper-negatives that were rendered transparent. The Scotch painter, David Octavius Hill, used this process to obtain faithful likenesses for the several hundred portraits that he planned to include in his huge canvas commemorating the founding of the Free Church of Scotland in 1843. Among the photographic studies, made with the primitive instrument and crude equipment at Hill's disposal, are to be found some portraits of amazing perfection. In carefully considered compositions and effective patterns of rich velvety blacks and brilliant highlights, the sitters are presented in natural, spontaneous poses, never suggesting photographic stiffness or artificiality. Hill was an isolated figure for over three decades. He stood by himself as the one great master of photoportraiture.

Professional photographers in America continued for many years to use the improved daguerreotype process. Though the exposures still had to be long, the sitter frequently is shown in a relaxed pose giving quite a pleasing and natural effect. The camera face had not yet arrived.

After the introduction of the photographic glass plate, there sprang up in a comparatively short time a tradition of artificiality and false values. Photography became a purely commercial trade, the studio an operating room and the operators mere mechanics without imagination or picture sense. The sitter had to be posed, the head was held firmly in a vise and the unfortunate victim was told to look pleasant. Then the retoucher went to work and removed with pencil and etching knife whatever trace of individuality and character might have survived the ordeal. Then prints were made on shiny paper and were handed out to the sitter, a dozen at a time, in various formats: "Carte de visite," "Cabinet," or "Imperial Boudoir," to be added to the family albums.

Portrait photography was in this state when I came to San Francisco over forty years ago. I was convinced that it must be possible to find another method of making portraits with the camera. I have told in Chapter III how I became interested in photography and how I decided to make it my life's work. I believe I was the first professional photographer to give people portraits that were more than mere surface records—pictures that in a pictorially interesting composition, in a carefully considered pattern of light and shade, showed something of the real character and personality of the sitter. In the finished picture I tried to subordinate unimportant detail and emphasize the essential characteristic features. I preferred the soft tones of a mat surface paper to the harshness of the glossy paper in vogue, and I found that I could obtain better results if I made my prints by projection—while permitted a wide range of control—instead of making direct contact prints. I have been using this method, more or less, to this day, though there are eminent photographers who do not approve of it. An article, "Rebellion in Photography," which I wrote for the *Overland Monthly* thirty-five years ago, expressed some of my theories which still hold good today.

Discarding all the sacred rules of photographic tradition, I had prescribed for myself a principle which I have religiously adhered to these many years: never to permit the sitter to be conscious of the exact moment when the picture is being taken, be it in the studio or out of doors. Even to the homemade family snapshot this rule ought to be applied. I still believe that it is impossible for anyone, young or old, to be one's real self when preparing an expression for the benefit of the camera, and it is likewise difficult for a person to feel at ease, to be relaxed and natural, in a studio that is solely adapted for photographic "operations" and is unlike any comfortable living room. Frequently when visiting photographers see my studio they exclaim, "What a fine library, and what interesting paintings! But where do you operate?"

David Octavius Hill

262

In spite of the tremendous improvements that have been made in everything pertaining to photography technically—camera, shutters, lenses, plates, and films—it is almost discouraging to have to confess that the work of the old Scotchman, David Octavius Hill, of ninety years ago has hardly been surpassed by any of the modern photographers. He had only the most primitive equipment at his disposal—no artificial lights, no rapid lenses or panchromatic plates—and yet he produced portraits that were revealing character studies and at the same time distinguished compositions of rich tonal scale. All his pictures were taken out of doors in soft sunlight. The modern worker who tries to obtain startling effects by the extravagant use of electric light at his disposal, shooting from all angles, might do well to remember that the sun, which nine decades ago enabled David Octavius Hill to make such masterpieces, shines for us too.

As Hill has proved, the excellence and perfection of the instrument used is not such an important factor for obtaining fine results. It is, of course, an advantage to have a camera with a fast lens and all the modern improvements enabling one to take pictures under almost any light condition. But it is possible to make photographs of real merit with a very inexpensive camera. The essential thing is to perceive a picture in what is before one, to choose an angle that will result in a pictorially interesting composition. The eye behind the camera is far more important than the lens in front of it.

Not long ago a well-known novelist, in looking through a portfolio of mine, exclaimed, "I wish I could take pictures like these but I'm only an amateur. What a wonderful lens you must have!" She was quite taken back when I asked her to show me her fountain pen, because I felt it must be a very marvelous one. Many of my successful photographs were made with an insignificant little pocket camera, when no other was available.

No matter what type of camera is used, it is necessary to make oneself familiar with its mechanism. The highly efficient modern miniature camera may require hours of study to master its intricacies, but then, after some experimenting, the necessary adjustments can be made almost automatically. One ought to be able to use a camera with the same ease and rapidity as the cowboy uses his gun. Too much preliminary fussing may lose a fine picture chance.

The late Clarence White was fond of repeating to his pupils a story that I once told in a talk at his school. An elderly lady had asked me to give her some lessons in photography. She "just loved art" and she was sure she would be able to make beautiful pictures. After a brief conversation I realized what a hopeless pupil she would be and I tried to deter her by quoting an absurdly high price for the lessons. "Oh, that will be perfectly all right," she replied. I had to think of another way of discouraging her. I explained that my method of teaching was a rather peculiar one. I told her I always made my pupils (I have never had any) practice with a pistol for several days so that they would learn quickly how to shoot without wasting any time in aiming. "Would I really have to fire a pistol?" she asked nervously. "Yes, that's one thing I insist on for the beginning," I told her. "No, I could never do that," she said, and departed disappointed.

It is within the power of anyone nowadays to use the camera successfully, even if one doesn't "just love art." The two great stumbling blocks that used to be responsible for so many failures of the amateur—the problem of gauging correctly the distance and the length of exposure—have been done away with by ingenious devices: one automatically gives the right distance; the other measures with unfailing accuracy the photographic strength of the light under practically all conditions, and indicates the right exposure required.

Unfortunately, there cannot be any mechanical contrivance that will guarantee a good composition. That the photographer has to find out for himself. It will require much patient experimenting, hours of waiting for the right light effect, ruthless courage to discard failures and a brave extravagance in using many films or plates for the same subject.

To Alfred Stieglitz of New York, more than to any other man, must be given the credit for the place photography occupies among the graphic arts today. He exercised a far-reaching influence through his own superb work, and perhaps even more through that sumptuous publication, *Camera Work,* of which he was the creator, editor and publisher. It contained reproductions —the most perfect ones ever to appear in any magazine—of the work of leading pictorialists and brilliantly written essays and comments by prominent critics. The exhibitions he arranged in the little Fifth Avenue gallery known as "291"—the home of the Photo-Secession Movement—were not only devoted to photography but to the showing of drawings and paintings with which New York was as yet unacquainted.

His whole life has been devoted to the task of gaining recognition of photography as an art. He told me the following characteristic episode. Edward Steichen, who had given up painting to devote himself to photography, had made a striking portrait of J. Pierpont Morgan, the elder. For some reason it did not meet with Mr. Morgan's approval, and Steichen gave it to Stieglitz who greatly admired it. One day, Miss Belle Da Costa Greene, the director of the Morgan Library, in looking through some of Mr. Stieglitz's portfolios, came across this portrait. "Why haven't we got this in our library? It's marvelous and I'm sure Mr. Morgan would pay

anything you asked for it." "It is not for sale," was the reply.
Miss Greene spoke about it to Mr. Morgan and told him what
Stieglitz had said. "Maybe if we offer enough for it we'll get it,"
he said, and authorized Miss Greene to offer Stieglitz a sum far
in excess of what a fashionable portrait painter would get for a
canvas. Again Stieglitz refused to sell it. "But," he added, "if Mr.
Morgan is willing to pay as much as that for it, he must have a
high opinion of its value. I will make him a present of it, provided that he has it hung for a year in the Metropolitan Museum
next to the painting Baca Flor did of him." He made this stipu-
lation, because he felt that it certainly would further the cause
so dear to him—the recognition of photography as an art. The
photograph was not hung in the Metropolitan.

The photographer whose profession it is to make portraits
of people will find it frequently hard, if not impossible, to please
his clients unless he is willing to make concessions which would
conflict with his ideas of integrity. I may say without boasting
that I have always managed to avoid this difficulty, unprofitable
as it may have been. In the first year of my photographic activities
in San Francisco, an incident of this kind occurred which I have
not forgotten. A woman had brought her daughter to be photographed. The girl had great beauty and a simple charm that was
quite unusual. Her hands were sensitive, with long tapering fingers. The picture that I made of her was a composition (including the hands) of extreme simplicity that conveyed something
of the rare natural charm of the girl. It was unlike any portrait
I had ever made before. When the mother saw it, the very qualities that appealed to me in the picture utterly displeased her.
"I wouldn't have that picture in the house," she exclaimed, and
departed angrily. Several of my artist friends admired the photograph and suggested that I send it to the London Photographic
Salon. It happened that Bernard Shaw, who was himself an enthusiastic photographer, referred to it, in a critique that he wrote,
as "the most unphotographic portrait." His remark was published
in the San Francisco papers, whereupon the mother came to my

studio and said that, after all, she liked the picture and wanted a dozen copies of it. "I am very sorry, but you cannot have them," I said. "What do you mean?" she asked. "She is my daughter." "Quite true," I replied, "but the picture is my picture. I did not mind your not liking it, but I did object to the way in which you expressed your dislike." She sent several of her friends to plead with me, but I kept her waiting several months. In the end, I relented and let her have the prints she wanted.

We hear and read so much these days about "candid camera" photographs, as if it were a startling innovation. I don't think that I have ever made any other kind. Even in the early days of slow lenses and slow plates, when it was much more difficult to catch a person unawares, on account of the necessarily longer exposures, I managed successfully.

In the attempt to avoid any conventional formula and to achieve at all cost a startling result, some of our modernists will treat a portrait chiefly as a motive for a compositional exercise in which a startling background, a weird camera angle, dark shadows and sharp highlights produce a fantastic pattern in which the sitter is merely an incidental factor. This may be a brave protest against the conventional commonplace arrangement found so often in the ordinary kind of studio picture, but it is not a solution of the main problem of photographic portraiture.

In these days, when there is hardly a home without a camera and the making of photographs has become a universal pastime, it is particularly difficult to make the public realize the difference between a picture that has artistic merit and distinction and a photograph that is just an indifferent record or a haphazard snapshot or just a stunt. They are all photographs. And frequently, by art critic and layman, the expression "only a photograph" is used. In one of the exhibitions at my studio a newspaper had sent the assistant art critic. He was very enthusiastic about the pictures, but he said, "I wish I could write the way I feel about your exhibition, but the boss told me not to praise it too much. 'Remember,' he said, 'they are only photographs.'" When I had an exhibition of my Greek pictures at the Guild Hall in East-hampton, Childe Hassam went twice to see them. "They are superb compositions," he said, "but what do these people here know about art?" He had overheard a visitor say to his wife, who was expressing her admiration for the pictures in enthusiastic terms, "Well, maybe, but remember they are only photographs!" Hassam told me that he went up to the husband and said, "I overheard your conversation. I suppose if it were an exhibition of Rembrandt etchings you would say, 'But they are only etchings.'"

Every photographer, amateur or professional, no matter how perfect his prints may be in range of tones, has always longed to be able to reproduce color. It is something that scientists have been working on for more than half a century. Even Daguerre at the very beginning of photography made some tentative suggestions which he published with the formulas of his invention. The first practical means of recording color photographically was the Kromscop, constructed by Frederick Ives, to whom photography is indebted for so many valuable and practical inventions and discoveries. The Kromscop was a rather clumsy affair in which three plates, having been exposed through three different color filters, were placed so that when viewed in this Kromscop box through the same filters, the eye would receive an impression as of one color transparency. It was through Professor Robert Wood of Johns Hopkins University that, at the turn of the century, I first learned about this process. This marked the beginning of my interest in color photography. The next step forward was the autochrome plate invented by the Lumière brothers of Lyon, which by one exposure after a series of simple manipulations gave one a glass transparency of astonishing color fidelity. The German Agfa color plate is constructed on the same principle and has of late years been perfected so as to give most satisfying results. Then, there was the Hess-Ives Tripak process, the first practical "one shot" color camera, which, embodying the same principles used in most modern and color cameras, gave prints not inferior to the ones made today by the latest improved methods.

The photographer whose eye has been trained to see the hues of nature in monochrome will find it difficult, when he tackles color photography, to see subjects as color compositions. As long as he gets color he is likely to be satisfied, regardless of any relation of values. A few workers have achieved amazingly fine results which are reproduced in many of our high-class magazines.

It is interesting to note however that color reproductions which were made almost a quarter of a century ago from the simple autochrome plate are sometimes neither technically nor artistically inferior to the work done today with modern improved methods. The frontispiece of the edition, illustrated by me, of *The Yellow Jacket,* George C. Hazelton's and Benrimo's delightful play done in the Chinese manner, is a color print reproduced from an autochrome that I had made in 1912. Its date might be 1936.

The color motion picture photographer is confronted with the same difficulty that the "still" photographer has to overcome. He must realize clearly that an entirely new approach is required before he will be able to successfully see as a color composition the scene he wants to record. Though some of the color movies shown recently have been eminently successful, especially in the outdoor scenes, a disturbing crudity and falsity of value in some of the interior scenes taken by artificial light will have to be rectified. Through an invention of two young musicians, Leopold Mannes and Leopold Godowsky, color motion pictures have been put within the reach of the amateur. The Kodachrome (Eastman) is based on an entirely new principle and permits the making of a color film without any special adjustments being necessary. Some of the films taken with this process by amateurs are surprisingly good.

Last fall I had occasion to go to Rochester to make a study of this process, at the request of Miss Anne Morgan, who was planning a six months' trip to the Orient and wanted it recorded on color films. It was especially necessary to ascertain how the new film would behave in tropical climate. In the course of my stay in Rochester I was given all the facilities needed for obtaining the desired information. One day Colonel Solbert, who is in charge of the technical department of the Eastman Company, told me of one of their latest enterprises: that they were now sending men all over the country to teach photography in the schools. He was quite surprised when I told him that in a talk I gave before the Bridgeport Art League in 1914, I had made the suggestion of teaching the use of the Kodak in the public schools. The Bridgeport papers gave it editorial notice. Thinking that if they considered it so important the Eastman Kodak Company might be interested, I wrote to Mr. Eastman, enclosing the clippings. I heard nothing from my letter. Colonel Solbert felt sure that the letter never got to Mr. Eastman, for he would not have overlooked such a valuable and far-reaching suggestion. The following year I received a press clipping from Kalamazoo, Michigan, telling how a leading citizen of the town, being impressed with my suggestion, had given money to one school to make the experiment and that both pupils and teachers were enthusiastic about it.

I firmly believe that the use of the small hand camera should be taught in our schools. It could be made elective so that the boys and girls who have not the sensitive hand to express themselves with drawing pencil or modeling clay would find in the camera a means of recording, in their own way, the beauty they would see in nature and all things around them.

The contests for amateur photographers which are arranged by our newspapers show how widespread is the desire to express beauty. The use of the small camera, intelligently taught, will enable our young people not only to see beauty in nature with a more sensitive eye but it will also make them appreciate with a deeper understanding the great works of art, which they may see in museums and galleries, thereby giving their life a new and fuller significance.

I HAVE NEVER BEEN BORED

WHEN I told Gelett Burgess that I was setting down my memoirs, he said, "You know, I've always wanted to write mine. But what about the women?"

"Well? What about them?" said I.

"Are you going to tell all?"

My answer to him was one that I have made to the many inquiries I have received from curious friends asking the same question. I have never told all. And I never shall. I do not like people who tell all.

I have never been able to understand why any man should be expected to disclose things in a book that he would never think of mentioning even to his most intimate friends. This is peculiarly true of his love affairs, which are usually implied by the phrase, "Telling All."

From the very silence of a man or a woman most fantastic legends may spring up. Speaking for myself, I have often thought it would have been interesting to have tried—no man could have succeeded—to live up to the reputation I had acquired.

I have had many attachments and they are beautiful memories. Some of them were deep enough to have tempted me to marry, had I not known myself too well. I could never recommend myself for a husband.

If my brothers had lived, my outlook on life might perhaps have been different. Although we were all bitten by the wanderlust, the bond between us was very close, and we would probably have settled down in some place where we would not have been too far from one another. They, perhaps, would have married, and the family feeling that was strong in us might have meant homes and marriage for the three of us. But they both died young, leaving me a solitary. Solitude can become a habit. And the responsibility I felt toward carrying on the Genthe name was not of sufficient urgency to turn me toward matrimony, about which I have very definite ideals.

My home life as a boy, and the true and touching devotion of my father and mother to each other, made the dignity and beauty of marriage as a sacrament a fixed idea in my mind. What I have seen of it, as it is so frequently practiced according to the modern mode, how thoughtlessly gone into and how flippantly dissolved, has made me feel that it is seldom the Eden I once thought it. Not long ago I went to a party given by a lady in celebration of her departure for Reno, where, after getting her divorce, she was to acquire another husband. She was quite amused by it all.

"Isn't it absurd?" she said. "Here I am going away to live for six weeks in a perfectly strange place, where a perfectly strange lawyer and a perfectly strange judge, neither of whom know anything about me or my husband, will sign a little paper ending everything between us. Isn't it a scream?"

There were other factors responsible for my remaining a bachelor. I could never marry a woman with money, and it happened that the women for whom I really cared and who perhaps cared for me, had fortunes of their own.

Putting these excuses aside and from the point of view of absolute candor, the main reason for my having remained single is that I have never been willing to give up my freedom. Through my persistence in going through life as a lone traveler, I realize that I may have lost something. But there has been compensation in the fine friendships which have enriched my life. In looking back I realize that these friendships, all in some way or other connected with my photographic activity, have meant more to me than any material reward resulting from my work. Quite a number of the old friends who had made life in San Francisco so pleasant for me have passed on, but I am grateful that some remain who make me long to return to the beautiful City by the Golden Gate. Other

California friends are now permanently settled in New York, and though it is hardly possible in this ceaseless strife and rush which living in New York means, to maintain the close contact that friendship demands and deserves, I succeed in seeing some of them more frequently than just once or twice a year, which is about the average frequency for New York.

In the hospitable home of Will Irwin to whom I have always been "Old Dutch," and his brilliant wife, Inez, I could always be sure to find good talk that was an exchange of ideas by intelligent people who were not afraid to think. The same I may say of John O'Hara Cosgrave and his sister Millicent who have known me longer and better than any other of my California friends. Their home in San Francisco was always open to me, and here in New York, after Jack's marriage to Jessica Finch (the founder of The Finch School—incidentally the only woman of my acquaintance who has a thorough knowledge of Latin and Greek), our friendship has continued unchanged. Cosgrave's deep and unerring wisdom has solved for me many a perplexing problem. The gatherings at their home are notable affairs, and I have never met at their table a person who was boring. The after-dinner talk is not always confined to the discussion of philosophical problems which are so dear to the author of *The Academy for Souls,* a book the profundity of which, I am sure, not many of his friends have grasped. I once remarked that he might say about his work what Hegel said of his followers: "Only three of my disciples have understood my theories, and even they have partly misunderstood me." Frequently subjects of a more material nature have been discussed. I recall an evening when among the guests were Dr. Alexis Carrel, Julian Street, Gene Tunney and Irving T. Bush, and the main theme of our serious discussion was the merits of the various vintages of white Burgundy.

The atmosphere of old-fashioned German home life that I find at the Edwin Ashtons, now permanently settled in New York, is restful and refreshing. To discuss with Emma Ashton some fine point of rendering a German phrase adequately into English—she has translated several works of modern German authors—revives my old philological instinct.

One of the first men I met after my arrival in New York in 1911 was Mitchell Kennerley, then very active as a publisher, before he became president of the Anderson Galleries. With his vast knowledge of books and his wide circle of acquaintances, he has been a stimulating influence throughout my New York years. Through him I have met a number of most interesting and delightful people who have become my friends: Eva Le Gallienne, Edna St. Vincent Millay, Zoë Akins, Bliss Carman, Jo Davidson, Christopher Morley—to mention just a few. To him also I am indebted for introducing me to that truly Bohemian restaurant of Christ Cella's. The excellent food and the congenial atmosphere of this place inspired Christopher Morley to found the "Three Hours for Lunch Club," a very civilized and quite un-American institution. Lengthy and delightful were the discussions we indulged in. Often there would be strenuous arguments, not always conducted sotto voce, and it was through my discussions with Jo Davidson that a great problem, of equal importance to photographer and sculptor, has been clarified for me: the convincing rendering of motion, especially dance movement, in art.

Another one of my good friends who loves to spend hours in discussing problems of art—and politics—is the sculptor Mario Korbel. The public knows him better through his garden sculptures of classic design and his graceful dancing figures than by his spirited portrait busts. A head that he did of me years ago in one sitting is now in the Whitney Museum. Mario Korbel, A. W. Bahr, the connoisseur and collector of Chinese art who has been my friend for twenty-five years, and I (we were known to our intimates as "The Three Musketeers") would generally be found at the end of a party engaged in lively discussion. If the subject was art or something related to it, I think that our remarks were more intelligent than when the talk drifted to politics. An evening at Korbel's studio will illustrate this. Most of the guests had gone. Prince Christopher of Greece, Charlie Chaplin and a few ladies

A GROUP OF RUSSIAN ARTISTS:
MOSKVIN, STANISLAVSKY, CHALIAPIN, KATCHALOFF, SORINE (who painted the Pavlowa Portrait)

CHRISTOPHER MORLEY   MITCHELL KENNERLEY

ARNOLD GENTHE ON "CHESTY"

BUZZER IV

who hoped to hear some more of Chaplin's delightful stories had remained. Unfortunately, the talk turned to politics. The argument became quite heated until the remark of a lovely lady, "words —just words," made us realize the absurdity and futility of such a discussion.

I always think with particular pleasure of the delightful evenings at the Walter T. Rosens'. As a rule there was music, often by world-famous artists. Sometimes Mrs. Rosen (Lucie Bigelow), ethereally beautiful, would play the Theremin. Named after its Russian inventor, it is unlike any other known musical instrument, having neither keys nor strings. It is a small cabinet with an antenna-like rod on one side and a metal loop on the other. An infinite variety of tones is produced by the movement of the player's hands which touch invisible sound waves in an electric-magnetic field, one hand controlling the pitch, the other the volume. It is a most mysterious instrument, and unless it is played by an expert musician who has mastered the very difficult technique, as Lucie Rosen has done, its value as a new mode of tonal expression cannot be appreciated. Sometimes, when Mrs. Rosen is not supported by a string quartette, Walter accompanies her on the piano in a masterful manner that astonishes even professionals.

At the Muschenheims' gatherings most of the guests belong to the musical world, artists of the Metropolitan Opera House or of the concert stage, Lucrezia Bori, Heifetz, Bodansky, Kreisler, Flagstaff and Toscanini, who is a very frequent guest. Here is one of the few homes where the Maestro feels like completely relaxing. It would be difficult to recognize in the charming genial guest the man who at a rehearsal the day before had worked himself into a state of dramatic and incredible fury, and who exercises such magic control over his orchestra.

Mr. John Hemming Fry, a very gifted painter and enthusiastic defender of classic art, is another friend of long standing. He has no patience with the vagaries of modernistic art, and in his paintings as well as in his writings (*The Revolt Against Beauty*) he is a staunch defender of the faith in the classic tradition and sound technique.

The bond that drew Edward Bruce and myself together is our mutual interest in Chinese art. I had known his beautiful wife Peggy when she was a little girl riding over the Stow Ranch near Santa Barbara. Bruce, at the time he was president of the Pacific Development Corporation, had a large collection of Chinese paintings and sculptures which are now in the Fogg Museum at Harvard. Then he decided to devote himself exclusively to painting. I have always believed that in his canvases of Vermont and California scenery he has felt very strongly the influence of the Chinese masters. We have had many delightful hours questioning just how much a modern American landscape painter may be influenced by the spirit of those great Oriental seers who lived a thousand years ago.

Of Albert Rothbart, one of the few bachelors among my friends, I see a great deal when he is not traveling about in distant corners of the world. We have many tastes in common but disagree about a sufficient number of things so as to make talk always interesting. I enjoy our friendly rivalry shown not only in candid camera experiments but at auction sales and on cross-country rides.

Few forms of sport have meant more to me than riding, and of games only billiards really interests me. Of cards I know nothing except that they make an admirable target for pistol practice. Unfortunately I have never developed any aptitude for golf, but for over fifty years I have been faithful to horseback riding. I learned early in life that riding meant more than just sitting on a horse and letting him go as he pleased. For one winter in Berlin I had for a riding master a man who had worked under James L. Fillis, the great trainer and master of high school riding, whose principles of equitation I have never forgotten.

For many years I managed to keep a horse of my own. The discipline, which the necessity of daily exercising the horse imposes upon one, is perhaps of even greater benefit than the actual physical exercise, and it never becomes monotonous, not even in the limited area of the bridle paths of the park or the enclosed ring of the riding academy. If one has trained the horse to be supple and obedient in all his movements so that he will yield to the slightest indication given by leg and hand, the rider will find a keen satisfaction in being able, with barely perceptible aids, to make the horse understand his will, and the horse will eagerly execute whatever is demanded of him. The fine companionship growing out of such an understanding between horse and rider is something not shared by any other sport.

The horse that was my faithful mount for twelve years in New York was "Chesty," a dark chestnut whom I had bought for a very small sum at an auction, where he appeared a spiritless, dejected-looking animal, badly trained, badly ridden. But since he seemed to have good bone and promising conformation, I took a chance. My equestrian friends were horrified. "You can't afford to be seen on that animal," they said. I spent many months of patient work with this horse, suppling and collecting him. He now had a sensitive mouth and carried himself proudly in well-balanced gaits. One day on the bridle path, I met one of my old friends who remarked, "What a stunning animal! He must have cost you a pretty penny. Where did you get him?" "He's the same horse you made fun of when I bought him at that Durland auction a year ago," I replied. I admit that he did not look the same.

Just as my love for horses dates back to my early childhood, so does my affection for cats. Their sheer physical beauty and consummate grace as well as the air of inscrutable mystery have always had a strong appeal for me. I prefer cats that have a deep purr and for that reason every cat I have owned was called "Buzzer."

Buzzer IV, whom I had with me for eighteen years, was a large, short-haired yellow cat—half Chinese, half Persian—looking more like a small tiger. He was very haughty, but never vicious, and he seldom condescended to make friends with strangers. In the course of years I made innumerable photographs of him, and some of the pictures, especially those posed with Billie Burke, Jane Cowl, Martha Hedman, and young Marguerite Churchill, were reproduced in the Sunday papers. Once a whole page (of the *Boston Herald*) was devoted to "Buzzer, The Most Photographed Cat in America."

He became even more famous through his correspondence with Oliver Herford's cat, Hafiz, which appeared in a magazine in Herford's column, "The Musings of Hafiz." Once he wrote: "I think the habit humans have of always wanting to have their pictures taken is silly. But living in a photographic studio, of course, I have mine taken frequently. The only time I don't mind is when I can have a cozy fragrant actress for a background." At another time he wrote to Hafiz: "I have recently laid out a mice hole golf course in my studio with rather stiff bunkers and hazards, for which the human niblick and mashie would prove utterly useless. As a rule I play at night. On account of the peculiar character of the course I can promise you a sporting game if you will join me some evening."

Buzzer was certainly an important figure in my studio and even today, years after his death, he is fondly remembered by young and old. I sometimes was accused of paying more attention to that cat than to people. Possibly I enjoyed his contented purr more than the idle chatter of an inopportune caller. I have not found another cat to take his place.

The greatest satisfaction I have derived from my work in photography has been my being able with the aid of my camera to help others enjoy the beauty I had seen and captured, whether it was in the human face, a street scene or a landscape. Some of my portraits have made their owners exclaim, "I would not part with that picture for anything." It is a pleasant thing to hear and makes me forget that in most cases the pictures which are now family treasures were at first received with scant enthusiasm, because they were so different.

Photography has never been for me a means of getting rich quick—or even slowly. Money has not meant enough for me to make a systematic effort to accumulate it. Making a picture has always interested me more than exploiting it. I have often failed to enter photographs in the International Salons of Pictorial Photography held all over the world, but I have never neglected an opportunity to exhibit my work in the Guild Hall at Easthampton, Long Island, where in ideal surroundings the pictures were shown to a sympathetic and intelligent audience, considerably adding to my own enjoyment of them.

Such appreciations of my work as were written by Henry Mc-Bride, Christopher Morley, Mary Roberts, Anna Strunsky, Josef Gregor, and V. Constantinidis, are of greater value and significance to me than gold medals and large checks.

Though for forty years my life in this country has been devoted principally to photography, I have never lost my inclination for study. I have spent more time with books than with men, and my reading has covered a vast field of subjects. The old philosophies as well as the new have been the constant subject of my study. From Confucius and Lao-tse and the Vedas, from Plato down to Spinoza, Hegel and Nietzsche, the search for a solution of the riddle of existence has been a never ceasing occupation. No matter what lofty thoughts and theories may be found in the writings of these great thinkers, no matter what the originality of their ideas, their brilliant and forceful arguments, when all is said and done one cannot help but admit humbly that the answer to most of the questions that perplex and puzzle us can be found in the books of the Old and New Testaments. The early missionaries in China were impressed with the similarity between Christian doctrines and the teachings of Confucius. I have in my possession one of the rare copies of a pamphlet published by the Jesuit missionaries (French, German and Spanish) in Peking in 1701 concerning an edict of the Emperor Kang-Hi in which at their request he had briefly set forth the principles of Chinese religion: the worship of Heaven, the teachings of Confucius, etc. The missionaries who had been accused by their Mother Church of too great a leniency toward the heathen Chinese now could prove that the principles of

Christian religion were not so very different from the Chinese.

The desire to surround myself with beautiful things has never quite left me, even after the San Francisco fire had so completely disposed of all of my possessions. I had never thought of them in terms of money but for what they called up of beauty and knowledge. I have learned the valuable lesson of how to own without possessing, though I am not content without having a few beautiful things around me. I can truthfully say that when I have had the opportunity to study at leisure the paintings of the great masters in the homes of collectors or in museums, I have had as much pleasure out of them as if they belonged to me. And more than once I have had the conceit to feel that I owned them because I knew them.

I am infinitely grateful to Destiny for sending me, so many years ago, to a country where I could pursue my way without becoming involved in things which were foreign to my nature. I have never regretted, not for a moment, nor in any way, that the scheme of life which had been planned for me so carefully and so definitely through generations, and by which I was to be a student and teacher within the confines of a German university, was changed to something so entirely different. Even if conditions in my native land had remained the same as they were in my youth, I could never have come to the new and true conception of human liberty which I have found in America.

In conclusion, I may say that though I have many friends who have given meaning to my life, I doubt that any of them really know me for the strange creature that I am. One came nearer to the truth than any when she said recently, "You certainly are a queer duck—a Don Juan, a Hermit Monk, a Chinese Sage, a University Professor—all rolled into one." Well, maybe. Of this I am sure: I have never been bored, and I daresay I have had as much out of life as is coming to any man.

INDEX

NOTE.—*Illustration will be found following the page indicated in this index by an asterisk.*

284

285

288

290